PREPARING FOR .NET ENTERPRISE TECHNOLOGIES

PREPARING FOR .NET ENTERPRISE TECHNOLOGIES

A Practical Guide for People, PCs, and Processes Interacting in a .NET World

Nelson Ruest
Danielle Ruest

ADDISON–WESLEY

Boston ■ San Francisco ■ New York ■ Toronto ■ Montreal ■ London ■ Munich ■ Paris
Madrid ■ Capetown ■ Sydney ■ Tokyo ■ Singapore ■ Mexico City

Many of the designations used by manufacturers and sellers to distinguish their products are claimed as trademarks. Where those designations appear in this book, and Addison-Wesley, Inc. was aware of a trademark claim, the designations have been printed in initial capital letters or in all capitals.

Microsoft, Active Directory, the BackOffice logo, .NET Enterprise Servers, Windows and Windows NT are registered trademarks of Microsoft Corporation.

The authors and publisher have taken care in the preparation of this book, but make no expressed or implied warranty of any kind and assume no responsibility for errors or omissions. No liability is assumed for incidental or consequential damages in connection with or arising out of the use of the information or programs contained herein.

The publisher offers discounts on this book when ordered in quantity for special sales. For more information, please contact:

Pearson Education Corporate Sales Division
201 W. 103rd Street
Indianapolis, IN 46290
(800) 428-5331
corpsales@pearsoned.com
Visit AW on the Web: www.aw.com/cseng/

Library of Congress Cataloging in Publication Data

Ruest, Nelson.
  Preparing for .Net Enterprise Technologies : a practical guide for people, PCs, and processes interacting in a .NET world / Nelson Ruest, Danielle Ruest.
    p. cm
  Includes bibliographical references and index.
  ISBN 0-201-73487-7
  1. Information technology. 2. Micrsoft.net framework. I. Ruest, Danielle. II. Title.

T58.5 .R84 2001
005.2'76—dc21   2001034108

Copyright © 2002 by Resolutions Enterprises
Resolutions Enterprises
171 St-Paul
Quebec, QC G1K 3W2
Canada
www.reso-net.com
EMF@reso-net.com

ISBN 0-201-73487-7
Text printed on recycled paper
1 2 3 4 5 6 7 8 9 10—MA—0504030201
First printing, October 2001

CONTENTS

v

PREFACE

When Addison-Wesley asked us to write this book, we were thrilled. We'd been working in the IT industry for over 20 years. During this time, we participated in a lot of projects, met people from every level of every type of organization, and lived through all sorts of work situations. Each and every experience had a single, unifying thread: *change and change management.*

This book enabled us to bring together many of the concepts and ideas we have gathered, identified, developed, designed, and put in place during our careers. Our goal is that it becomes a guide that can help you, we hope, to understand change and to transform your organization into one that can live with constant change, whether it is technological or human in nature.

Living with constant change is important to all of us who work with computers. A 2001 Statistics Canada survey revealed that more than 57 percent of working Canadians worked with a PC. Of these, more than 80 percent worked with a computer every day. This trend is the same in the United States, and it doesn't stop with the workforce. Computers are becoming even more pervasive in our everyday lives.

This world of constant change is the reason for our focus on people, PCs, and processes. Knowing, understanding, and mastering everything about your organization, its objectives, and its purpose are essential when you are implementing IT change if you want to be able to profit from it and, especially, help your users benefit from it. This book helps you get there.

In this book, we propose a unified Enterprise Management Framework (EMF) for distributed technologies. This Framework can help people and organizations make better sense of the IT world. The book is presented in two parts. First, it helps you identify the need for change in your IT infrastructure. It also identifies specific tools you can use to ease the change process—to manage the change.

Second, it helps you prepare for the EMF and implement it as a comprehensive IT change management strategy.

This book is also a planning tool that can help you make the transition to .NET Enterprise Technologies, a world where all elements are tied together and every element may impact the others, a world where it is important—if not crucial—to ensure that every modification you bring to your network does not impact existing processes in a negative manner. Here, IT change is not only constant, it is *perpetual,* because IT components are always on the move.

We included more than 100 illustrations that help define the processes we describe. Because many of the processes can appear fairly complex at first, these illustrations help simplify them. These processes work: Each and every one has been implemented in whole or in part in real-life situations.

Information is power. The more you know, the better your decisions will be. That's why we feel managers and IT professionals—and even users—should be aware of the processes we describe. One of our main goals is to bridge the gap between the vision users have of a computer system and the technical approaches IT professionals take to prepare and deliver them.

We sincerely hope you find this book as rich and rewarding as we have. For us, this book is the culmination of a dream: helping people interact with PCs. Your comments will always be appreciated because they can only help improve the way users around the world interact with computers.

Acknowledgments

We would like to thank everyone who participated in the creation of this book, especially our clients and our partners, who helped us learn so much about change management. We'd also like to thank our reviewers for their insightful comments.

Companion Web Site

Several of the items in this book can also be found on our companion Web site: http://www.Reso-Net.com/EMF. Among the resources you'll find there are

- All of the forms displayed in this book, especially those in the appendixes (available in Adobe Acrobat format)
- Some of the complex images in the book (available in JPEG and/or EPS for printing in a larger format)
- Additional items to assist you in your change management processes

Enjoy the book!

Danielle Ruest and Nelson Ruest

INTRODUCTION

The .NET Infrastructure Roadmap

We rent a lot of cars. It's simple. What's really wonderful about cars is that they all work alike. Of course, there are variations, but in general, if you know how to drive, you can get into a car—any car—and drive off within five minutes at most.

All cars are made of the same basic parts and always include a common interface: a steering wheel, a transmission, gas and brake pedals, four wheels, and so on. Unless you're in a country like England where everything is the other way around, you can get behind the wheel of any type of car and drive off quickly.

Why isn't it the same with computers?

Computers are similar to cars. They all have the same basic components: a screen, a CPU, disk drives, a keyboard, a mouse, and so on. Where they differ is the *interface*.

Computers, even computers of the same type with the same operating system, have a strong tendency to be different from one another in terms of how people interact with them. Take Windows, for example. It is the single most common user interface in the world. Yet it is so versatile that very few Windows systems offer the same basic interactions with the user. This is sometimes even the case within the same organization.

In departmentalized organizations, each department has a tendency to perform its own PC analysis and deployment, including the entire interface design and accompanying services. Why is this the case?

Is it because people think PC means "personal computer"? Perhaps. In fact, in organizations of all sizes, PC should mean "property of the company." If that is the case, companies should treat the PC as a strategic organizational

Personal Computer versus Property of the Company

People like to have a sense of ownership over the tools they use. It gives them a degree of security. Just as you wouldn't take away a favorite hammer from a carpenter just before the "big job," don't try to tell a computer user that there is nothing "personal" in a computer.

One of the important concepts to get across to users is that the computer is an appliance, just like a telephone. What's personal or personalizable on a computer is *logical* rather than *physical*. Elements such as the desktop, Start and Programs menus, Quick Launch areas, and screensavers help give us a sense of propriety without being focused on the computer itself.

It is important for corporations that implement "locked-down"[1] systems (Windows NT Workstation or Windows 2000/XP Professional) to ensure that each user has a clear understanding of what he or she can personalize on this system. If the focus is on *logical* rather than *physical* ownership, organizations and users can come to terms.

asset that provides the same basic set of services and a single unified interface to all corporate users.

That is what this book is about: *the human factor in technologies*. It's about how people interact with PCs. How PC interfaces can be designed to simplify this interaction process. How PCs can be managed according to proven processes that provide given responses to given situations. How a corporate IT department is, in fact, a service provider. How a corporation can truly achieve valuable returns on investments (ROI) and how total cost of ownership (TCO) is *not* a myth.

Humans interact with computers in a vast number of ways. The elements described in Figure I.1 are some of the most important ones.

This book focuses on implementing distributed environments with examples from Microsoft Windows technologies. Why? Because they are the most widespread computer technologies in the world.

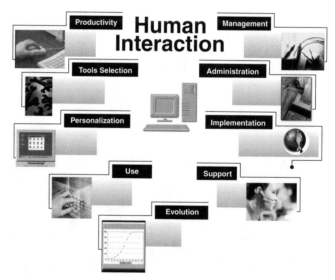

FIGURE I.1 Human interaction with computers covers several different aspects.

---

1. A "locked-down" system is a PC that has specific components whose access is locked to the user. For example, the user cannot change configuration settings, cannot install software, and cannot uninstall software. True locked-down systems are only supported by Windows NT or Windows 2000/XP or higher because they are supported by the NTFS File System.

It's not our place to tell you to buy Microsoft technologies; this book does not aim to join the debate between Microsoft and other information technologies. But if you've already made the choice—if Microsoft technologies are part of your infrastructure; if despite everything, you have to live with Microsoft technologies; or if you're looking at a future Microsoft implementation—it *is* our place to help you understand how to benefit from their use.

Preparing for .NET Enterprise Technologies is about the complex interactions between people and PCs. It is about how you deploy new technologies while still permitting your users to go about their business. It is about how you can create a structural model of the services your information technologies are designed to provide. It is about how you can adapt your approaches to people in order to provide a quality service that enhances the computing experience for everyone involved.

Even though the process methodology included in this book focuses on examples from Microsoft implementations, it can be applied to *any* distributed technological environment. It describes a universal approach that actually achieves TCO and obtains valuable ROI with distributed technologies.

After years of existence in the industry, Windows is still widely misunderstood. Several myths surround this operating system. Most are unfounded and completely avoidable. With over 20 years of experience with project implementations of Microsoft and especially Windows technologies, and with over 145,000 users affected by these implementations, we have noted that organizations using these technologies always face the same basic problems.

- How can you implement a distributed system based on a "simple" technology like Windows and actually turn it into a corporate computing environment that provides stable and constant service?
- Why is it that every Windows user is familiar with the "blue screen"?[2] In fact, people are so familiar with this concept that Microsoft even used it in their advertising campaign for Windows 2000 Professional.[3]

---

2. A "blue screen" occurs in Windows 9*x*, Windows NT, or Windows 2000 when there is a critical error that causes a process to stop completely and thus "hang" the computer.

3. This advertisement first appeared in *E-Week* magazine in November 2000.

- When should you deploy new Windows technologies?
- Where should you look to improve quality of service within a Windows world?
- What should you consider when you want to limit the impact of ever-changing versions of Windows on businesses and users?

This methodology, or rather, this *Enterprise Management Framework (EMF)*, provides a series of consistent and easy-to-follow processes covering everything from initiating communications with your user base to the structure of training programs in the organization. It includes proven project approaches for the deployment of technologies. It focuses on a complete understanding of the underlying services framework required in a distributed organization. It also describes a special certification approach that can ensure the stability of Windows systems.

The Scope of the Book

The .NET EMF is concentrated on a new generation of Microsoft software: the .NET generation. It takes into account new feature sets from technologies that have become the basis of the Internet today. This new model is designed to meet the challenges of the modern IT world: 24/7 availability, simplicity of management, and a new client/server model. Many software manufacturers, including Microsoft, have taken this new orientation.

Bill Gates, chairman and chief software architect for Microsoft, states it clearly: "What will the next generation of the Internet look like? Many of us envision an online world where constellations of PCs, servers, smart devices, and Internet-based services can collaborate seamlessly. Businesses will be able to share data, integrate their processes, and join forces to offer customized, comprehensive solutions to their customers. And the information you or your business needs will be available wherever you are—whatever computing device, platform, or application you are using."[4]

---

4. Taken from a Microsoft advertisement that appeared in *E-Week* magazine in June 2001.

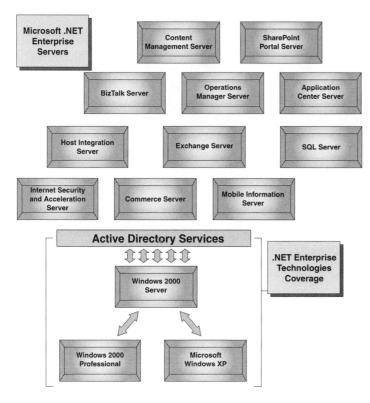

FIGURE I.2 This book focuses on underlying infrastructures for .NET.

Microsoft .NET is about speed and agility of service development by sharing Web-enabled services. It is a very powerful scenario that requires one underlying truth: The infrastructure that supports these processes and services must be stable. That is what this book is about.

Preparing for .NET Enterprise Technologies helps you map out the infrastructures you need *before* you implement Microsoft's .NET Framework and/or .NET Enterprise Servers, as shown in Figure I.2.

Given Microsoft's development strategies in the past, this framework should be valid as is for at least the next five years, helping you grow and adapt with the new Microsoft product strategy: the .NET Framework. But to do so, you'll need to rethink some of the ways you work with information technologies today.

If you are using Windows technologies, the examples in this book will help you prepare a new IT framework that will

Lasting Technologies

It's true! One of our clients designed a Windows NT network in 1996. Today they are still using the same network despite the arrival of new technologies. Their upgrade is limited by available budgets, but nevertheless, their original network design was such that they don't really need to upgrade or modify its structure until new business drivers demand it.

Windows 2000 and Windows XP

Microsoft expects to release Windows XP Professional in 2001. As a result, the examples cited here cover both Windows 2000 and XP.

Microsoft Technologies

We'll cover each of the Microsoft technologies mentioned here in more detail throughout the book.

Reading Map

You'll find a Reading Map at the end of this Introduction. This image will help you identify which chapters in this book are important to your role within your organization.

The Sources of Our Recommendations

This book covers a wide range of information. The subjects we discuss originate with conversations and actions we have undertaken during the course of our careers with a variety of IT audiences: users, technicians, project managers, training staff, communicators, IT managers, and others.

be ready to accept and use the services of Microsoft's .NET Enterprise Servers. It focuses on a directory service and an underlying structure for PCs and servers in preparation for network evolution. In our Microsoft examples, we cover Active Directory, Windows 2000/XP Professional, and Windows 2000/.NET Server or Advanced Server. All of these pave the way for Microsoft .NET Enterprise Servers and the .NET Framework.

If you're not using Windows or you're using Windows only at the PC level, you can still use the concepts in this book. You will need to transfer the Windows examples to your own networking technology, be it Linux, UNIX, or something completely different. The concepts are universal.

The EMF

This is not specifically a technical book, but it does offer technical content. It is aimed at network administrators, systems managers, software developers, and business managers who need to understand how IT supports business processes. It is also aimed at users, who must often live with the systems as they are.

This book addresses all of these groups. Because each group has its own particular interests, it won't be necessary for every group to read each chapter. Different groups will want to focus on different chapters, although we recommend that everyone at least skim through the entire book.

This book should serve as a guide, a tool that IT and management personnel can use to understand and manage change within underlying IT systems. It provides a structured approach to change management. The EMF provides a unified method through which you can view technologies, technological projects, and change management in a .NET world.

The first chapter, "An Ever-Changing World," focuses on defining change, especially IT change, and identifying ways that can make it easier for people to live with.

Chapter 1 is also where we introduce the QUOTE System. This methodology enables organizations to take a single, generic approach to any change situation. This five-step method can easily be adapted to any type of analysis, project, problem identification, or evolutionary process.

From then on, the book uses the QUOTE System to identify how you can personalize the EMF and make it your own. It begins with a situation review and needs analysis. This analysis enables organizations to identify what their business-related IT needs actually are.

Once the needs are identified, they help define an IT framework. This framework will serve as the basis for the Global Architecture, a tool that provides assistance in the understanding of business IT needs and their evolution. This is the foundation upon which the EMF is based.

Next, we begin the Framework elaboration. We describe the actual technologies that will be included in the Framework and the global and/or specific role each will play, as well as the interaction levels between each technology. This helps us map approaches and needs to technologies. Here we draw the service architecture for both PCs and servers. At this stage, we outline the objectives or *targets* for the IT framework deployment.

After we describe these technologies, we review the principles that are involved in their design, interaction, and management. Three primary principles are covered: standardization, rationalization, and certification. This finalizes the essence of the Framework.

Once we've outlined the EMF, we validate each of its components and organize its structure—both need to be focused on specific service offerings. This framework for distributed services requires a series of different substructures to be implemented:

- Support processes for administrative practices
  - Software lifecycle management
  - Software and hardware certification
  - Presentation layer definition
- Standardized management processes
  - Administration practices
  - Development guidelines
  - Support tools and techniques
- Preparatory processes
  - Inventory procedures
  - Component certification
  - Machine staging
  - Application deployment approaches
  - Implementation approaches

Finally, we describe how to deploy the framework and begin its use within the organization through:

A Day in the Life of a User

Using a computer in business is a way of life today. For many, this is a new challenge they must face because they are unfamiliar with the tool. Perhaps the best way to become familiar with this tool is to outline the tasks you must perform with it on a daily basis. Here is an example of this outline for most information workers:

1. Arrive at work. Start the PC if it is not already running; unlock it if it is.
2. Check for new e-mail. Answer the most pressing e-mail, add To Do items to the task list, and assign priorities and due dates.
3. Print today's Task and Meetings list, including item priorities.
4. Establish today's priorities. If meetings are involved, verify that they are still on and that everyone is aware of them.
5. If documentation is a require-ment, verify or create docu-ments as needed with a word processing, presentation graphics, or spreadsheet tool.
6. Lock computer session during breaks or meetings.
7. Lock computer at the end of the day. Don't close the session or shut down the PC unless it is official policy.

Structuring your workday in this manner should simplify the way you work with PCs.

- Project management structures
- Communications programs for all levels of the organization
- Training programs for all staff levels
- The principles required to support the evolution of the Framework

The appendixes and the sidebars provide a series of tools, such as questionnaires, forms, standards, and standard operating procedure strategies, all of which can be used in each phase of the EMF preparation process.

A Chapter Roadmap appears at the end of each chapter. This image provides a graphical summary of the concepts covered in the chapter.

Each chapter also includes several items to help illustrate the concepts involved: anecdotes, case studies, examples of deliverables from various projects, flowcharts, and diagrams. This book is a guide and should be treated as such. You can read it in its entirety or simply go directly to the chapter that explains what you need to know. You can even just use the appendixes and apply them to your own project.

Remember, the focus of this guide is the people factor: *the human factor in technologies*. We do not limit the human factor to end users. Each and every member of the organization interacting with computers has something to add to the personalized EMF you will prepare.

THE .NET ROADMAP

Use this flowchart as a guide to understand the concepts covered in this book.

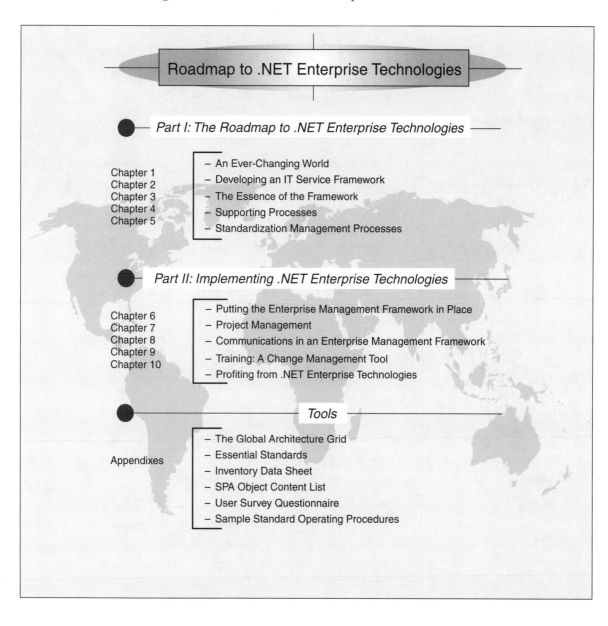

Roadmap to .NET Enterprise Technologies

Part I: The Roadmap to .NET Enterprise Technologies

Chapter 1
Chapter 2
Chapter 3
Chapter 4
Chapter 5

– An Ever-Changing World
– Developing an IT Service Framework
– The Essence of the Framework
– Supporting Processes
– Standardization Management Processes

Part II: Implementing .NET Enterprise Technologies

Chapter 6
Chapter 7
Chapter 8
Chapter 9
Chapter 10

– Putting the Enterprise Management Framework in Place
– Project Management
– Communications in an Enterprise Management Framework
– Training: A Change Management Tool
– Profiting from .NET Enterprise Technologies

Tools

Appendixes

– The Global Architecture Grid
– Essential Standards
– Inventory Data Sheet
– SPA Object Content List
– User Survey Questionnaire
– Sample Standard Operating Procedures

THE .NET READING MAP

Use this flowchart as a guide to identify which chapters are important to you. We strongly recommend that you at least glance through the supporting chapters for your group.

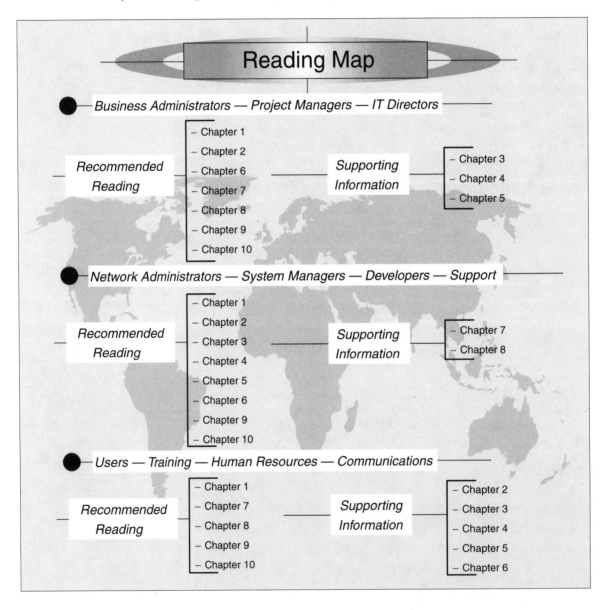

PART I

The Roadmap to .NET Enterprise Technologies

.NET Enterprise Technologies consist of a complex collection of different interaction levels all focused on information technology (IT), business objectives, human resources, and organizational processes. The .NET roadmap begins in Chapter 1 with a look at how people react to change and what IT professionals can do to minimize the impacts of change in their organizations.

Chapter 2 examines how information technology can support the processes identified in Chapter 1. If change is to be managed and its effects minimized, IT has to be more responsive to user and organizational needs.

To do so, IT professionals must fully understand how the Enterprise Management Framework (EMF) is constructed. This is the focus of Chapters 3 and 4. Chapter 5 provides an elaboration of the EMF's basic principles. These principles become the pillars of the Enterprise Framework IT professionals can use to move to .NET Enterprise Technologies.

Finally, Chapter 6 examines how the EMF will change the very structure of existing IT services.

CHAPTER 1

An Ever-Changing World
Finding Stability in a Continuously Changing Environment

We often have a tendency to fit people into two camps:
— The smart ones . . . those that see things our way,
— The others . . . those that just don't want to understand.
—Translated from "Le changement planifié"
by Collerette and Delisle

It often seems that way, but it doesn't always have to be the case. People all have the same basic needs. One of the major constants in IT environments, and one that is often forgotten as due dates slip and deadlines arrive, is that *people* are always involved. Incidentally, it's often when you implement a new system that you encounter the type of situation described in the introductory quote.

People sometimes take hard positions when they are faced with change, especially massive change. Camps form and lines are drawn. Most, if not all, IT projects face this challenge. Why is this? Why does a major change affect people this way?

Human Nature

Human beings all search for a certain amount of stability in their lives. They want a home where they can be king or queen. They want a steady job. They want to be able to apply a measure of predictability to their lives. But, unfortunately, most people soon realize that stability is ephemeral. And sometimes it simply can't be achieved.

Essentially, people want to be able to control their lives to some degree. But the nature of society today—the nature of life itself—is one of constant change and evolution. What's worse, the rate of change in our lives is increasing.

Take information, for example. In our grandparents' time, news didn't travel very fast. Today, we get more news during our breakfast routine than many of our grandparents did in an entire year. Much of this information requires us to make decisions. Is it important to me? How will it affect me? Do I have to take action? For many, living with this increased rate of change is very difficult.

According to Abraham Maslow, a well-known psychologist, people's basic needs fit into five major categories. These needs are described as a pyramid because of their degree of importance and interaction with each other. For example, if people's physiological needs are not met, their self-actualization needs will simply not be important to them. This concept is illustrated in Figure 1.1.

This doesn't mean that computer projects or implementations have to fulfill all of these needs. What it implies though is that we have to pay attention to each other's basic needs when we interact with each other. And, if possible, we should try to satisfy each one in some form, be it minor or major, before passing on to the next. This is one of the keys of successful IT implementations.

Following are the needs IT professionals should focus on when planning to implement a technological change:

- *Activity:* People need to be able to take action; it gives them a measure of control over a situation.

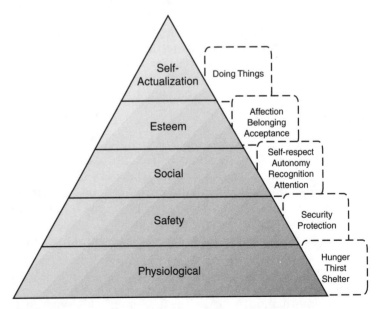

FIGURE 1.1 Maslow's Pyramid of Needs. This pyramid describes what people require to be able to achieve a level of comfort.

- *Security:* People need to maintain a degree of security at all times.
- *Protection:* People need to know that the group to which they belong protects them.
- *Stability:* People require that at least some basic elements of their lives are stable.
- *Structure:* People like things that are organized because they are easy to understand.
- *Community:* People enjoy feeling part of a community; they tend to gather together.
- *Belonging and acceptance:* People need to feel that they belong to a group and are accepted by it. People also need to be able to trust in others.
- *Self-esteem:* People need to be able to maintain their self-esteem in every situation.
- *Self-respect:* People need self-respect. They need to be able to be proud of their accomplishments.
- *Autonomy:* People like to be able to do things by themselves.
- *Recognition:* People need to be recognized for their worth.
- *Appreciation:* People need others' appreciation—it helps bond them to a group.
- *Competence:* People need to know that their knowledge has worth.
- *Self-actualization:* People need to accomplish objectives in a manner they feel is rewarding.

Each and every project you undertake doesn't have to be all things to all people, but when you deal with other people, you should be aware of their needs just as they should be aware of yours.

Basic Personality Types

It's helpful to understand the basic personality types of people you may encounter during projects and other IT situations. According to the principles of Adult Learning and Sports Coaching, there are four basic types of people:

- *Directors:* People who clearly know what they want and don't have time to lose

Essential Needs in an IT World

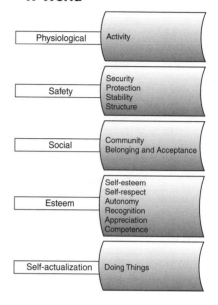

Needs are described in order of importance, with the most important need at the top.

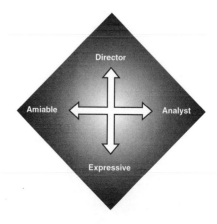

Most people fit into this personality quadrant. Each of us shares traits from three of the attributes at most.

- *Expressives:* People who seem to know everything or at least always have something to say
- *Amiables:* People whose major desire is to be accepted by others or who need to please others
- *Analysts:* People who feel most comfortable when tasks are given to them in a list that outlines what needs to be done and what actions to take

Of course nobody fits exclusively into just one of the previous categories, but these four personality types form a quadrant that indicates how each type interacts with the others.

Paying attention to personality types can help you in your interactions with them. You can quickly learn to recognize what type of person you are dealing with in a given situation and respond to that person in a manner that is appropriate to his or her need. This is the first definition of *service*.

If you want to understand personality types a little more, do the following role-play exercise.

Learning about People

One of the best ways to learn about the four personality types is to role-play. Imagine yourself as one of the four types. Identify which behaviors you would use to project this image to other people. Then, after you're comfortable role-playing the four basic types, try to look at others and categorize them. Finally, learn how to satisfy the needs of each type.

There is no better advantage when you're in a new situation than being able to quickly spot these personality types, especially when you are the *change agent*.[1]

Change in IT

Nowhere is change more prevalent than in the IT world. In IT, everything changes all the time. There are always new versions of products and there are always new deployments to perform. Many, if not all, of us have lived through DOS, Windows 3.*x*, Windows 9*x*, and Windows NT, and many are now going through the implementation of Windows

---

1. The *change agent* is the person who initiates change.

2000 or Windows XP. Soon, all of us will live in a .NET[2] world.

In fact, the only constant in technology, the only element you can absolutely rely on, is *change*.

IT change is not limited to organizations. Today, IT change reaches into our very lives. A great example of this is the year 2000 problem. The change brought about by this IT problem affected most of the population on the planet. And it was only the beginning.

IT touches us all. We all use banking machines. We all buy with Interact or other direct-payment technologies. Our cars use computers to fine-tune motor operation. Every information or knowledge worker uses some type of PC, PDA, or other automated information system. More and more of the general population are using the Internet. Even those who think they are most removed from information technology use it in some way almost every day.

Our entire society faces change, IT-related or not, at some point in time. How do we deal with change? What are the tools and techniques we can use to facilitate change in our lives? Must we resist, or should we just go with the flow?

The answers to these questions prove valuable to IT organizations because they are always faced with change. For instance, IT professionals often become experts on a given technology. They may be quite proud of their accomplishments, and they have every right to feel that way. But this feeling of accomplishment is usually short-lived because of the ever-changing nature of technology.

Technicians who were experts on Windows NT have had to face this issue. Windows 2000 is built on NT, but it is entirely new code with new functionalities, new methods, new operating techniques, and new capabilities. Each and every Windows NT technician has had to or will have to undergo a period of mourning, a period of resistance to change, because each will need to undertake a new learning process to regain his or her expert status. And, of course, during that time the technician feels no better than anyone else does in a change cycle.

Change situations are the same for everyone—IT professionals who need to learn a new technology are no

Training for Windows 2000

For technicians who are not familiar with Windows NT, Microsoft recommends a five-week training program for Windows 2000.

---

2. Microsoft has announced that Windows XP, code-named "Whistler," is to be released in October 2001. They are already hard at work on the following versions, code-named "Longhorn" and "Blackcomb."

exception. They begin with a stable situation: They are familiar with Windows NT. Then they go through a thawing of their inner knowledge: At first, they believe they don't know anything about Windows 2000, but as they move along, they discover that much of it is like NT after all. And finally, they return to stability as they begin demonstrating their newly gained knowledge. This process is illustrated in Figure 1.2.

The Emotional Cycles of Change

Whether we're ready or not, change exists and will always exist at several different levels in our lives. It affects each of us to a different degree based on the ease with which we can adapt and the support of the group we belong to. One thing is certain, we will go through a mourning period whether we are the initiator or the target of change.

Everything begins with a new outlook: "Nothing is permanent, except for change."

Change always affects us directly. Our first reaction when we are faced with a change is emotional: Once again, we must live through *another* change! But if you are the initiator of the change, the emotional aspect is simple and easy because you want to create change—you are the *change agent*.

Change agents use a proactive approach that begins before the change is to take place. A proactive approach is best for IT environments because it deals with problems *before* they arise. Examining information systems or situations and determining ways to improve them is often one of the best ways you can facilitate change and ensure that your systems provide the services they are designed to. This is the second definition of *service*.

Proactive and Reactive Approaches to Change

Following are the proactive and reactive approaches to change. Note the differences between them.

Reactive Approach

1. In a stable state, unprepared for change.
2. Change occurs.
3. React to the change event with panic and resistance.
4. Stability returns after the turmoil from the reaction is over.

Proactive Approach

1. Watch for change, examine change factors.
2. Identify coming change.
3. Prepare for the coming change.
4. Change arrives; engage planned reaction.
5. Stability returns after the reaction is complete.

The difference is clear: Being proactive means being prepared.

You are in a stable state when change arrives.

Things blow up. There is a thaw and things are in motion.

The change is accepted. Stability returns.

FIGURE 1.2   Going through a change situation

But beware of changing for the sake of change!

If you are the object of change, one of those destined to receive the "benefits"[3] of change, your first reaction to it is resistance. Why? Because people who tend to be the objects of change don't expect it. In their search for stability, they have erected defense mechanisms that lull them into thinking that change will not occur, that life is stable.

When people are the objects of change, their reactions are often unconscious, but they probably consist of the following three elements:[4] cognitive, emotive, and behavioral.

- The *cognitive* element refers to the ideas and beliefs people apply to their role in or their sense of belonging to the group or the situation to which the change applies.

- The *emotive* element consists of the emotions people feel toward the loss of their sense of belonging.

- The *behavioral* element refers to the way in which people react when faced with change.

It's easy to understand why people react this way: They are faced with what they deem is an attack on several of the elements that form their basic needs.

- The obsolescence of their knowledge ("Must I relearn everything once again?")

- The distortions their own perception of the situation brings ("Did he just say what I think he said?")

- Their previous experience with change of this type ("Do you remember the last time they did this?")

- Fear of the unknown ("What will happen to me?")

- Economic or social reasons ("Will it affect me directly? If so, how?")

The previously listed factors form the core of resistance. They will not change and we will not be convinced until a good deal of effort has been expended by the change agent to provide us with information.

What's worse is that until these efforts have been expended, people who resist change will expend efforts of

Divide and Conquer

It is important to note that when an organization is faced with change, there is a strong tendency for people to form camps. Camps draw lines and challenge each other. This can never be good for the organization as a whole.

Beware of any consultant or manufacturer that encourages you to form camps within your organization. It is sometimes obvious that his or her only goal is to make a sale, no matter what happens to your IT environment's cohesiveness.

---

3. Whenever we're faced with change, we must first determine if it will be beneficial to us personally. Thus "benefits" are not clear until we have had a chance to absorb the impacts of the change.

4. Collerette and Delisle, "Le changement planifié."

Positive Resistance

Resistance to change isn't always negative. Sometimes resistance serves to make change agents stop and take a second look at what they are proposing. This second look often makes them realize that what they are proposing needs adjustment.

their own in its resistance. They will bring to bear their influence within the organization. Their position in the organizational chart will also have an impact on the level of resistance they can bring to bear. And the control they have on resources required to bring about the change will be applied to stop or hold back the change.

Whatever our individual reactions to change, we all undergo an emotional cycle that always includes the same basic processes (see Figure 1.3). It's just human nature.

Stability within an Ever-Changing Environment

One of our most basic needs is stability. No matter what, we want things to stay the same. It may not be perfect, but at least we're used to it. In a world of constant change, stability is hard to come by. But there are ways to create stability. One of the best is to learn how to manage uncertainty. We must live in a changing world, but we can learn to tame it.

Taming change is at the heart of the science of *change management,* a deliberate effort we can apply to change an unsatisfactory situation. Because change is constant, change management must also be constant. Stability within change means always being ready for change.

A Welcome Change

- Uninformed Optimism (Initial enthusiasm)

- Informed Pessimism (It will never work!)

- Hopeful Realism (Maybe)

- Informed Optimism (There is a light at the end of the tunnel.)

- Completion (Supporters of the change)

An Unwelcome Change

- Immobilization (Total shock)

- Denial (This isn't for me!)

- Anger (I don't want to!)

- Bargaining (Maybe not me.)

- Depression (Why me?)

- Reevaluation (Well, maybe me?)

- Acceptance (Supporters of the change)

FIGURE 1.3 The Emotional Cycle of Change. Whether we like it or not, we all face the emotional cycle of change. Think about it. Your own experience with change will teach you that this is the case.

> ## Change and the Change Agent
>
> Change agents are ready for change. As initiators, they are often the ones who bring change into their own and others' lives. But even change agents sometimes have difficulty handling change. For instance, who has ever been comfortable with tax increases, especially if they seem unfounded?
>
> Understanding that change isn't always pleasant enables change agents to mitigate the impacts of change as often as possible, making change easier for everyone involved.

Change often occurs in cycles. New versions of software appear annually or semiannually. Revolutionary new products can emerge on the market more randomly, but if they are part of a product family, they usually appear in five-year cycles.

Windows is a good example of the latter. Windows 3.*x* was available in the late 1980s. Windows for Workgroups arrived a couple of years later, but it didn't offer anything revolutionary with the exception of new networking technologies. Windows 9*x* brought major technological change to the product family in 1995 with a completely new interface and major improvements on underlying components. Windows NT 4.0 arrived a year later as a follow-up to Windows NT 3.*x* with the look of Windows 9*x*. Figure 1.4 illustrates the evolution of Microsoft's Windows operating systems.

> According to Microsoft, 25 million lines of code make the difference between Windows 2000 and Windows NT 4.0 greater than the difference between Windows for Workgroups and Windows 95.

Almost five years later, Microsoft released Windows 2000. This product is a major change from Windows NT. It offers new concepts and features (such as Active Directory) and leaps beyond the limitations of its forbears. The upcoming Windows XP and Windows .NET Server will finally provide a single, unified code for all flavors of Windows: CE, Personal, Professional, Server, Advanced Server, and Datacenter Server. "Blackcomb" is even further in the future, but it is not expected to bring any major revolution in the way Microsoft Windows technology works and operates.

Change Management Processes

The only way to achieve stability within change is to develop a series of management processes that you can apply to change situations. A structured approach enables you to adapt to change or even adapt the change to your needs.

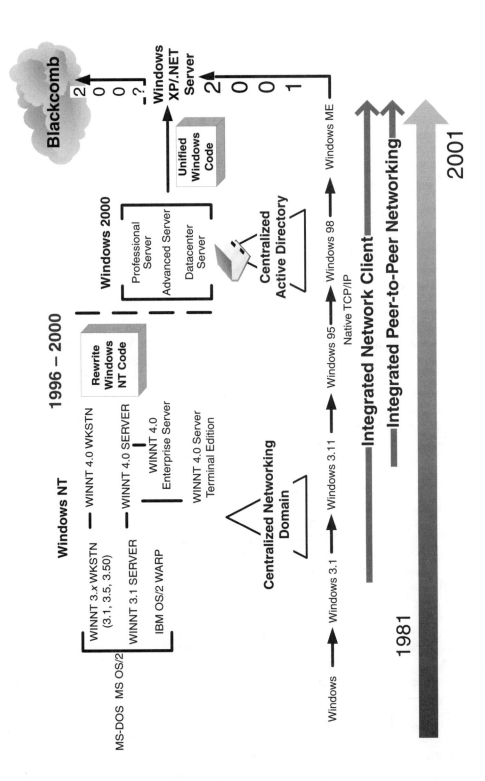

FIGURE 1.4 Microsoft Operating System Evolution. Microsoft operating systems tend to change according to five-year cycles. With Windows XP, Microsoft finally unifies all Windows code into a single source.

This approach includes four distinct phases:

1. *Diagnostics Phase:* In this phase, you identify and describe the unsatisfactory situation you want to change. You also describe the situation the change is to bring. You identify the resources you can apply to support the change, and you predict the different types of resistance you should expect, especially those that can be influenced or mitigated. This phase consists of an evaluation and a comprehension of needs at various levels, it is also known as a *situation review and needs analysis.*

2. *Planning Phase:* In this phase, you select the forces upon which you want to act. This phase serves to define and structure the objectives you want to attain. It is designed to identify appropriate actions or strategies for each objective, positions to be taken, and solutions to adopt. It ends with a complete plan, including deadlines, milestones, and task definitions for each person implicated in the plan. In this phase, you'll need to think of partnerships with the appropriate players who will have to act upon the change.

3. *Execution Phase:* In this phase, you ensure that appropriate follow-ups are undertaken throughout the implementation of the change. The follow-ups use defined criteria to evaluate the change being implemented. In this phase, you focus on the introduction of technologies and techniques that aim to facilitate the way people can adapt to the change. These technologies and techniques must be simple and easy to learn in order to achieve their goals.

4. *Evaluation Phase:* This phase completes the change management cycle with a complete postmortem review to ensure that all objectives have been met with minimum negative impact.

Figure 1.5 illustrates the change management process.

The QUOTE System: A Structured Approach for Change Management

Resolutions Enterprises uses a change management approach—the QUOTE System—that is slightly different than the traditional approach described in the last section. The QUOTE System is based on five steps instead of four.

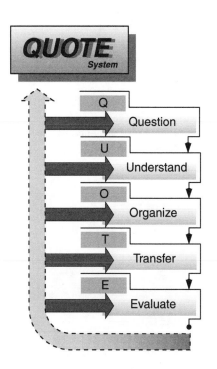

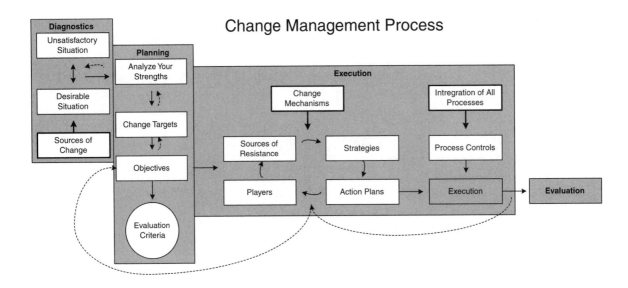

FIGURE 1.5 The Change Management Process.[5] The phases of change management form a single, unified process that is recurrent at all times.

The QUOTE System's Question Phase

This book is focused on the QUOTE System. The Introduction and Chapters 1 and 2 introduce the Question Phase of the QUOTE System because these phases are focused on *discovery,* the process of identifying change situations.

1. *Question Phase:* This is the diagnostic, or discovery, phase. In this phase, you need to identify several factors in the change situation. The first is that the change is occurring. The second is the scope of the change. The third is where the change originates. The fourth is what you already have in place. The fifth is how what you have in place will be affected, and so on. It is essential in any change situation to take inventory of what you already have.

2. *Understand Phase:* This is the planning phase. Now that you have gathered all of the information on the change in the Question Phase, you can start planning how you can influence the change. In this phase, it is essential to fully understand how new technology features will impact the elements in place within the organization.

3. *Organize Phase:* This is the first part of the execution phase. In this phase, you focus on testing and piloting the elements of the solution you identified in the Understand Phase. Because IT change tends to affect large sections of an organization—if not the organization

---

5. Collerette and Delisle, "Le changement planifié."

as a whole—it is important to validate all solutions before you implement them.

4. *Transfer Phase:* This is the second part of the execution phase. Now that you have tested all solutions and modified them according to the test results, you can transfer the solutions to all of the sections of the organization that are impacted by the change.

5. *Evaluate Phase:* Finally, you need to evaluate the change you implemented to understand how it can continue to evolve within your organization. In this phase, you focus on reinitiating the discovery phase and ensuring that your organization can grow with the solutions in place. This is also the time to revalidate all of the support methods you put into practice to ensure they provide the structure required to allow system evolution.

When you think about it, you can use the QUOTE System in almost every change situation, personal and organizational.

Using such an approach in your everyday life can offer you a measure of stability within this changing world. Using this approach in your organization ensures that organizational or IT change is always structured. This method can greatly simplify and reduce the impact of organizational change in corporations of all sizes. For this reason, we will use this structure throughout the rest of the book. Now that you have discovered that IT change is constant, you can proceed to the inventories you need to create in the Question Phase.

Going with the Flow

Whether your team includes 50 or 5,000 people, taking care of their needs as much as possible when you implement change will reduce costs, help you more easily achieve your goals, and mitigate the change's impact on organizational productivity and business processes, not to mention the ease with which the change will take place.

"Going with the flow" means being prepared. If you're rafting down a river, you don't have much of a choice when the speed, direction, or level of difficulty changes. You brace yourself, try to anticipate what will happen, and react appropriately. That's what you need to do with change.

Learning from Change

"It gets easier every time."

This is a statement most of us are familiar with. And it's true. Change does get easier to deal with every time you go through it. The key is to derive lessons from change. Organizations especially should always perform an evaluation after implementing a major change.

Change isn't destabilizing. It's a part of our lives. Uncertainty is prized as well as feared. Don't be the object of change—initiate it. Become a change agent, or at least be ready for change. And if you do initiate change, think of others. Think of the changes over which you have no control and those that you yourself have had to experience. "Do unto others as you would have done unto you" is the third definition of *service*.

A World of Service

In today's world, things are expensive. All of us, rich and poor alike, want (or need) to make our dollars go as far as they can. And when it comes to service, we like to buy quality. If you have a choice between a very friendly and personable service provider and one that doesn't look you in the eye, chances are you'll choose the former and you'll keep going back.

The same applies to corporate IT services. The difference is that you don't have a choice of whether to come back or not. If it's good, that's great. If it's not good, too bad—you're stuck with it.

So far, we've covered three definitions of service:

- Respond to people in a manner appropriate to their need.
- Use a proactive approach to change.
- Act toward others the way you'd like them to act toward you.

These definitions are important because today we live in a world of service. In Canada, the service industry represented more than 68 percent of the gross national product in 1998. In the United States, it represented more than 64 percent of employment sources.

In such a competitive marketplace, only the best can profit. And in a service industry, "the best" often means the most courteous, the most dedicated, and the most pleasant. It is no wonder that the latest craze in the IT industry is e-commerce. The e-commerce industry has grown from a virtually unknown source of revenue for many to one of the most promising industries of the future. But even in e-commerce, organizations have started wondering how to compete.

It's simple: If your Web site is not user-friendly, well thought out, or even nicely designed, people won't come

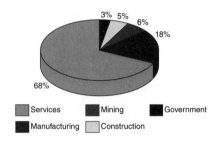

The service industry in Canada represented more than 68 percent of the Canadian gross national product in 1998.

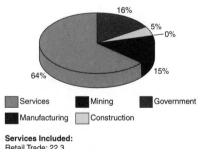

Services Included:
Retail Trade: 22.3
Finance, Insurance, and Real Estate: 7.2
Wholesale Trade: 6.8
Transportation and Public Utilities: 6.4

In the United States, the service industry provided more than 64 percent of jobs in 1998.

back to it. And a basic principle of business is that if your company doesn't generate repeat business, it won't survive. This principle is one of the reasons for the appearance of a new trend within e-commerce: *customer relationship management (CRM)*. Not only is a well-designed e-commerce site a good place for a user to visit, but it becomes even better when it recognizes the user.

MSN (http://www.msn.com/) is a good example of CRM in action. Using Microsoft Passport technology, MSN offers to record your preferences and even provides a secure store for your credit card number when you use Passport to shop online. This CRM approach makes MSN interesting and practical to users.

In a more traditional approach, Starbucks, the Seattle-based coffee vendor, offers a very compelling service: You can go to any Starbucks in the world and purchase a cup of coffee brewed in exactly the same way as you would find at any other Starbucks. This predictable, familiar experience is one of the reasons for Starbucks' phenomenal success.

Defining Service

The *Concise Oxford Dictionary* defines the word "service" as, among other things, "work done to meet a general need; work done on behalf of an employer; benefit conferred on or exertion made on behalf of someone; expression of willingness to confer or make these; performance of function by machine, use; assistance; provision of what is necessary; assistance or advice given to customers after sale of goods."

From the word "service" comes the word "serviceable," which is defined as "willing and able to render a service." In the global marketplace, this definition should be changed to "willing and able to render a *high-quality* service" if success is a factor.

Given the reorientation of North American and worldwide industries toward service, both of these terms should be entrenched in our vocabulary today—they should be part and parcel of our daily culture. It is clear that most of us are involved in some way, shape, or form with the service industry.

Service in an IT World

If a definition of service is "work done to meet a general need; provision of what is necessary," then IT is a service

Customer Relationship Management

What is *customer relationship management (CRM)*, you ask? Here's an example:

If your Web site can remember customer visits, it can provide special promotions to that customer and only that customer. If someone visits a particular page displaying one of your products and doesn't buy it, your site is not responding to demand. The more customers visit your site, the more you know they are interested.

A good CRM system tracks customer visits, and after a certain number of visits, it offers a special promotion to the customer. This special offer may be the thing that inspires the customer to make that vital transaction.

Of course, the entire CRM process must be automated. Otherwise, how could you possibly keep track of the millions of visits you expect on your e-commerce site? A sound CRM system offers automated service as one of its basic functions.

User Is a Four-Letter Word

IT professionals want to help. Most of them go beyond the call of duty to help out a user in a given situation.

But many IT professionals have some negative preconceptions about users—the title phrase of this sidebar says it all. Who in IT has never heard this phrase? Why is that?

By using terms and phrases such as this in our everyday language, we unconsciously form opinions about the people we work with.

The "Soft" Aspects of System Design

The "soft" aspects of system design tend to focus on human interaction with PCs. For example, it is important in the deployment of a new operating system, such as Windows 2000 or Windows XP, to ensure that the design of the desktop is well thought out and meets the needs of the user community.

Meeting the needs of the user community often takes second place for IT professionals, because designing the deployment of an OS on multiple systems is a major undertaking in and of itself. What both groups need to understand in such a dialogue is that IT and the enterprise are responsible for the selection of technologies, while users' responsibilities are to identify and communicate their business needs.

because information systems provide an important set of services to organizations—services that support the business functions of the organization's user base. It is no wonder that one of the key elements of a network is the *server*. This machine offers a clear set of services to the IT community.

But it is not just machines that offer services to the IT community. Computer services are supplemented by services provided by the people who surround and support them. Unfortunately, this is one area where the notion of "serviceable" is not necessarily present. This is understandable. When computers were first invented, they were extremely complicated to use. The people who supported the services provided by these systems were continually learning how to use them, just as the users were. Because no one had worked with these machines much before, it was hard to define customer approaches.

But things have changed. Computer systems are just as complex, but they have become much more user-friendly, and computer services are much more complete. And, given that people are becoming increasingly more comfortable with computers, users feel as if they have something to say in the way systems are conceived. IT personnel can no longer remain in an ivory tower and expect to provide service without encountering some form of user resistance if they don't check with users first.

Just like change, IT should not be viewed as an end in itself. IT is a service. If it is to survive in the Information Age, an organization must ensure that its IT services meet users' demands, not just in terms of volume, but also in terms of content and especially in terms of approach. Too often, IT personnel plan new technology implementations without any regard for the "soft" aspects of system design: the needs of the user base. This isn't necessarily by design. Often, IT personnel look at the complexity of new technology implementations and by default focus on their technological aspects. When asked if they consider how various implementation elements will impact users, they either say that they don't have time if deadlines are to be met or that it's not a concern because they "know" their users.

In fact, they often aren't paying attention to the soft aspects of system design for three reasons.

- The technological content of a new version of software is so complete that dealing with it during implementation is a job in and of itself.

- They don't know about or aren't aware of the soft aspects of the new software version.
- They themselves are resistant to change.

Many major IT projects don't make enough allowances for soft aspects. When organizations realize that information technologies provide a core set of services to their business processes, they will begin to focus on soft aspects. But the focus needs to be constant; it cannot simply occur during implementation projects. It must be an ongoing process.

Because IT is a service, it must be bound by a clear set of rules that take into account what a service truly is and how a service can be a success. Face it, if your IT service doesn't respond to business needs, your organization can go bust.

Consultant versus Advisor

Most organizations today require the use of consulting firms. The complexity of new technologies alone makes this a must. In addition, organizations aren't always involved in migration projects or major systems design. Consulting firms provide focused technical expertise that can save considerable time and money during a project. But consulting firms are not all alike. Organizations should learn to identify the difference between *consultants* and *advisors*.

A traditional consultant's role is to deliver whatever the customer wants. When the customer says, "Do this," the consultant answers, "Yes!"

When the customer says, "Do this" to an advisor, on the other hand, the advisor's response is "Why?" By asking this question, the advisor forces the customer to clearly identify what he or she is requesting. This redefinition of the request often leads to a more productive and complete implementation. Requestioning then becomes part and parcel of the process used to implement new services.

Organizations should strive to know the difference between consultants and advisors and when to call on each to mitigate the impact of change.

Case Study:
Implementing a Major IT Change

Organization Type	Public Sector
Number of Users	10,000
Number of Computers	13,000
Project Focus	Migration from an Obsolete NOS to Windows 2000
Project Duration	2 Years
Specific Project Focus	Maximizing the Use of Internal Resources
Administrative Type	Decentralized

In its migration from an obsolete network operating system to Windows 2000, this organization decided to focus on the use of its internal IT staff rather than the use of consultants. Of course, consultants were called in, but their role was to support and orient the customer rather than to perform the migration work.

Because most of the IT department personnel had worked for the organization for at least ten years, they felt they "knew" their customer base. And like everyone else, they had become set in their ways. This wasn't the first implementation of its kind that they were performing, and they felt they knew what they were doing.

The first phase of the project focused on designing the new systems architecture. The IT staff faced several challenges. Not only was the network operating system being replaced, but the operating system of every PC was also being replaced. They decided to perform clean installations on each PC. To do so, they required a configuration management and PC staging tool. Rather than search the marketplace for such a tool, their initial group of consultants proposed to design it for them. The result was a new approach to PC preparation.

Problems arose when the centralized architecture group came to implement the new tool. Because they "knew" their user base, they "forgot" to verify that the new approach would be functional within their organization. Because the organization used a decentralized PC administration, they had already put in place systems to perform PC management. In fact, two such systems were already in place. The new tool did not integrate with either of the systems, and local administrators were left with *three* different tools to manage and operate.

Isn't the purpose of new technology to simplify tasks and workloads?

Harmonizing Change in IT Environments

IT projects must focus on more than just technology: They must also focus on the service they offer. And as a service offering, they should strive to limit impacts and meet business needs. Like any change situation, an IT project has to focus on people and business processes if the change is to be successful.

The key to a seamless change implementation is to focus on the needs of individuals while introducing change. Because we live in a world where change is a constant—not to say the only constant—we need to try to make change as painless as possible, not only for others but also for ourselves. This is the fourth definition of *service*.

If you want to ensure the success of your IT services and thus the success of everything that depends upon them, the first priority of technology must be the human factor.

Case Study:
Moving to a New Operating System

Organization Type	Private Sector
Number of Users	1,500
Number of Computers	1,500
Project Focus	Migration from an Obsolete NOS to Windows NT 4
Project Duration	6 Months
Specific Project Focus	Migrate Applications to Windows NT
Administrative Type	Centralized

In its migration from OS/2 to Windows NT, this organization decided to focus on the automation of all system construction in order to ensure centralized control in its 650 points of operation. Because they had sound experience in OS/2 and because Windows NT was just an extension of OS/2,[6] the IT staff involved felt they were familiar enough with the system to "know" how it worked.

Of course, they hired consultants. The consultants were put in charge of the system build automation. But the consultants were from familiar firms with which the client had developed their OS/2 systems and processes. Thus, the project began to focus on doing things in familiar ways. Because OS/2 was much less popular than Windows, they were in the habit of developing tools and techniques internally instead of searching for products on the open market or searching for existing functionalities.

A review of the systems automation prepared by the project team demonstrated that several elements and functionalities that existed already within the NT framework (but were absent from OS/2's) were reprogrammed. All of this programming was useless because NT already supported the functionalities.

When migrating to new technologies, it is always important to ensure you understand *all* of its existing and new functionalities.

6. Windows NT has often been called OS/3 because it emerged from the progression of the joint development efforts Microsoft made with IBM for OS/2 version 1.2.

CHAPTER ROADMAP

Use this flowchart as a guide to understand the concepts covered in this chapter.

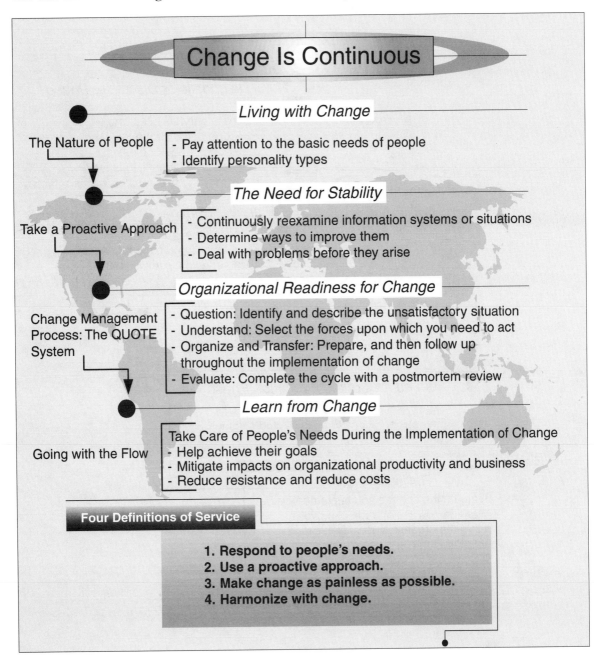

Change Is Continuous

Living with Change

The Nature of People
- Pay attention to the basic needs of people
- Identify personality types

The Need for Stability

Take a Proactive Approach
- Continuously reexamine information systems or situations
- Determine ways to improve them
- Deal with problems before they arise

Organizational Readiness for Change

Change Management Process: The QUOTE System
- Question: Identify and describe the unsatisfactory situation
- Understand: Select the forces upon which you need to act
- Organize and Transfer: Prepare, and then follow up throughout the implementation of change
- Evaluate: Complete the cycle with a postmortem review

Learn from Change

Going with the Flow
Take Care of People's Needs During the Implementation of Change
- Help achieve their goals
- Mitigate impacts on organizational productivity and business
- Reduce resistance and reduce costs

Four Definitions of Service

1. Respond to people's needs.
2. Use a proactive approach.
3. Make change as painless as possible.
4. Harmonize with change.

THE GENERIC QUOTE ROADMAP

Use this flowchart as a guide to the processes covered in the QUOTE System.

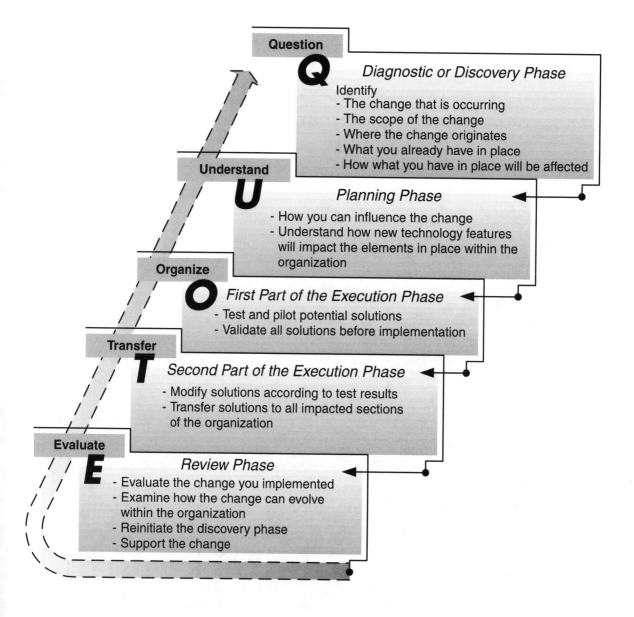

Question

Q *Diagnostic or Discovery Phase*

Identify
- The change that is occurring
- The scope of the change
- Where the change originates
- What you already have in place
- How what you have in place will be affected

Understand

U *Planning Phase*

- How you can influence the change
- Understand how new technology features will impact the elements in place within the organization

Organize

O *First Part of the Execution Phase*

- Test and pilot potential solutions
- Validate all solutions before implementation

Transfer

T *Second Part of the Execution Phase*

- Modify solutions according to test results
- Transfer solutions to all impacted sections of the organization

Evaluate

E *Review Phase*

- Evaluate the change you implemented
- Examine how the change can evolve within the organization
- Reinitiate the discovery phase
- Support the change

CHAPTER 2

Developing an
IT Service Framework

We live in Quebec City, Canada, in a province that is just above the state of Maine. At least twice a year, we travel to Vancouver, which is at the other end of the country. We don't go often, but we like it a lot. It enables us to see the breadth of the country.

One of the things we like the most about Vancouver and the entire West Coast in general is the approach many businesses have toward service. Take, for example, our favorite Vancouver restaurant. As we mentioned, we only go to Vancouver twice a year or so. But every time we go to this restaurant, we receive exceptional service.

The first thing they do while you're sitting at the bar waiting for a table is take your credit card to run a tab. The next thing you know, they know your name (they obviously read it on the credit card). Then, we don't know how they do it but they remember your favorite drink. If you haven't been there before, they'll chat you up to get to know you. The next time you come in, they'll remember you and treat you like an old friend.

In a marketplace that is as competitive as the Vancouver restaurant industry, making people feel at home is clearly one of the best ways to get repeat business. We like this restaurant: The food is good (especially the black bean quesadillas) and the ambiance is particularly friendly.

For us, this restaurant is a great example of the concept of "service."

As you have seen, quality service is the foundation of a strong and directed IT department. But before you can define how to put such a service strategy in place, you need to understand what the service structure for IT needs to be.

The QUOTE System's Question Phase

In this chapter, you'll continue the Question Phase through discovery. Now that you understand the people you deal with and how you deal with them, you need to identify what you are to deliver to them.

What is essential in an IT infrastructure? Which services are required in order to fully support knowledge workers?

Defining IT Services

In the Introduction, we presented the concept of human interaction with computers. This concept outlined nine different ways in which people interact with computers. As you saw, several of these deal primarily with the end user, but many also deal with administrators, managers, developers, support personnel, trainers, communicators, planners, and others. An IT service infrastructure must respond to the needs of each and every one of these types of interactions. Thus, the IT service offering must first be *conceptual,* as shown in Figure 2.1.

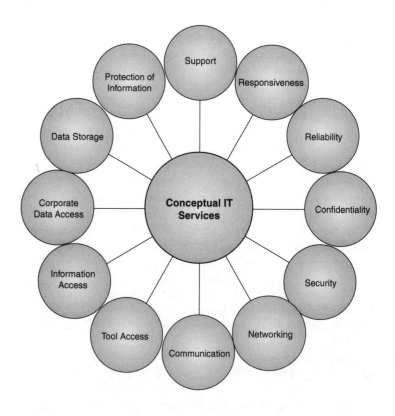

FIGURE 2.1   Conceptual IT Services. The use of a conceptual map of IT services provides a guideline for the design of those services.

The basic services required for an IT infrastructure are as follows:

- *Responsiveness:* The entire IT infrastructure from PC to network must provide appropriate response times in order to enhance the user's computing experience. Responsiveness should *never* be an obstacle to productivity.
- *Reliability:* Computer systems should always work when they are needed. Whether you offer 24/7 access to your computing systems for your staff or not, these systems should always work when people use them.
- *Confidentiality:* Users should feel that the information they work with can be confidential if it needs to be. This is not an outlet for personal abuse, but rather a feature that must be available if it is required for business purposes.
- *Security:* All information that is private to the organization must be secure at all times. This means that access to this information—whether from intranet or extranet sources—must be protected from external as well as internal prying.
- *Networking:* Users need to be able to interact with others through their point of access, whether that is a dumb terminal or a PC workstation.
- *Communications:* Users need to be able to communicate both internally and externally. This means that whatever the form of the message users want to diffuse, an IT service will be available to support it.
- *Tool access:* Users need to have access to appropriate tools at appropriate times. This does not mean that they can simply choose whichever tool they want to use. It means that if users require a specific function from a tool, the corporation is ready to respond in a reasonable amount of time.
- *Information access:* Users need to be able to access the information they need to perform their work. This means that both internal and external information sources should be available to them.
- *Corporate data access:* Internal and external users must be able to find appropriate corporate data when they require it.

- *Data storage:* Users need to know that the information and data that they produce will be stored in proper locations with the space required to support their needs.
- *Protection of information:* All information produced within the organization must be protected and recoverable at all times.
- *Three-tiered support:* Users need to receive support for the use of IT tools and for problems that occur with their systems. They also need advice for solving IT problems when appropriate.

Conceptual IT services form a basic framework for the delivery and management of information technology. From this framework, you can start to extrapolate the guidelines for IT service delivery. These guidelines will help shape the very nature of the IT service you intend to deliver.

The Driving Principles of Quality IT Service

The best way to deliver quality service is to define basic directives that can orient the service in all situations. These directives form the driving principles for IT. An organization that makes use of IT services must define and delimit how they will be delivered in order to be able to validate the level of quality being offered to its resources. This, of course, must always be in line with the requirements of the organization's mission.

Diversity within the Organization

Organizations use IT infrastructures to support their internal business objectives. For most organizations today, an IT infrastructure means the implementation and support of a *distributed environment,* a network supported by a series of centralized servers, additional data repositories such as mainframes or minicomputers, and decentralized points of access to that network usually in the form of PCs (or workstations).

For many organizations, this means a variety of tools and even a variety of operating systems. It is surprising to discover that most organizations still use different operating systems on their PCs. In our marketplace, most organizations have and support Windows 95, Windows 98, and Windows NT Workstation within their networks. This diversity of systems can only increase costs and reduce effec-

Operating System Diversity

One of the important factors in the operation and administration of distributed environments is *maintenance.* Every organization that uses more than one operating system on its PCs is faced with systems obsolescence. If your network includes Windows 95, Windows 98, and other operating systems, it usually means that you cannot guarantee that all systems are up-to-date. For one thing, Windows 95 itself is an obsolete system. Windows 98 became obsolete when Microsoft released Windows ME in the summer of 2000. We will see the obsolescence of Windows ME with the arrival of Windows XP.

Even if those systems weren't obsolete in and of themselves, each offers a secondary version. For example, Windows 95 included the original edition and two "patched" versions: OSR1 and OSR2. How can you guarantee that your systems all use the latest version if diversity is at the core of your network?

tiveness, because it is simply humanly impossible to know everything about every system. When an organization uses different systems, it cannot master them all. To do so, the organization must put in place and pay for different teams of professionals with the sole purpose of supporting one and only one of the systems in place. Or the organization can pay for "experts" who know only a portion of each technology's capabilities.[1]

Standardizing on a single PC operating system (OS) is costly. There is no doubt that replacing a variety of systems with a single, unified OS is expensive and time-consuming, but the advantages are clear: Everyone works with the same tools and everyone uses the same approaches.

One of the major problems in organizations today is the diversity they must support. Because people have a tendency to focus on the "personal" aspect of a PC, they often insist that they have the right to determine the tools they will use on "their" computer. But, in fact, the PC must be viewed as an *appliance*—a tool applied as a means to an end.

To understand this concept you must return to the basics. Why do people use computers in organizations? Is it for their personal pleasure or to perform work that meets business goals and objectives? For example, when a new person arrives in an organization, that person will often have his or her own preferences and work habits. If the person is used to producing documents with WordPerfect, he or she will request this tool even though it is not a corporate standard because the person feels that's the only way he or she can be productive. Organizations often acquiesce to employees' requests because they want to respond to their needs. Does this mean that individual needs override corporate needs?

In fact, there are corporate needs that must override employees' personal needs. When new employees request a specific product, it is because they fear change. They are already in a fragile situation because they feel the need to prove themselves in their new job. They fear that the ar-

Opportunities for IT Change

Standardizing networks is a costly undertaking. There are two major situations where standardization can be implemented.

The first is when an organization is faced with the update of all of its computer systems because it wants to move to a new OS. This is one of the best times for implementing OS standardization because all systems will be affected.

The arrival of Windows 2000 is such an opportunity. It is an even better opportunity than usual because of the breadth of change it brings to the Windows environment. More than 100 new features or improvements are included in Windows 2000. These changes are significant. But what is even more important is the nature of Windows 2000. For the first time in its history, Microsoft offers a true enterprise-ready OS for both servers and PCs.[2]

The second situation in which standardization can be implemented is during an organizational merger. This occurs a lot in the business world when partnerships form or acquisitions are made. In the public sector, it occurs when political decisions are made.

---

1. Even the most knowledgeable professional cannot know everything about every system.

2. In the first quarter of 2001, Sunbelt Software and the Giga Group performed a survey on customer satisfaction with Windows 2000. In their findings, the Giga Group indicated that Windows 2000 was the best version 1.0 of an operating system ever delivered by Microsoft. You can find more information about this at http://www.win2knews.com/ (search for "Giga Group").

rival of new tools along with the new situation will produce a negative impact on their initial performance appraisal. These fears are completely normal given what you learned about change situations in Chapter 1. What the organization needs to understand is that giving employees a nonstandard tool will not help them in the long run.

Your desire to help should not focus on enabling newcomers to be different, but rather on helping them quickly integrate within the organization's work methodology. You need to help newcomers focus on how to perform their work, not support their alienation from others.

Standardization, Rationalization, and Certification

If you are to understand how to treat a computer as an appliance, you need to understand and implement three key concepts within your organization.

- Standardization
- Rationalization
- Certification

These three concepts help you define your IT services. They are key to the delivery of structured IT services within any organization.

Standardization is at the core of any cost-driven delivery of IT services. *Standardization* means that everything is the same. Of course, you cannot take this definition literally. It would be costly, for example, to provide a complex drawing program such as Microsoft Visio to everyone in the organization, especially because it is most likely not something everyone would use.

In IT, standardization means that at the core of all IT services, you find a single and unique approach. If everything is the same at a given level of the IT infrastructure, you can ensure consistent service delivery. For example, simply ensuring that all PCs use the same OS with the same level of service pack will greatly help the repair process for support personnel because they will always know and understand the starting point of any problem-solving situation. In fact, they can also devise and prepare standard responses to the most common problems, thus reducing problem resolution time and cost. Standards also provide the basis for evolution. Because you are working from a

The Standardization Scope

Standardization must cover the breadth of IT activities. For example, organizations often use more than one consulting firm to support the IT department. Each firm has its own way of doing things—its own approaches. Integrating all of these approaches into the organization can be well-nigh impossible.

Instead of adapting the organization to the consulting approach, the corporation should design a standard approach for in-house consulting that meets its own needs.

common set of services, it becomes easier for you to look at their improvements.

Rationalization helps support the standardization concept within IT. By *rationalization* we mean a reduction of diversity. This reduction is primarily focused on the tools in use within the IT structure. This means that instead of selecting a tool based on familiarity or personal preference, you choose it because of its *function*. For example, if you need a word processing program, you should select a single and unique word processing program. This ensures that all information produced with this tool is reusable by the entire corporation.

It is simply amazing that organizations still use more than one tool per function today. The cost of using different tools for the same function, whatever the reason, is a cost that organizations should simply refuse to bear. If you take word processing as an example, you can quickly see that any organization that supports and accepts the use of multiple word processing programs must bear the cost of having information in deposits that do not support corporation-wide information diffusion and reuse. Despite Microsoft's best efforts, WordPerfect documents do not always work properly in Microsoft Word. Producing information in one software format that is not corporation-wide definitely limits its use to a specific category of users: those that use the same software. Yet reuse is one of the basic principles of information management.

It is clear that most organizations today understand this concept in terms of office automation because Microsoft Office has become the most popular office automation suite on the market.[3] What is less clear is why organizations have not extended this principle to all other software products in use within their IT infrastructures.

Certification deals with the methods put in place to prepare tools for deployment. By introducing a certification process before deploying hardware or software technologies, organizations can take proactive measures to ensure stability.

Standardization, rationalization, and certification go hand in hand with quality IT service. If these principles are not implemented in an organization, the organization is likely to face the following problems.

---

3. Microsoft Office is not only the leading suite on the market, but it is the leading suite by far. Office accounts for at least 90 percent of new office automation suite purchases today.

The Rationalization Process

You can find a complete list of activities for performing a personalized software rationalization in Chapter 4.

Mainframes as an Example

When managing distributed systems, IT professionals should follow the lessons learned with mainframes. In a mainframe environment, everyone depends on the same processing power. If it fails, everyone is unable to perform. Thus, managers and administrators of such large environments have designed and implemented structured strategies for implementing change.

In a mainframe environment, you don't implement multiple tools for the same function. You basically choose one software product per function. This has advantages and disadvantages in a mainframe world. To users, software selection is often poor, but system stability is very high.

In distributed environments, there is a much better software selection because so many more products are available. In addition, natural selection processes tend to produce clear winners. You should use this availability of powerful tools to select the one that fits your needs best. You can achieve stability by taking a standard approach to the tool's use, deployment, and administration.

- It will have difficulty maintaining and updating the corporate network. Too many products mean multiple zones and levels of expertise within the IT department. Some products will be very well known and will thus be well supported, but others will not be well supported due to lack of knowledge or support resources.

- Most support situations will require "one-on-one" relationships. This means that because diversity is the key, each problematic situation needs to be diagnosed by itself and cannot be related to other situations occurring in the network.

- Information sources will be disparate. If users choose the way they store and produce information, they are the only ones who have access to it. Corporation-wide integration of information sources will be impossible.

- If diversity is a factor, it will be almost impossible to remotely manage and administer distributed systems. How can you implement a management tool, such as Microsoft Systems Management Server,[4] unless it is designed to support complete diversity?

- If diversity is a factor, it will be extremely difficult for the network to evolve and change when new and revolutionary technologies are introduced in the marketplace. The cost of tracking the evolution of diverse products will limit the productivity of the organization.

- If diversity is a factor, it will be impossible to aim for information sharing through internal development. Developers will follow their own personal guidelines and each internal application will be an island.

- Reliability will be difficult—if not impossible—to achieve. A computer system that must host a plethora of products is much harder to design than one that supports only a few specific tools. Stability and reliability are very hard to achieve when diversity is a factor.

IT problems are expensive. It simply does not make sense to live with these problems if you don't have to. Using an Enterprise Management Framework (EMF), you can avoid the types of problems described in the previous

Acceptance of the EMF

Using the EMF by itself doesn't guarantee success. You have to make sure it is accepted and adopted by the entire organization. The best tool for this is *communication*.

---

4. Systems Management Server provides four key services: inventory, remote control, software metering, and software delivery in heterogeneous environments.

list and improve your productivity at all levels. People in your organization will be able to focus on their tasks and won't get sidetracked by issues that simply shouldn't exist in your network.

The first step is preparation and planning. Even for this, you need a structured approach. This is the Question Phase of EMF design.

Using a Strategic Plan for Change

Standardization can be defined as follows: "A group of *technical rules* resulting from the *agreement of producers and users* and whose aim is to *specify, unify, and simplify,* with the objective of *increasing productivity* in a specific area of human activity."

This definition implies that a group of rules encompasses the breadth of IT activity within a corporation and all of the people who interact with it. If this is the objective, standardization must be supported and implemented through a strategic plan. Such a plan will require a vision and guiding principles in order to be able to evolve once implemented.

Because IT provides a service to the corporation, it must be able to respond to demand. But as we have seen, a quality service goes beyond demand: It predicts demand. It is important to include in your strategic plan an approach that will support a partnership between IT and its various clients: individual users and the corporation as a whole. This partnership will require mechanisms for the expression of new ideas, for the identification of critical new technologies, and for the immediate integration of those new ideas and technologies within the corporate IT infrastructure.

This approach will change the role of IT. It will enable IT to proactively suggest solutions *before* problems arise, all within the technology framework that has been selected and is supported by the standardization process. As such, it is important to define this framework and identify its components.

Defining the Vision

Every strategic plan requires three core components:

- A vision

Strategic Planning Today

Corporate timescales have changed. In the early days, corporations could plan for several decades and actually expect the results they predicted. But with the rate of change in IT today, it is no longer possible. At most, corporations can plan ahead for two to three years and somewhat reliably predict outcomes.

Given the increased rate of change, organizations' plans need to be much more flexible in order to foresee change.

Designing Your Strategic Plan

You can find a list of activities to design a personalized strategic plan in Chapter 7.

- Objectives
- Driving principles

The first step in designing a strategic plan is establishing a vision. Given what we know about people, given our need to control IT costs and limit impact on users, and given the business need for IT systems, the vision of IT should be as follows: *"Provide a complete set of IT services that supports users in their tasks, supports the organization in its objectives, and evolves with business needs while maintaining tight control over costs."*

A secondary, corollary statement is also essential to support this vision: *"Understand the specific needs of your user community. These needs are expressed through individual requests."* This means that IT departments should always use a basic testing technique for every request to ensure that their response fits within the confines of the organizational framework. Otherwise, they will fall into the traditional approach and find they are once again responding to requests by individuals not corporate needs.

Objectives for a Strategic IT Plan

It is impossible to list here all of the objectives that will drive a strategic IT plan because most organizations have their own vision, but it is likely that the objectives for the strategic IT plan would include the following:

- *Increase systems stability.* Eliminating the "blue screen" from the network enables users of all levels to concentrate on their work and not on their system.
- *Reduce interventions among users.* The purpose of IT is to support business objectives. If the IT department is always delivering new services in an unstructured way, it is constantly disrupting the business workforce. In addition, users need to be able to stabilize their level of knowledge before new features can be introduced productively.
- *Reduce intervention delays.* If a given amount of stability is introduced into the network, support personnel will be able to focus on real problems rather than on problems caused by diversity.
- *Reduce system complexity.* Introduce a selection process not to limit functionality, but rather to introduce stability.

- *Control total cost of ownership (TCO)*. Implement structured approaches, such as standard operating procedures, to ensure that costs are truly controlled.
- *Implement network management tools*. By introducing inventory, alert management, systems administration, and software delivery tools within the network, IT can have centralized control of the network infrastructure.
- *Facilitate system evolution*. By implementing a total enterprise management approach, IT can introduce new functionalities through regular schedules and without workforce disruption.
- *Review IT investment strategies*. This review will allow for new and innovative approaches to cost control. IT is a service and should be charged as such to other departments within the corporation.
- *Introduce the concept of corporate software*. The corporation should own all software in use. If a user requires a specific product for his or her tasks, and the requirement is valid, the corporation should acquire this tool.

These objectives support the strategic vision and enable it to evolve.

Defining the Driving Principles of Change

The strategic plan for IT must include driving principles. These principles control the approaches used for change management within IT. They are all-encompassing and affect every level of the organization.

Controlling the Impact of Change

Implementing corporation-wide standardization and rationalization approaches impacts all user levels within the organization. The best way to implement these approaches is often with the arrival of new technologies. For example, the release of Windows 2000 and its following versions is significant enough that it can allow the implementation of an EMF.

Principle 1: Use a Win-Win-Win Approach

Because IT affects the organization as a whole, every project implemented by IT should focus on using a win-win-win approach. This approach ensures that the concerns of everyone affected are taken into consideration during a project. Everyone has something to gain.

Specifically, this means that the approach should consider the following groups.

- *Users:* This group should gain through the implementation of productive tools that will enable them to focus on the work they do instead of the tool they use to do their work.
- *The IT department:* This group should gain through the simplification of network administration processes that should lead to a reduced number of interventions at the user level and reduced lag time for interventions.
- *The corporation:* This group should gain through a definite increase in productivity at all levels and reduced operating costs.

The approach should be slightly different at each of the three levels of intervention.

- *Users:* This group should benefit from an approach that will enable them to focus on their needs and functions within the organization.
- *The IT department:* This group should benefit from approaches that enable them to design systems that respond to user and business needs and that support structured interventions that focus on systems evolution instead of problem repair.
- *The corporation:* This group should benefit through the implementation of a new bond between IT and corporate users.

Principle 2: Implement Complete and Interactive Communications Processes

IT should be transparent and provide complete information to all levels of the corporation at all times; a continuous communications process should be in place. People should not learn of critical aspects of a project or of an IT implementation at the last minute. If this is the first time a strategic plan is put into place, the communications process should begin with an information-gathering stage involving a significant sample of users of all levels and of all functions within the organization. In fact, users should be the ones who perform this information collection.[5]

---

5. This process is described in detail in Chapter 8.

The information collection will enable IT to fully understand user and corporate needs.

Principle 3: Form a Specific Service Contract between IT and Its User Base

The objective of IT is to put into place effective services
that respond to organizational needs. The service contract
between IT and its user base must be clearly defined and
leave no room for ambiguity. In order to avoid ambiguity,
IT needs to clearly define all of the terms that will be used
in the service contract.

Principle 4: Define a Common Vocabulary

IT needs to use terms that are clear and, if possible, concise
when defining its service contract. In order to do this, it is
often important for IT professionals to remove themselves
from their own situation and take a global view of their
role within the organization.

Examples of common vocabulary terms are as follows:

- *Empowered user:* This term is often misunderstood by
  IT. An empowered user is an autonomous user, not a
  self-service user. The user should never have to be a
  computer technician. It is not a user's role to repair a PC
  or install PC software. IT should provide powerful tools
  whose functions are to assist users in the accomplishment of their tasks. "Empowered user" means that the
  user can perform his or her tasks without any obstruc-
  tion or interruption.

- *Roles within the service contract:* The following three
  roles need to be defined: IT department, IT service desk,
  and user.

  - The *IT department* is a service provider whose role is
    to provide advisory and leadership services to the user
    base.

  - The *IT service desk* is the user base's single point of
    contact with IT. All user requests should go through
    the IT service desk.

  - The *user* is an IT customer who has specific needs.
    These needs must fit within the corporate IT structure.

These three roles help shape the strategic IT plan. IT
must respond to the demands of its customers, and user
requests are no longer treated on an individual basis,
but rather within the context of a global IT strategy.

- *Service policy:* Given clear role definitions, IT can begin to define a service policy. This policy must cover the following elements:
  - Empowering users means enabling them to perform work without interruption of service.
  - IT's new role is to help define the needs of its user base and recommend solutions.
  - IT must form a business partnership with its client departments.
  - As a service provider, IT must provide quality tools and services to its customer base.
  - IT's responsibility is to provide tools that are responsive and easy to use.
- *Service levels:* Finally, IT must define the service levels it can offer to its user base. These service levels must be based on stability and robustness. The higher the stability, the better the guarantee of service IT can provide. If you take the example of a PC workstation, the more the environment is locked, the greater its stability. The more flexible it is, the less stable it is. This concept is illustrated in Figure 2.2. If this concept is to work, it is extremely important to identify what is locked and what is

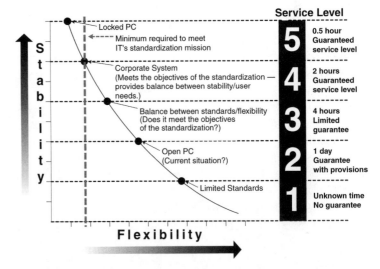

FIGURE 2.2 Stability versus Service Level. Stability and flexibility have a direct impact on the service levels an IT department can guarantee.

not. Locking the wrong elements can cause a lot of damage to the relationship between IT and users. A clear definition of the locked elements is an absolute must.

Most organizations today are at Level 2 in the diagram in Figure 2.2 because they still use PC operating systems that do not support the implementation of stability.[6] The goal of every organization should be to aim for Level 4. This level ensures a given stability but enough flexibility to allow for ease of evolution.

Principle 5: All IT Systems Are Corporate Tools

This principle means that PCs and other IT tools belong to the corporation and not to individuals. Users have the right to personalize some elements of their PCs, but these are logical, not physical, elements. Standards must be put in place at all IT service levels to ensure a measure of control and stability.

Principle 6: Follow Industry Standards When Acquiring, Using, and Administering IT Infrastructures

All organizations should put in place and manage their IT services according to the precepts of the IT industry if they want to implement systems that support business competitiveness. Several industry organizations provide guidelines for IT implementations. Some of the most pertinent guidelines are discussed in the next section.

Principle 7: Centralize Corporate Systems Whenever Possible

This principle does not imply that organizations that use decentralized administration structures must change. It means that in a client/server infrastructure, as much as possible should be centralized on the server, especially for corporate systems. Servers are easier to update and upgrade than workstations, especially in a .NET world.

Microsoft, for example, offers the ability to perform in-place changes through its ASP.NET approach and with the support of tools such as Application Center Server 2000.

---

6. Windows 95 and 98 do not support this level of stability because they do not sufficiently support system locking in the way Windows NT or 2000 do through NTFS, the 32-bit file system.

Through its centralized execution of applications, Windows 2000's Terminal Services also allow software centralization.

Using decentralized applications means distributing the location of the system's executable code. Placing this code on PCs means being willing to support a more complex update process. In some cases, though, this may be the only approach that meets an organization's business needs.

Principle 8: Rationalize All Product Selection within the Corporation

The corporation, not individual users, should be the one to select tools. However, the corporation should support a recommendation procedure if users feel a tool is necessary to their work. A specific IT role should be put in place for tool selection. Tools should be selected by function, and only one tool should perform any given function. Market share and vision should be selection factors. This approach will foment information exchange and reuse within the corporation.

Principle 9: Unify All Applications within the Corporate Network

A unification process should be undertaken along with the rationalization process. All users should be migrated to the selected tool for any given function. This will most likely require the implementation of conversion programs in order to recover existing corporate information.

Principle 10: Implement a Virtual Computing Environment

Every user should be able to use any point of access (or workstation) in the corporate network and be immediately productive.

Principle 11: Implement Zero Administration for Windows Principles in IT Management

The Zero Administration for Windows (ZAW) principles support total network management and form part of the basis for the EMF. If your corporate network is composed of a distributed environment running under Windows, you will need to specifically focus on administrative task automation and remote workstation management. The principles of ZAW are covered later in this chapter.

Rationalization and Change

Your corporate rationalization processes must be able to adapt to change. Some exceptions will always be required.

The Virtual Computing Environment

This concept will be fully detailed in Chapters 4 through 6.

Principle 12: Be Prepared for Network Evolution

Once the network has been standardized, IT must put in place an EMF. This Framework will support a controlled, yet constant, network evolution.

Principle 13: IT Is the Single Point of Service

Every request that concerns any field covered by IT services must be directed to the IT department. It cannot be addressed by any other part of the organization.

Principle 14: IT Is Not an Island

There must be a continuous communications process between IT and the other sectors of the organization with which it must interact. This communications process must also involve training and communications resources, as well as user and management representatives.

These principles are supported by additional concepts as described in the following sections.

Acquisition Guidelines

Every IT infrastructure component, hardware or software, for workstations or servers, must be based on specific guidelines that should include the following:

- A set of standards must be defined for all software and hardware components. Most organizations would not acquire obsolete hardware, yet many still use obsolete software.
- All hardware should be purchased in lots wherever possible. This will reduce diversity in all components—PCs and servers alike. Purchasing PCs in lots of 100 or more[7] enables an organization to prestage the PC with its version of OS, which reduces deployment costs.
- All hardware should be purchased according to the latest industry guidelines. One of the most important industry standardization efforts in hardware is the Wired for Management initiative, or rather, the Networked PC. Each

---

7. This depends, of course, on the size of the organization. If a corporation has between 1,000 and 5,000 users, lots of 100 or more are acceptable. If the organization has more than 10,000 users, lots should be considerably greater than 100. If your organization is on the smaller side, you should still aim for lots as big as you can get.

If It Isn't Broken, Don't Fix It!

The title of this tip is a great rule of thumb, but like every other principle, it all depends on where and when it is applied. In terms of software, it is amazing to see the number of organizations that still use DOS-based software.

It is true that software conversion and evolution implies cost, but so does obsolescence. Some organizations want to stick with a given product because they feel it does what they need it to do. What they don't realize, or what they aren't ready to face, is that an obsolete tool often holds back the evolution of the network. Organizations often overlook the costs they incur every time this product must be configured to work on a new OS. DOS programs are difficult to adapt to Windows 95. They are even harder to adapt to Windows NT.

The Evergreen Lease

With the rapid evolution of hardware and software in the marketplace, it is interesting to note that most organizations today still buy all of their IT equipment.

Given the need to control costs and maintain stability within budgets, it is surprising that the evergreen lease is not more prevalent. Why buy a computer when you could lease it for a few years, and then exchange it for an up-to-date model, all at the same cost?

Because software and hardware evolve so quickly today, major software manufacturers now offer software *subscriptions* instead of purchases. Why not? Software is only rented anyway, because you have to constantly update it with patches and other improvements.

Licensing and Software Assurance

In 2001, Microsoft modified its licensing structure to move to the subscription model. This change means that software licenses are no longer acquired—they are rented. Contracts last for three years, and clients must purchase the latest product versions at the end of that time. In addition, clients can purchase software assurance if they want to have access to guaranteed upgrades.

In this environment, it is very important for organizations to have a structured change management process such as the EMF.

hardware component in designed for remote management, which is a must today in any corporation. Microsoft publishes the specifications for this initiative at http://www.microsoft.com/technet/hw/arch/15netpc.asp?a=frame. This information is updated every year as technology changes. This is much more important to corporations than the minimum requirements of an OS.

- All software should run natively on the OS. If it is a 32-bit operating system, the software used on it should be a 32-bit version. If the OS is 64-bit, the software should be 64-bit as well. Evolution is part and parcel of IT systems.

- Every software product that provides services for a given number of users should be centrally managed and deployed through automated procedures. An organization can determine the extent of this policy. For example, if a software product has a user base of ten or less, manual installation could be acceptable in order to reduce costs.

- All applications in use should permit the exchange of information with applications providing the same or other functions. Information exchange should be a key factor in application selection.

- All applications should use the same basic interface wherever possible. Because most organizations provide an office automation suite to their users, it makes sense that this set of tools is the most well known by the user community. Organizations should capitalize on this knowledge bank by selecting other commercial applications that use the same or a similar interface and by designing corporate applications according to their suite's interface design.

These guidelines will help support the standardization and rationalization processes.

IT Service Use Guidelines

In addition to guidelines for acquisition, the corporation needs to redefine IT service usage. This redefinition should include the following guidelines:

- All IT services should be used according to corporate guidelines. The PC is an extension of the IT infrastructure and as such provides access to the services IT offers. The EMF must include usage guidelines.

- Home use of IT services should be available only if it is officially supported and properly structured.
- Personal software should not be used within the corporate IT infrastructure. If a tool is required for a specific task, the corporation should acquire it.
- User data should be protected centrally. All permanent user data should be stored on servers and backed up on a regular schedule.

If standardization, rationalization, and certification are implemented through an EMF, IT must take the responsibility of supporting these principles. This means that the Framework must be defined in such a way that it includes the evolution of the standardization, rationalization, and certification principles.

Managing Total Cost of Ownership

Total cost of ownership (TCO) is a well-known term that has been applied in all sorts of situations by hardware and software manufacturers. But in fact, TCO is a science, not a marketing approach. TCO is made up of two distinct elements:

- *Direct costs:* These are costs that are defined through budgets, including
  - Hardware (PCs, servers, cabling, routers, bridges, storage, backup systems, and so on)
  - Software (PC, server, network management, and so on)
  - Network operations (personnel budgets for system maintenance, operation, and administration)
  - Productivity operations (personnel budgets for all information work)
  - Corporate development (customized, in-house development to meet specific business objectives)
  - Communications (all IT communication efforts)

In many cases, organizations do not have a global picture of these various budgets. It is important to consolidate these budgets in order to master all direct costs.

Corporate Budget Reviews

Many corporations have decentralized IT budgets. That is, individual departments are responsible for the acquisition and purchase of their own PCs and software. This approach makes it difficult to implement standardization and rationalization. "If I pay for it, I will choose it" is the attitude IT managers are faced with.

Corporations need to redefine their approach to IT budgets. It is fine to decentralize budgets, because it is one of the best ways to make departments accountable. But in a standardization process, it is important to understand that IT must provide a core set of services and standards to all departments. Thus, budgeting should change from a right to select everything to the provision by IT of a basic PC including a given set of local and networked services.

When a department purchases a telephone for a new employee, the employee doesn't usually get to choose the brand or any options other than those offered by the centralized telephone system. Why should it be different with a basic PC?

Total Cost of Ownership

One of the reasons it is so difficult to control TCO is the way some IT budgets are designed.

Some organizations still limit IT budgets and distribute the lion's share of the overall IT budget to client departments. This is fine so long as IT can charge back for the services it delivers. If not, it becomes difficult to control TCO because sources of spending are distributed, and often IT managers must use portions of their budget to pay for large projects in small portions. The danger of the latter is that there can never be any coherence to a project if it is managed in this fashion.

- *Indirect costs:* These are costs that are incurred but not directly budgeted. These costs are harder to evaluate, but they should include

  - *User self-support:* A user will futz around trying to find out how to fix something, or worse, the user will ask a colleague and interrupt the colleague's work as well as his or her own work.

  - *Unclear support services:* If IT does not provide a clear, three-tiered support program and policy, including user-skills support, users will often install their own versions of software on their system because they are familiar with those tools. This causes some minor gains in productivity, but it mostly results in losses due to increased complexity in the system itself.

  - *Nondirected training:* A user will futz around trying to find out how to do something, or once again, he or she will ask a colleague.

  - *Unplanned system halts:* This category includes productivity losses when a system halts or hangs for any given reason.

These indirect costs can constitute up to 50 percent of the TCO. They need to be controlled if the organization wants to master TCO. The EMF provides for control of these costs.

Some basic acquisition guidelines will help minimize costs. For example, organizations should purchase corporation-wide licenses for every tool their entire network of users will use. These can include tools such as office automation suites, antivirus software, network access software, compression utilities, and so on.

In addition, corporations should acquire software maintenance programs along with the software itself. For example, Microsoft .NET Enterprise Servers[8] is composed of several different tools: Windows 2000 Server, Internet Security and Acceleration Server, SQL Server, BizTalk Server, Commerce Server, Host Integration Server, Application Center Server, Exchange Server, and more.

A .NET Enterprise Server license becomes productive as soon as an organization makes use of at least four .NET products. In addition, a .NET maintenance license helps

---

8. This product was formerly known as Microsoft BackOffice.

ensure that the organization is always up-to-date because it is obvious that Microsoft cannot make these products evolve at the same speed. New versions of each component appear throughout every year. Individual purchases cannot ensure that the IT infrastructure is always up-to-date.

The rationalization process can also be used to reduce costs in license acquisition, because most manufacturers offer competitive upgrade pricing. An organization can take advantage of these cost reductions when rationalizing a set of products, such as word processing programs. The organization can save by exchanging licenses from the old product for licenses of the new standard at a reduced price.

If an organization wants to reduce costs, it must implement a strategic plan that is supported by principles and guidelines.

Zero Administration for Windows

Given the complexity of distributed environments, several manufacturers have joined together to form the Distributed Management Task Force[9] (DMTF). This organization has outlined several series of standards aimed to simplify centralized IT management and to reduce overall TCO.

Microsoft has implemented its own version of the principles outlined by the DMTF standards: the Zero Administration for Windows (ZAW) initiative. It is an internal initiative whose aim is to reduce costs while simplifying Windows administration. With Windows NT, ZAW was mostly composed of principles, but with the coming of Windows 2000, ZAW has become one of the driving factors for the core feature set of this new version of Windows.

The objectives of ZAW are to

- Balance the economics of PCs with the centralized control available on mainframes
- Provide management tools for mission-critical, server-based applications
- Provide tools that support centralized IT management while profiting from a distributed processing environment
- Provide tools that can integrate the management of the new wave of Internet-based applications with that of older, mainframe-based applications

9. You can find DMTF information at http://www.dmtf.org/.

ZAW is composed of the following 15 principles:

- Centralized PC management
- Centralized network administration
- Remote OS delivery in distributed environments
- Remote application and service pack delivery in distributed environments
- Support for a virtual workspace
- Central data storage
- Simplified PC replacement
- Local caching of user data and applications on the PC
- PC configuration validation at start-up
- PC configuration freeze (or lock)
- Web-based enterprise management
- Graphical script management
- Integration of the desktop management infrastructure (DMI)[10] to all management tools
- Centralized network access administration
- Access control through group policies

All of these principles are evident in the feature set of Windows 2000 or Windows XP (see Figure 2.3). IntelliMirror technology supports most of these, but there are also the basic scripting approaches included in Windows 2000 Server and Active Directory, Remote Installation Services, and the Management Initiative undertaken by Microsoft with NetIQ Corporation. Today, Windows 2000/XP offers the possibility of complete software lifecycle management for all levels of a server or a PC.

The Move to an Enterprise Architecture

Information technology has evolved over the years. In the 1980s, organizations moved to information systems on a piecemeal basis, as shown in Figure 2.4. Business units developed their own systems and put in place the infrastructures required to support them. IT was in charge of segregated environments.

---

10. DMI is one of the hardware standards to come out of the DMTF. Wake-on-LAN technology is an example of DMI.

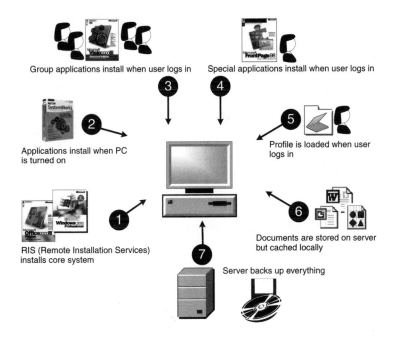

FIGURE 2.3 Windows 2000/XP Software Lifecycle Management. The entire PC staging and repair process is managed in seven steps. Everything is stored on a server and is automatically backed up.

Then in the 1990s, organizations started to rationalize their infrastructures by moving to distributed networks of PCs, as illustrated in Figure 2.5. Business systems continued to use different technologies to develop and support the systems they required. IT was in charge of semi-integrated environments.

Today, organizations are beginning to realize that they require complete integration if they want to control costs, as shown in Figure 2.6. Incidentally, .NET technologies are finally mature enough to offer complete support of differing business objectives. As such, the enterprise architecture offers one unique infrastructure that integrates both IT infrastructures and systems development and support. IT has finally become a strategic corporate asset.

To support the .NET enterprise architecture, you need a .NET EMF.

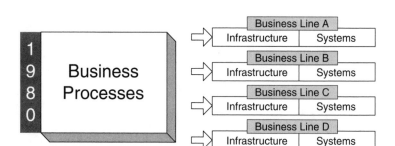

FIGURE 2.4   Organizations began by implementing systems on a business-line basis.

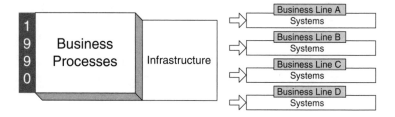

FIGURE 2.5   IT infrastructures were unified in the 1990s.

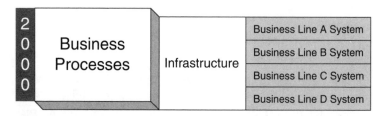

FIGURE 2.6   Enterprise architectures bring the most stability by unifying business and IT functions.

The Foundation of a Change Management Strategy

Building the EMF can be a complex undertaking that may seem arcane to all but the initiated. Because building a framework is an architectural undertaking, you can compare it to building a home. To begin building a home, you need a foundation. Then you can add walls and a roof, interior partitions, plumbing, power, and all sorts of other services. You must use a structure because you must be sure that everything fits together. But first and foremost you need an action plan: a strategic plan for IT.

The starting point for the framework of this house must be the plan. In the case of an EMF, this plan is the Global Architecture, which is composed of a series of principles, orientations, processes, rules, and standards that will guide the organization through the acquisition, construction, modification, and implementation of its IT resources. In fact, it is the result of the Question Phase of the strategic plan.

The Global Architecture

An IT infrastructure includes all types of different components. These include hardware, software, protocols, development methodologies, database systems, operating systems, applications, administrative and management systems, and much more.

With the arrival of distributed client/server systems, the major focus of the Global Architecture must be interoperability, scalability, and portability of the applications, their subcomponents, and their output throughout the entire IT enterprise. This approach helps preserve all IT investments. It also serves as one of the starting points for the elaboration of the framework surrounding the Architecture.

Your organization's IT framework must be able to meet the challenge of distributed technologies, so it must be constantly reviewed and reoriented. But for this review to occur, you need to be able to clearly identify its elements. For this, you need to have complete and thorough inventories of all of its components.

To more easily understand the design of a Global Architecture, you can use a grid like the one shown in Figure 2.7.

The grid in Figure 2.7 consists of 20 cells.[11] Its headings vary depending on the architecture model used, but one that works well includes the following headings across the top:

Building a Home

The steps for building a home are familiar to anyone who has built anything from a tree house to a snow fort. They always break down as follows:

1. Start with a plan for your home building project.
2. Design your architectural plan: how things will fit together.
3. Now the physical building can begin. Lay down the foundation, and then add the walls, the flooring, and the roof.
4. Put in all the services (plumbing, power, heating, light, cabling, and so on).
5. Finally, finish the inside and the outside of the frame.

The Global Architecture

You can find an empty grid including definitions of the content for each cell in Appendix A. It supports the elaboration of your own Global Architecture.

Appendix A also includes a list of the contents of the inventories required to support the Global Architecture. In addition, this inventory list can be used to initiate an Active Directory migration.

---

11. This grid is adapted from the Zachman model for IT architectures. Zachman uses a 30-cell model. This 20-cell model is simple while still achieving the required goals because each cell is modified by time.

Data, Information, and Knowledge

Data refers to the facts on hand; *information* is obtained from the processing of data; and *knowledge* is derived from the interpretation of *information*.

A Global Architecture focuses on data because the process of obtaining knowledge from data is at the core of the Architecture itself.

- Network
- Data
- People
- Tasks

The grid also includes the following row categories:

- Scope
- Enterprise
- Influences
- Systems
- Technologies

Each of the items in the headings influences each of the cells it touches. For example, Network denotes all of the physical components of the infrastructure; Data consists of all of the facts that make up the organizational sources of information; People are the cogs in the wheel of the organization; and Tasks relate to how People interact with each other and with both the Network and the Data.

Global Architecture	Network	Data	People	Tasks
Scope				
Enterprise				
Influences				
Systems				
Technologies				

Time →

FIGURE 2.7 The Global Architecture design grid

The grid's column headings are put into relation with each of the rows. The rows identify the specific coverage of each column. For example, Technologies identifies the hardware components of each column; Systems focuses on the logical components; Influences identifies the area of influence for the element; Enterprise covers the interaction models for each element; and Scope is its breadth of coverage.

Organizations undertaking the design of an EMF need to identify for themselves the content of each cell. Ownership for each cell has to be assigned to specific groups within the organization. Interacting groups and departments for each cell also have to be identified.

An example of a completed grid is displayed in Figure 2.8. It shows the types of elements that should be included in each cell. (This is an example only.)

Once the Global Architecture is designed, it should not be allowed to stagnate. Responsible groups need to constantly review and renew the contents of their cells.

Each cell interacts with each of the cells adjacent to it.

Global Architecture	Network	Data	People	Tasks
Scope	Geographic	Mission-Critical	Departments	Enterprise Goals
Enterprise	Logical Structure	Schema	Workflow	Logical Links
Influences	Network Architecture	Data Model	Security Policies	Business Plan
Systems	Distributed Services	Distributed Services	Human Interface Devices	Applications
Technologies	Physical Structure	Physical Distribution	Geographic Distribution	Organizational Chart

Time →

FIGURE 2.8 An Example of a Global Architecture. Each cell has been filled with the component that best identifies its content. Interactions of the cells with each other create the framework for the Global Architecture.

Global Architecture Equals Inventories

As mentioned before, knowledge is obtained from interpreting information. Information itself derives from the processing of data. For an organization to fully understand the breadth of its EMF, it must know itself. Many organizations do not have complete inventories of all of their IT assets, including people, PCs, and processes. Most have portions of these inventories, but not all.

The concept of a Global Architecture is principally an inventory exercise. It is the starting point for organizational knowledge of IT assets. Your inventories should be precise, succinct (as much as possible), and accurate.

Inventory Contents

Your Global Architecture inventory will include all sorts of information: diagrams, organizational charts, maps, lists, spreadsheets, databases, documents, and so on. In addition, it will include global and detailed views of your systems.

Defining the Global Architecture

You must examine several elements of the corporate and IT structures in order to identify the elements of the Global Architecture. Some of the elements this particular inventory should cover include:

- The network architecture
- The geographic distribution of the network
- The network's physical structure
- The network's logical structure
- WAN-based distributed services
- The data schema
- The data model
- Mission-critical data
- Distributed services that support the data model
- The physical distribution of data
- Personnel
- The organization's department structure
- Workflows within the organization
- Corporate security policies
- Human interface devices (HID) and designs
- Personnel geographic distribution
- Logical links within the organization
- Corporate goals
- The corporate business plan
- The corporate organizational chart
- Applications used to support the corporate mission

The results of this examination fit within the 20-cell grid presented previously.

The Foundation of the Global Architecture

Because you're building a home, you need to begin putting together the structure now that you have the plan. As with a home, you begin with the foundation. The foundation supports every other part of the home, so it must be strong and it must include all the critical elements of the organization. Again, its elements must be inventoried and those inventories must be maintained.

The elements contained in the foundation should include the following. All can be found within the organization itself.

- Interrelations between groups
- The corporate mission
- Sources of information both internal and external
- Information flows within and without the organization
- Human interactions in the organization
- Documented information
- Guidelines for evolution of the framework
- Corporate management and management approaches
- Technological administration processes
- Communication processes
- Training practices and policies

The foundation supports the Global Architecture (see Figure 2.9). In the analogy of a home, the foundation is the basement and the Global Architecture is the flooring.

Next, you can lay down the framework and follow that with the outer structure, never forgetting that while the outer structure will be what is most apparent, the entire structure is supported by internal flows and energy sources (see Figure 2.10).

Applying the Outer Structure to the Framework

As mentioned earlier, the Framework is composed of three core elements: people, PCs, and processes. In addition, the infrastructure elements of the Framework are both physical and logical. These items form the outer structure in our home analogy.

The infrastructure includes items such as strategic alliances, both within the corporation and with external partners. Because the Framework deals with technology, it is important to be able to supplement your own internal visions with those of industry leaders. These should be your strategic partners.

Every internal strategic positioning must include external choices or the selection of external products. Strategic IT partnerships are vital to the survival and adaptability of the Framework. They also have a major impact on the validity of IT investments.

Using Appropriate Skill Sets

It is important to include the appropriate skill sets in this exercise. Two skill sets are crucial:

- Technological expertise
- People and business expertise

Both skill sets are required because the design of a Global Architecture is not only technical. If it is to function properly for the organization, the Global Architecture must include human factors along with the technological ones. Two new roles are defined.

Enterprise Architect

Organizations are already becoming familiar with the concept of a chief information officer (CIO). Of course the CIO plays a critical role in the design of the Global Architecture. But along with the CIO, the organization requires an enterprise architect.

The background of this architect is different from that of traditional IT architects. The enterprise architect benefits mostly from a sound understanding of the complex interactions between IT components and all levels of the organization. In fact, the enterprise architect understands the human factor in technologies.

Workflow Architect

In addition, the organization requires a workflow architect who has a complete understanding of the complex interactions between all levels of the organization and is technical enough to be able to vulgarize technical concepts. In fact, the workflow architect focuses on the human factor in technologies.

The two positions bring people, PCs, and processes together in the Global Architecture.

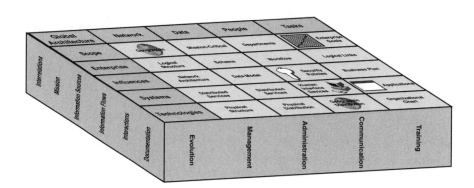

FIGURE 2.9   The EMF Foundation. The home begins to form as you add the foundation. Each of the foundation elements helps support the Global Architecture.

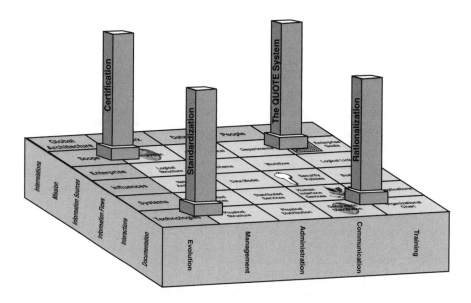

FIGURE 2.10   The Initial Framework of the EMF. Now that the flooring is supported by the foundation, the initial framework can be laid down. The concepts of standardization, rationalization, and certification, along with the QUOTE System, will form the supporting structure for the entire framework.

It is thus extremely important that the core strategic partners be visionary, because these partners will lead your organization into the future, and any wrong choices today will have major impacts tomorrow.

Strategic partnerships also impact the other elements of the infrastructure. On the physical side, they impact

- Physical components
- Geographic interrelations of the physical components
- Communication links
- Operation and administration of these components

On the logical side, strategic partnerships impact

- Operating systems for PCs and servers
- Distribution of IT services
- Usage principles for the services
- Operating and administration principles for the services

The final element of the infrastructure is the evolutionary vision. How will IT technologies and services evolve with time and need? Figure 2.11 displays the final version of the .NET EMF.

Is Your Partner Visionary?

To determine if your partner is visionary, answer these questions:

1. How did the partner become visionary?
2. What is his or her level of expertise in the matter at hand?
3. What is his or her level of credibility?
4. Was he or she right in the past?
5. Are his or her predictions today realistic and can they be realized?

A Scalable Framework Vision

The design of a Global Architecture can be complex, but it provides a complete methodology for the identification of each and every IT component within the corporation. It is the basis of your EMF. Once you've designed the Frame-

The Scope of Windows 2000

An EMF was useful in a Windows NT environment because it enabled organizations to structure processes in IT management. But its application to Windows NT was limited because Windows NT's own technological scope was limited.

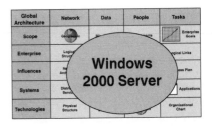

The scope of Windows NT affected only part of the Global Architecture.

Windows 2000 and Windows XP are true enterprise-ready operating systems. Configuration management, Active Directory services, security, and networking improvements increase its scope to cover the breadth of the Global Architecture.

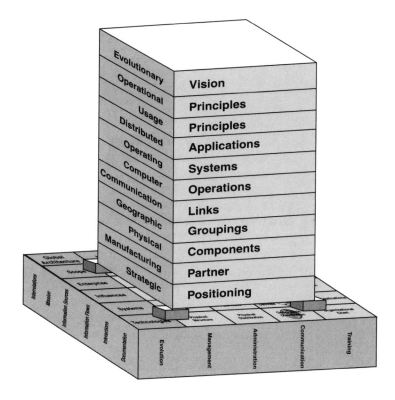

FIGURE 2.11 The Final Version of the .NET EMF. The home is complete. The outer layer includes the elements that will be dealt with during the administration of the EMF.

Using a Home-Building Analogy

The use of a home-building analogy enables you to put all of the components of the Global Architecture into perspective. It also visually demonstrates the tight level of interaction required by all the components.

Windows XP

Windows XP provides a strong argument for distributed systems with its integrated Terminal Services. Through Terminal Services, users will be able to lock their corporate PC at the end of the day, go home, and log on to their corporate PC through the Internet to continue working on a project. The next morning, they can unlock the PC and continue their work.

work, you can use it to support the business objectives of your corporation and render the corporation more effective in terms of information management through the application of technology.

Distributed environments are important. More and more organizations are coming to rely on them. Just like mainframe systems, distributed environments must be stable because they provide support for core business functions.

Every information business has one key asset: people. Distributed environments are a benefit to information businesses because they put the power where it is most needed: in the hands of information workers. The distributed environment IT model is organic. It offers services based on local resources, whether they are desktops or regional servers. It can interact with legacy systems and legacy data deposits without additional development investments on mainframes. It can be subtle enough to quickly respond and adapt to sophisticated user requirements. And, through the EMF, it can offer complete stability in much the same way mainframes have for the past 30 years.

Using the QUOTE System

Windows is one of the most frequently used technologies on the market. Nevertheless, users cannot say that their Windows experience has always been the most pleasant. Not even Microsoft can make that claim.

This "negative" Windows experience may be a result of the lack of interaction between the various groups that live with IT within a corporation. Each group tends to focus on a single aspect of the system as it is prepared, used, and evolves within the organization. By including people, PCs, and processes, the EMF helps you view and understand all of the elements that can support stability.

Now that we have laid the foundation for the Framework, we can proceed to examine the core set of services it requires and the core set of processes that enable it to deliver stability, robustness, and performance in a distributed world.

We introduced the QUOTE System in Chapter 1. This system contains five basic steps and is a process that you can apply to any change management situation. Designing an EMF is managing change. Thus, we will use this system throughout the upcoming pages to structure our approach to Framework design.

The first stage of the QUOTE is the Question Phase. By focusing on inventories, this chapter continued the Question Phase after the introduction of the nature of change in Chapter 1. In this book, we act on some, but not all, of the elements of these inventories. Our focus is on those that can affect how we manage change within diverse IT organizations.

This focus becomes evident in Chapter 3, as it begins with a discussion of the Understand Phase with an outline of the solution elements of the Framework.

Case Study
Four Ministry Merger

Organization Type	Public Sector
Number of Users	1,200
Number of Computers	1,200
Project Focus	Ministry Merger
Project Duration	6 Months
Specific Project Focus	Merger of Disparate Ministry Technologies
Administrative Type	Centralized

Political decisions are often controlled more by potential increase in popularity than by business need. When this is the case, disparate ministries are often merged at what seems a whimsical thought from a newly elected administration.

In this project, four disparate ministries were merged into one. Each of these four formerly independent ministries used a different network operating system (NOS). One used Banyan Vines StreetTalk, another used Digital VMS, the third used an outdated version of Microsoft Windows NT, and the fourth used Microsoft Windows for Workgroups. The objective was to migrate all networks into a single, unified NOS: Microsoft Windows NT version 4.0. In addition, it was important to ensure that all units learn to operate in the same way.

The organization used the QUOTE System to first identify all of the elements and practices of each network. Then, keeping the elements that seemed appropriate, a new Global Architecture was designed. This Architecture included components from each of its predecessors. Network drive mappings came from StreetTalk, server management practices came from Windows NT, PC management came from Windows for Workgroups, and data structures came from Digital VMS.

The result was a single, unified architecture that responded to the needs of the new organism. The advantage of this architecture was that it recovered sound elements from each of the source systems, so users did not have to relearn everything. The things users liked were recovered and other elements were improved.

The core element of this project was recovery of existing components and communication of this fact to all users. Resistance to change was kept at a minimum because people could easily find familiar things in the new environment.

Case Study
PC Software Rationalization

Organization Type	Public Sector
Number of Users	3,500
Number of Computers	3,000
Project Focus	PC Enterprise Framework
Project Duration	18 Months
Specific Project Focus	Reduce the Number of Software Applications in the Network
Administrative Type	Decentralized

When this project began, the organization used eight different operating systems and more than 1,100 software applications on its PCs. Support costs were very high and no end was in sight. In fact, users had so many PC problems that rebooting was their answer to all problems.

A complete inventory of all software applications was performed. This inventory was collated from four different sources: Intel LANDesk, Microsoft Systems Management Server, a Paradox database, and a login script executed on each PC. Each inventory included different information. Even the same categories in each product had different data. The result was a list of 1,100 applications. Rationalization was performed by function and breadth of use.

- 1,100 applications were on the initial list.
- After investigation, 532 of the applications were identified as being actually installed on a PC.
- After removing multiple versions of the same product, 432 applications were listed.
- After a reduction based on function,[12] only 295 applications were left.
- Of the 295 applications, further analysis demonstrated that

---

12. Function applies mostly to software categories: spreadsheets, word processing, graphics, and so on.

- 76 were in use by servers
- 38 were in use by non-PCs
- 181 were PC products in actual use

Further negotiation with users led to a final list of 138 PC applications.

Case Study
Designing an Active Directory

Organization Type	Public Sector
Number of Users	50,000
Number of Computers	50,000
Project Focus	Active Directory Design and Implementation
Project Duration	1 Year
Specific Project Focus	Integrating the Diverse Parts of an Extended Organization
Administrative Type	Decentralized

This organization had over 2,200 different points of service to its customer base. Each of these points of service offered one of five different sets of services. Each thought it was unique and had little in common with the other. Because the integration could not be imposed, the organization had to use cooption and collaboration as rallying points.

The project team designed a blueprint for the integration. Each point of service could make its own choice from several possible integration scenarios. The blueprint was divided into four sections or decision points.

The first point focused on the selection of the number of forests and trees in the directory. Ideally, a single organization has a single forest and a single tree. This simplifies management because of the hierarchical concept of a directory service. Every major policy can be applied from the top down if it has been designed properly at the top level *before* the integration of its subcomponents.

The second point dealt with the attribution of subcomponents or containers, such as domains and organizational units. Organizational units are contained within a domain. A domain delimits a specific security policy. Establishments that required a certain level of independence would select a domain. Establishments that were managed from a point outside the establishment would be given organizational units that were placed within a management domain.

The third point focused on service level agreements. It included namespace management and positioning of core directory service points such as domain controllers (user authentication), domain name services (directory service locations), and global catalog services (finding people, PCs, printers, shared folders, and so on).

The fourth and final section dealt with information transfer within the directory. It was based on network topology and replication traffic that must travel over the wide area network (WAN).

The resulting blueprint is illustrated in Figure 2.12.

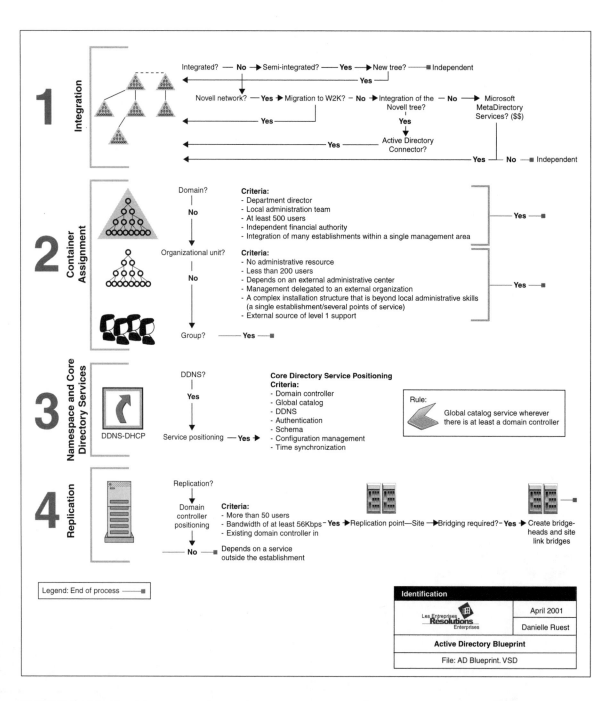

FIGURE 2.12   This blueprint can be used in any organization that wants to move to a directory service such as Active Directory. The blueprint must be used in conjunction with the inventory list described in Appendix A.

CHAPTER ROADMAP

Use this flowchart as a guide to understanding the concepts covered in this chapter.

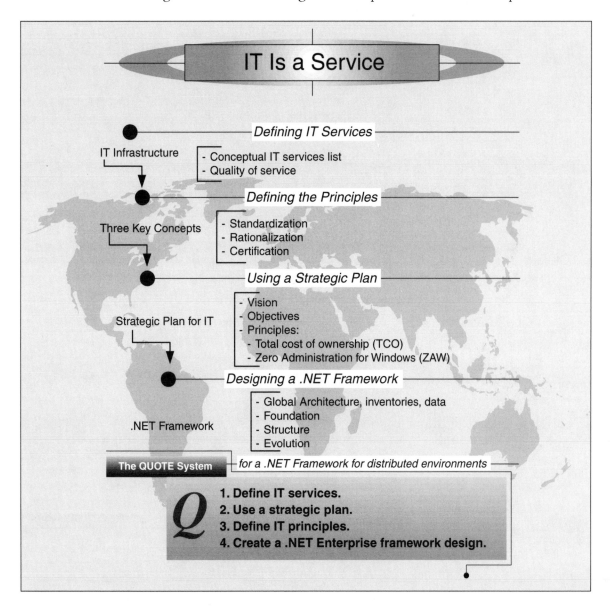

IT Is a Service

Defining IT Services

IT Infrastructure
- Conceptual IT services list
- Quality of service

Defining the Principles

Three Key Concepts
- Standardization
- Rationalization
- Certification

Using a Strategic Plan

Strategic Plan for IT
- Vision
- Objectives
- Principles:
  - Total cost of ownership (TCO)
  - Zero Administration for Windows (ZAW)

Designing a .NET Framework

.NET Framework
- Global Architecture, inventories, data
- Foundation
- Structure
- Evolution

The QUOTE System *for a .NET Framework for distributed environments*

Q
1. Define IT services.
2. Use a strategic plan.
3. Define IT principles.
4. Create a .NET Enterprise framework design.

CHAPTER 3

The Essence of the Framework

Designing the IT Services Infrastructure

> Business is going to change more in the next 10 years than it has in the last 50.... If the 1980s were about quality, and the 1990s were about reengineering, then the 2000s will be about velocity.... Business process improvements will occur far faster. When the increase in velocity of business is great enough, the very nature of business changes.
>
> —*Bill Gates*, Business @ the Speed of Thought

Managing IT in today's fast-paced business world is a complex process. Managing distributed environments is even a greater challenge because each component seems separate. Viewed individually, the components of a distributed environment seem isolated.

You can build PCs in a certain way. You can provide services on servers in another. You can provide support without reference to other IT divisions. This works so long as you remain within your own field of expertise. But its limits are quickly identified when you need to interact with others.

Microsoft's .NET Architecture

Microsoft has made several efforts to help IT professionals identify the interrelationships between elements of a distributed system. Their first initiative was the BackOffice Product Suite. It was launched along with a new visual concept, the Digital interNetwork Architecture (DNA), as illustrated in Figure 3.1. The DNA formed the working components of a *digital nervous system*—a structured IT environment where all the components interacted with each other in much the same way a human nervous system does. When tied to BackOffice, the DNA made sense. It displayed the role of every component and that component's potential interactions with others.

Microsoft's DNA demonstrates how the client, rich or thin, interacts with server and legacy systems to form a

The QUOTE System's Understand Phase

In previous sections of this book, you learned about the Question Phase of the QUOTE System, which involves identifying issues and problems that organizations face and inventorying what is within organizations today.

This chapter deals with the Understand Phase. In this phase, you'll begin to explore potential solutions. You have defined the problem. You know there are technologies and processes that you can apply to control and profit from your distributed environment. This is the phase for initial solution definition.

All of the solutions we elaborate here are based on the initial discovery process for the EMF.

The content of this chapter is rather technical. When defining technical services, it is important to discuss them at some point. All readers should still browse through this chapter because it outlines core concepts that everyone can understand.

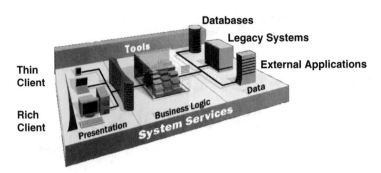

FIGURE 3.1   Microsoft's Original DNA Concept. In Microsoft's original DNA concept, you can begin to see the interrelation between all the components of a distributed architecture.

complete unit. The glue that holds this together is the *infrastructure,* which is composed of physical network elements and system services both driven by business logic.

In this picture, the client can be *thin*—a terminal responding to computing services centrally located on a server—or *rich*—a full-fledged PC running its own applications as well as giving access to centralized services. Applications can be internal, commercial, or a mixture of both. Databases serve as the corporate data repository. These databases can be stored at any level of the system so long as they remain sharable and recoverable.

With Windows 2000, Microsoft modified the DNA approach to have it become the .NET Framework. For most corporate environments, this means the continuation of distributed systems. The major difference between the DNA and the .NET structures is the latter's focus on Web-based technologies and Web-structured reliability and performance.

In a Web environment, technologies need to be running at full 24/7 reliability. Demand is constant because time zones no longer affect service use. Because the Internet is available to the entire world, your customer base has become global. With its new Web orientation, Microsoft has developed tools and technologies to manage, upgrade, and service server-based applications and operating systems while continuing to provide 24/7 service.

With the rewriting of Windows NT code, Microsoft was able to take Windows 2000 to a new level. Using principles based on Windows NT, Microsoft enhanced the Windows code structure to include more growth, more stability, and

The Rich Client

Though the thin client is a popular concept today, it has not become a reality within corporate networks. Most people who continue to use distributed environments focus on rich clients: PCs including several local software components that must be upgraded and maintained on a regular basis.

This is not a bad strategy. The advantages of a distributed architecture and its potential gains in productivity are clear. What is less clear is how to achieve stability within this environment.

more extensibility. Server versions of Windows 2000 include Windows 2000 Server, Advanced Server, and Datacenter Server. Terminal Services are built into the Windows code as its clustering functionality. Windows 2000 is the glue that ties the entire distributed structure together.

Microsoft also introduced .NET Enterprise Servers to support the services required by the .NET Framework. Microsoft proposes the following services for .NET Enterprise Servers:

- Host and mainframe integration to provide access to legacy systems

- Internet security and acceleration for external network boundary protection

- A relational database system integrated into the system directory

- A messaging and groupware system that provides a unified storage system for the very first time

- Market-ready commercial services

- Underlying infrastructure services based on an XML transaction model

- Robust load balancing at three levels: network, application component balancing, and data repository clustering

- An application management and deployment service

- A mobile system management service

Products bearing functional names provide all these services, as illustrated in Figure 3.2. More services will be available as Microsoft expands on its .NET services structure. But this service structure continues to tie together all of the elements of a distributed environment. Interactions with users now extend from PDAs and other mobile devices to rich clients. The underlying OS is Windows 2000 or XP and every additional service is simply an extension of the OS's architecture.

The .NET strategy is quite powerful. More services and further extensions will appear as Microsoft continues to make it evolve. But the core of the model remains the underlying infrastructure. Integrating all of the .NET products and ensuring common management and administration strategies is the challenge we face if we want to profit from this

Datacenter Server and the Thin Client

As mentioned earlier, thin clients have not yet become standard within organizations. Perhaps the reason for this is that the centralized processing model is not one that you usually think of when you think of Windows. A server that hosts multiple user sessions in terminal mode must be quite robust. This may have been impractical before the advent of Windows 2000 Datacenter Server. Now with Terminal Services integrated to Windows code and with the sheer size of a 32-processor Datacenter Server, we may see a return to thin client concepts.

This trend gives even more meaning to the EMF. If all services are centralized, absolute system stability is a must.

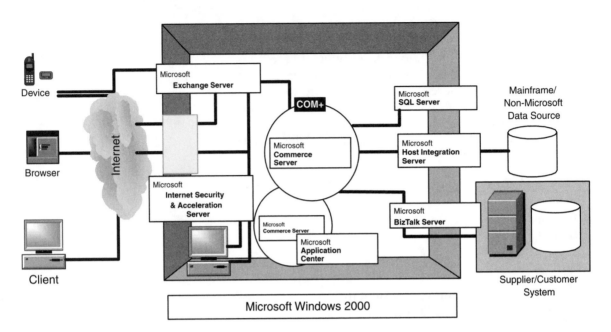

FIGURE 3.2 The new services structure supporting .NET

The Microsoft Operations Framework

Microsoft based its Operations Framework, part of the MSF, on principles derived from IT Infrastructure Library (ITIL). ITIL offers comprehensive documentation on IT best practices. You can find out more about ITIL at http://www.itil.co.uk/.

model. To help us do so, Microsoft has begun to offer some of these strategies through its Microsoft Solutions Framework (MSF). This is the first time Microsoft services and recommendations delve seriously into the deployment, administration, and operation of IT services.

Several core components are specifically presented in the Microsoft Operations Framework (MOF).[1] Both the MSF and/or the MOF are available only through the use of Microsoft Consulting Services or though official Microsoft training. We will use these frameworks as points of reference throughout this book, but we will also cover more basic concepts.

A Distributed Services Architecture

One thing is clear in both Microsoft's former and present architectures: Every element of the architecture is related to the others. For you to fully understand this relation and the elements of this relation that are crucial for proper management and administration, you must first define which IT services you require.

---

1. You can find more on the Microsoft Operations Framework at http://www.microsoft.com/mof.

Chapter 2 identified the list of conceptual services required by the user base. This list focused on two primary sources: the information worker's needs and the needs of an IT-driven corporation.

The information worker requires stable services, access to data, access to appropriate tools, access to other people, confidentiality and protection of information, as well as full-fledged support.

The corporation requires productivity, security, knowledge reuse, protection of information, managed costs, stable services, and the appropriate level of interaction within and without each business unit.

In order to meet these needs through the provision of IT services, IT departments need complex technologies and complex organizational structures to manage them.

The list of services IT must cover is more complex than the conceptual IT list. It tends to focus on technologies and includes more detail.

The list of IT services covers the following elements:

- *Physical components:* This category covers every hardware component of the IT infrastructure, including cabling, WAN and LAN equipment, servers, PCs, PDAs, additional input and output devices, storage and recovery technologies, and more.

- *Operating systems:* Each physical component that includes processing capability, such as routers, switches, servers, PCs and PDAs, requires an operating system. Windows, for example, covers PDAs, PCs, and servers, and interacts directly with routing equipment through the Routing and Remote Access Service extensions built into Windows 2000.

- *Networking:* Both LAN and WAN networking are services that must be provided and supported by IT.

- *Communication:* People must communicate with each other and with systems. Systems must communicate with each other.

- *Directory services:* As the core element of a security strategy, directory services must be designed to respond to organizational and business needs. The design of Active Directory, for example, is a process that should involve both the IT and human resource departments.

- *Security subsystems:* Security must be prevalent at all levels of the IT infrastructure from people processes to server and WAN access.

Conceptual IT Services: A Recall

The list of conceptual services identified in Chapter 2 includes

- Responsiveness
- Reliability
- Confidentiality
- Security
- Networking
- Communications
- Tool access
- Information access
- Corporate data access
- Data storage
- Protection of information
- Three-tiered support

The Science of Cybernetics

Cybernetics is a science that specializes in decomposing systems in order to see how they work. In this science, it is possible to focus on minute details. Focusing on small details is good, but it is also important to be able to take a step back in order to view the whole picture when planning systems.

- *Input and output services:* It must be possible to produce and collect data in a variety of formats.

- *Internet services:* Internet services cover everything from the management of intranet applications to access to the Internet, to the software required at the client and at the server, to the development models required for intranet and extranet systems. This is one of the key elements of Microsoft's .NET approach.

- *System and object management:* The IT department must provide systems that manage all of the components, physical and logical, of the distributed environment.

- *Data repositories:* Storage is required for all corporate data.

- *Document repositories:* Storage is required for all corporate documents.

- *Data protection:* Backup and recovery techniques and procedures are required for both data and documents.

- *Transaction services:* Because data transactions are critical to an organization's business, the validity of these transactions must be protected at all times. Transaction services provide an additional layer to the processing of data. By verifying the validity of each transaction and committing it only when it is complete from end to end, transaction services ensure stability within the data.

- *Workflow services:* The information processes and departmental interactions must be supported by the system. In fact, the system must be able to assist and sometimes enhance the execution of workflow interactions. These services must also support document management processes.

- *Commercial applications:* The system must be able to provide the support of commercial applications. These applications can provide the corporation with best-of-breed systems and tool sets that support the corporation's business processes.

- *Corporate applications:* For business needs that are not supported by commercial applications, the corporation may require custom applicative solutions. These custom solutions can provide the corporation with tool sets that more directly support the corporation's business processes.

IT Services: A Summary

The list of services that IT must manage includes

- Physical components
- Operating systems
- Networking
- Communication
- Directory services
- Security subsystems
- Input and output services
- Internet services
- System and object management
- Data repositories
- Document repositories
- Data protection
- Transaction services
- Workflow services
- Commercial applications
- Corporate applications

When you map these services to the conceptual requirements of the user base, you can see that everything begins to fit together nicely. Because the categories listed previously do not cover the entire spectrum of the list of conceptual services, IT must provide additional services in the form of processes. To meet the conceptual requirements, IT must develop structures that support the following.

- *Responsiveness and reliability:* IT needs to ensure that all distributed systems are available on a 24/7 basis with little or no downtime.

- *Confidentiality:* In addition to security, IT needs to apply confidentiality processes.

- *Three-tiered support:* IT needs to support the organizational community's use of its services at every level. The responsibility for this support structure can be shared between IT and client departments, but IT needs to be the driving force behind this service.

Now that we have a list of potential IT services (see Figure 3.3), we need to create a "picture" of the components at both

Information Processing Tools	Corporate Applications (Intranet and Extranet)		
	Transaction Services	Workflow Services	Commercial Applications
Storage	Data Protection		
	Data Repositories	Document Repositories	
Distributed Services	Communications	Directory Services	Security Subsystems
	Input and Output Services	Web and Internet	System and Object Management
Networking	LAN		
	WAN		
Basic Services	Physical Components		
	Operating Systems		

FIGURE 3.3 The Structure of IT Services. IT services can be divided into the categories displayed here. This is a conventional map of technical IT services.

extremities of the architecture: the client and the server. Other architectural elements will come into focus as we examine the interactions between clients and servers later on. We'll also review how people interact at each end of the client/server spectrum, that is, how users interact as clients and how IT professionals interact as administrators.

Using a Structural Model

In order to better understand what is required for the architectural elements of PCs and servers, you can use an existing and well-known services model and modify it to suit the needs of distributed environments.

The International Standards Organization's OSI Networking Reference Model is a good source model to use because it is based on several principles. It describes networking between clients and servers through a series of layers, but each layer has its own set of functional services. Interactions between layers are based on using common services, and interactions are limited to the layers immediately adjacent to any given layer.

The service layers for network communications are

- Application
- Presentation
- Session
- Transport
- Network
- Data Link
- Physical

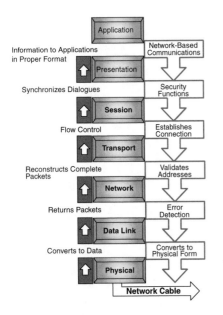

This image illustrates the OSI Networking Reference Model.

The illustration of this model displays the interactions between the different layers of the OSI model. This model has become a familiar one to most IT personnel today because it is at the base of all networking communications.

An OSI Networking Reference Model for PCs and Servers

It is possible to create a layered model for IT services based on the OSI Networking Reference Model. In this model, each layer offers a given set of services to the others. Each layer interacts with the others and each layer has a specific function. This layered model can be applied to the core elements of a distributed environment, PCs, and servers. It can also show the levels of influence each of the three key players (users, IT, and the organization as a whole) has over each layer.

In this model, we'll redefine OSI to mean "Open Systems Infrastructure." Our new model focuses on the service point of access (SPA), which is usually a PC or a server. We use the term "service point of access," because PCs and servers form a point of interaction between the network and a user. The content of an SPA can be divided into nine layers similar to those of the OSI Networking Reference Model. The content of each layer can be supported by the standardization, rationalization, and certification concepts.

The nine layers of the new IT Model for Service Points of Access include

- Physical
- Operating System
- Network
- Storage
- Security
- Communications
- Commercial Applications
- Presentation
- Corporate Applications

Each layer is defined in detail in the sections that follow.

Physical Layer

The Physical layer covers PCs, servers, cabling, printers, scanners, and all other physical components of the IT infrastructure. In terms of the model, standards are set for each. For example, the breadth of this layer for SPAs (PCs or servers) should cover

- Processor and speed
- RAM storage capacity
- Minimum RAM requirement
- Drive bay capability
- Minimum hard disk storage
- Networking components

Physical Layer Ownership

It is important to include the concept of ownership for each of the layers. As discussed earlier, ownership is shared between users, IT, and the corporation.

Two groups own the Physical layer: IT and users.

IT Standards = 10%

These standards outline the minimum components for either servers or PCs.

Specialized User Requirements = 90%

Task-based user requirements determine the additional components added to the base outlined by IT. For PCs, this means the inclusion of additional technologies such as CD players or writers, smart card readers, biometric recognition technology, and so on. For servers, this means additional technological components required to meet the server's specific function.

- Power management (ACPI)
- Video capability
- Additional input and output components (CD readers and writers, DVD players, keyboard, mouse, USB, IEEE 1394, and so on)

For PCs only, the SPA should cover

- Maximum hard disk storage

Operating System Layer Ownership

Two groups own the Operating System layer: IT and the corporation.

IT Standards = 50%

These standards outline the OS type and version, service pack and hot fix levels, as well as driver libraries.

Corporate Requirements = 50%

The corporation outlines what is required from the OS by defining business needs and opportunities.

Operating System Layer

The Operating System layer covers primarily PCs and servers, but it is also important to ensure proper levels of other operating systems (such as those within routers) in order to increase the degree of interoperability between physical components. For PCs and servers, this layer should include

- Windows OS (preferably Windows 2000 or higher)
- Appropriate level of service pack and/or hot fixes
- Manufacturer-certified drivers for all peripheral equipment
- All dynamic link libraries (DLLs) required to support corporate applications (includes runtime versions of libraries such as Visual Basic, Microsoft Access, and Visual Studio)
- Corporation-wide OS complements such as typefaces, regional settings, and so on

Networking Layer Ownership

Two groups own the Networking layer: IT and the corporation.

IT Standards = 50%

These standards outline the structure of the services offered by the layer and how they will be administered.

Corporate Requirements = 50%

The corporation outlines what is required from the network by defining business needs and opportunities.

Networking Layer

The Networking layer covers all of the components that tie the network together, including

- *Unique networking protocol:* This protocol should be TCP/IP.
- *LDAP directory structures for Windows 2000:* This component is a standard Active Directory structure for all domains, groups, and organizational units that control what users "see" on the network.
- *Unique object naming structure:* All network objects, PCs, servers, printers, and file shares should have a unique naming structure.
- *Unique scripting approach:* All scripts should be unified and should be based on a single scripting language.

- *Certified scripts:* All scripts should be code-signed[2] to ensure validity.

- *Legacy system access:* A unique set of components should be used to access legacy systems. This set of components should focus on the underlying networking layers that are required to establish links with the legacy systems.

- *Remote access and virtual private networking:* This layer should include all components for either remote access or virtual private network access to the corporate network and any other external system required by users.

- *Remote object management:* Every component required on the end-point object, such as a PC for remote management and administration, should be part of this layer because the network is what ties the distributed system together. With the advent of Active Directory and the control it offers over PCs, this layer now includes networking client drivers. It should also include drivers for PC management (for example, SMS and DMI) and drivers for logical object management, such as corporate programming components or programming support technologies.

Storage Layer

With the advent of the new storage area networks,[3] the Storage layer extends to cover

- *Physical components:* These components include SANs, disk subsystems, network storage systems, and backup technologies.

- *Storage software:* These systems must administer and manage storage elements.

- *File services:* For Windows 2000, file services include Distributed File Services, a technology that integrates all file shares into a single, unified naming structure, which makes it easier for users as well as replication technology to provide fault tolerance in a distributed environment.

Storage Layer Ownership

Two groups own the Storage layer: IT and the corporation.

IT Standards = 50%

These standards outline the storage type and its supporting technologies.

Corporate Requirements = 50%

The corporation outlines what is required from storage by defining business needs.

---

2. *Code signing* means inserting a valid corporate public key infrastructure certificate within the script code. This certificate can be recognized by network objects such as PCs and thus ensure that only validated scripts can run in the network.

3. *Storage area networks* refers to a substorage system that is separate from PCs and servers. This is a complete unit whose sole purpose is to store data and documents.

"Blackcomb" Objectives

One of Microsoft's objectives for Blackcomb, a future version of Windows, is a unified storage system for all data. It is a considerable undertaking, but one that will greatly unify the storage layer if it works.

- *Indexing services:* All data must be indexed and searchable.
- *Databases:* Because data has many forms, the Storage layer must support its storage in any form.
- *Transaction services:* The Storage layer should control transaction services because these services validate all data stored within databases.
- *Data recovery practices and technologies:* All data must be protected and recoverable.
- *File structure:* The file structure of all storage deposits, local (on the PC) and networked, must use a single, unified structure. This structure should support the storage of both data and applications.
- *Unified storage:* If at all possible, implement a unified storage technology that enables users to store rich data in many formats under the same structure. Microsoft Exchange 2000 is an example of this type of technology. It enables the unified storage of documents, graphics, videos, sound clips, electronic mail messages, and electronic forms, all within a single, unified virtual storage space.

For PCs, this layer should also include

- *Data replication technologies:* Data that is stored locally on a PC to enhance the speed of data access should be replicated to a central location for backup and recovery purposes. For Windows 2000, this means putting in place an offline storage strategy, part of the IntelliMirror feature set.
- *Temporary data storage:* The PC disk drive should be used as a cache for temporary data storage in order to speed up PC performance.
- *Single, unified tree structure:* All PC disk drives should have a single, unified tree structure so that users do not have to relearn it. In addition, all PC management tools should be stored as subdirectories of a single, hidden directory.

Security Layer Ownership

Two groups own the Security layer: IT and the corporation.

IT Standards = 50%

These standards outline all of the IT security practices and supporting technologies.

Corporate Requirements = 50%

The corporation outlines what is required from security by defining business needs.

Security Layer

The Security layer includes a variety of elements aimed toward the protection of corporate business assets.

- *Ownership of IT assets:* A security strategy outlines ownership levels within the IT infrastructure. If a person is the owner of a PC, he or she is responsible for it in any way he or she deems fit. But if the corporation is owner of an asset, employees must follow unified rules and guidelines concerning security.

- *User profiles:* Each user should have a personal profile that can be stored centrally. This central profile can be distributed to any PC used by the person.

- *Group policy:* Group policies enable the unification of security approaches within a distributed environment. By applying security through policies, IT departments ensure that settings are the same for any given set of users.

- *Access rights and privileges:* Each individual user should be given specific access rights and privileges.

- *Group management:* Wherever possible, this should be done through the use of groups.

- *Centralized access management:* All security parameters for the corporate IT system should be managed centrally through unified interfaces, if at all possible.

- *Nonrepudiation technologies:* Every user of the system should be clearly identifiable at all times and through every transaction. For Windows 2000, this means implementing a public key infrastructure for the distribution of personal certificates.

- *Internal and external access control:* Access to the corporate network should be controlled at all times. This includes all technologies that assist access control, such as proxy or firewall agents, SecurID technologies, smart cards, biometric recognition devices, and so on. For Internet access control with Windows 2000, this means implementing Microsoft Internet Security and Acceleration Server.

For PCs, the Security layer should also include

- *Confidential storage:* Because PCs (especially portables) are not permanently tied to the network, it is important to ensure the confidentiality of any data stored locally. With Windows 2000, this means implementing the Encrypting File System (EFS).

Communications Layer Ownership

Three groups own the Communications layer: IT, the corporation, and users.

IT Standards = 40%

These standards outline the communications technologies and supporting practices.

Corporate Requirements = 30%

The corporation outlines what is required from communications by defining business needs.

User Requirements = 30%

Users need feedback outlets. These outlets must be part and parcel of the Communications layer.

Communications Layer

The Communications layer deals with elements of the network that support communication in all of its forms.

- *E-mail:* E-mail technologies include a variety of electronic communications tools, such as electronic mail, chat, discussion groups, public folder sharing, and more. For Windows 2000, this means implementing Microsoft Exchange Server.
- *Workflow technologies:* Because workflow is a form of communication and is often based on electronic mail technologies, it must be part of the Communications layer.
- *Shared conferencing:* Virtual conferencing is a tool that should be available to users to reduce physical meeting costs. For Windows 2000, this means implementing Windows Media Services.
- *Internet browser:* Browsing technology is becoming a strong communications tool inside and outside the corporation. This includes all associated subtechnologies, such as media players and script engines.
- *Broadcast technology:* IT, the corporation, and individual departments must have a means of communicating vital and timely information to their respective users. This requires some form of broadcast technology.
- *Group and individual agenda scheduling:* Because time management often incurs a communications process, the network should support agenda scheduling at individual and group levels. The latter should include the ability to schedule objects such as meeting rooms, video projectors, and so on.
- *Legacy system access:* If terminal emulation is a requirement, this layer should include a single, unified terminal emulator application.

Commercial Tool Layer

This layer includes two principal elements.

- *Common Commercial Applications:* This sublayer consists of tools in use by the entire user population.
  - *Information production tools:* Office automation tools such as Microsoft Office should be available to every user that requires their use. These tools are normally deployed to every IT user. Deployment of these tools

includes both client and server components if the automation suite is to be controlled centrally.

- *Generic graphics tools:* All users should be able to illustrate concepts and create drawings. Illustration is a basic communications tool and it must be part of a core set of PC tools. On servers, this means implementing technologies that enable the indexing and sharing of illustrations and drawings as well as the capture of configuration information.
- *Service packs:* All common tools should be regularly updated as service packs are released for them.
- *Lexicons and vocabularies:* All lexicons and corporate vocabularies should be unified to ensure the consistency of all output.
- *Commercial utilities:* All common commercial utilities such as Adobe Acrobat Reader, WinZip, and Internet search engines that are required by the entire user base should be included here.

• *Specialized Commercial Applications:* This sublayer consists of tools in use by smaller groups within the user population. This part of the layer is called the Horizontal Software Layer (HSL), because these tools are in use by personnel from various departments and their distribution cuts across multiple departments. The content of this sublayer is listed below.

- *Restrained clientele applications (RCAs):* Commercial tools required by the user base, but not by all users.
- *RCA management by function:* Wherever possible, RCAs should be managed and deployed through functional groupings. For example, the group Web Publishers should all have access to Microsoft FrontPage.
- *Functional regroupings:* The corporation should endeavor to categorize RCA commercial software users by function as much as possible. This should enable the corporation to identify groups of applications required by each IT role within the corporation. Examples of IT roles include generic user, information worker, application enhancer and database developer, project manager, report generator, and so on. Limiting the number of these groups will simplify system administration. Of course, it must be tempered with cost. There is no sense deploying a software application to someone who simply doesn't need it.

Commercial Tool Layer Ownership

Ownership identification for this layer is divided into two parts: common applications and specialized tools.

Common Applications

Two main groups own the Common Applications layer because it is common to all systems:
    IT and the corporation.

IT Standards = 50%

These standards outline the common commercial toolkit and its supporting practices.

Corporate Requirements = 50%

The corporation outlines what is required from common tools by defining business needs. Here the corporation also represents users because common user needs are taken into account.

Specific Applications

Three groups own the Specific Applications layer: IT, the corporation, and users.

IT Standards = 50%

These standards outline the common framework supporting specialized tools.

Corporate Requirements = 30%

The corporation outlines what is required from special tools by defining business functions—roles each user plays within the IT community.

User Requirements = 20%

Users outline their functional and specific needs to the corporation within corporate guidelines.

Presentation Layer Ownership

Three groups own the Presentation layer: IT, the corporation, and users.

IT Standards = 40%

These standards outline the presentation approach and supporting practices.

Corporate Requirements = 30%

The corporation outlines what is required from presentation by defining its mission and business strategies for meeting it.

User Requirements = 30%

Users outline personal requirements that fit within the standard framework and business requirements.

User Interface Design

You can find excellent coverage of what is required when designing a Windows user interface in Volume 2 of *Microsoft Win32 Developer's Reference Library*, which is available from Microsoft Press.

You can also browse articles on the subject at the MSDN Online User Interface Center (http://msdn.microsoft.com/ui).

Corporate Desktop Design

We'll discuss the specifics of corporate desktop design in Chapter 4.

Presentation Layer

The Presentation layer is the interface layer. For users, it most often involves the desktop. For IT, it involves the administrative interfaces for all PCs, servers, and services.

One of the advantages of Microsoft Windows is that its design is based on one principle: common user access. This is a defined set of rules that lay out how people interact with PCs. It defines menu interfaces, keyboard shortcuts, and mouse movements, and sets standards for their method of operation.

Users who are familiar with Microsoft Word, for example, have since its inception in the early 1980s used the same set of keyboard shortcuts. None of these users has had to relearn any basic keystroke since the program first became popular.[4]

The advantage of Microsoft's common user access approach is that there is a standard interaction mode within Windows' own Presentation layer, but corporations should move beyond the default Windows desktop and specifically enhance Windows' defaults with their own desktop designs.

On the PC, the Presentation layer should include

- *Desktop design:* The desktop should offer a single, unified design to all users. All users should be familiar with this design because it is the default design activated at any new logon within the network. This design should be divided into specific desktop zones that each contain unique information.

- *Local versus central desktop control:* Users should be aware of the elements they are allowed to modify within the desktop design.

- *Active Desktop:* Windows 2000's Active Desktop brings Internet technologies directly to the PC desktop. The information displayed on each desktop can be categorized by group. This means that all financial employees can have the finance department's Web page displayed on their desktop at logon while systems administrators can have a support Web page applied automatically at logon on any system.

---

4. This isn't absolutely true. Microsoft did change the Save As function from F2 to F12 at some point to bring it in line with other Office applications, but no other keys where changed.

- *Common shortcuts:* All basic shortcuts on the desktop should be the same on all systems within the system category. For PCs, it should be one thing; for servers, it should be another.
- *Common menus and Quick Launch areas:* All tool access should be standardized and all menu subcategories should be reduced as much as possible. When applications install, they tend to install a series of extraneous shortcuts such as "Visit our Web Site for Free Offers." These shortcuts are not required within the corporate network.

On the server, the Presentation layer should include the same approaches as on the PC, but with an administration focus. Thus, administrative and troubleshooting tools would be displayed in the menus instead of the productivity tools on the PC.

Corporate Tool Layer

This layer includes mission-critical tools and processes. It is dubbed the Vertical Applications layer (VAL) because its user base consists of specific departments. User bases are vertical because they are all contained *within* a department.

- *System role:* Each system, server or PC, should have a defined system role, including security and directory servers, PCs as networked access points, application servers, storage systems, and so on.
- *Departmental groupings:* All departments need to track their users and provide them with appropriate corporate tools through departmental groupings.
- *Application development:* Proper toolkits should be made available to all business functions of the enterprise. These toolkits should be based on all of the standards outlined in all of the underlying layers.
- *Confidentiality of information:* Departments must be able to ensure proper access control for centralized corporate systems.
- *Support to the mission:* In addition to mission-critical applications, this layer includes all tools that provide support to the mission, including financial and administration systems.

Corporate Tool Layer Ownership

Three groups own the Corporate Tool layer: IT, the corporation, and users.

IT Standards = 40%

These standards outline the common framework supporting corporate tools.

Corporate Requirements = 30%

The corporation outlines what is required by defining its mission and the business strategies designed to meet its mission.

User Requirements = 30%

Users outline personal requirements that fit within the standard framework and business requirements.

This image illustrates the new model for PCs and servers.

A Complete Model

The layered approach to IT services provides a simpler model to follow than the traditional approach because it is familiar.[5] By dividing each level of IT service into nine layers and identifying which forces influence the design and conception of each layer, you begin to see people, PC, and process interactions at a more basic level—that of technology.

Graphically, the new model for PCs and servers represents a design that is very similar to the OSI Networking Reference Model with the addition of two layers. This model begins to demonstrate how you can construct and present IT technologies in understandable ways. But much about these technologies is not represented in this type of diagram. A separation of all the services into layers enables you to imagine that each layer can be independent with its own management model and its own approaches to service delivery.

In fact, even though all of the layers are related to each other in specific ways, some have a stronger relationship than others. By examining the clientele of these layers, you can begin to see that some layers need to be delivered to the entire user population, whereas others have restrained clienteles. The clientele factor must then influence the nine-layer model—it needs to transform the model to divide it into sections that are meant for everyone and others that are meant for specific groups of users, as shown in Figure 3.4.

We need to restructure the model into an illustration of five basic layers. This new diagram can now serve as a map for system design and deployment.

The IT Model for Service Points of Access

As you can see in Figure 3.5, the final IT Model for Service Points of Access (both PCs and servers) regroups several layers into a single unit because all of the elements within this core set of services, or *service kernel,* are common to all systems.

The Commercial Tool layer must be divided into three parts.

---

5. As mentioned before, the OSI Networking Reference Model is familiar to most IT professionals.

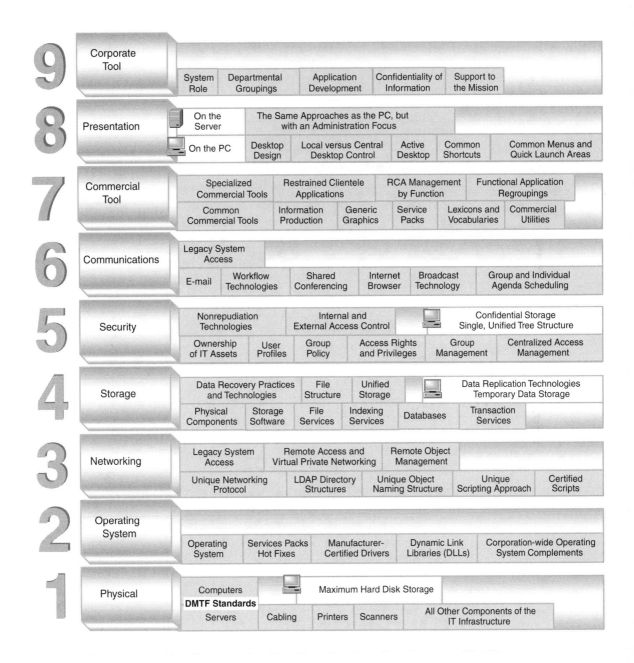

FIGURE 3.4 A Complete Model for SPAs. This image illustrates the nine layers of the IT Model for Service Points of Access. Items including the PC icon (🖥️) focus on PCs only.

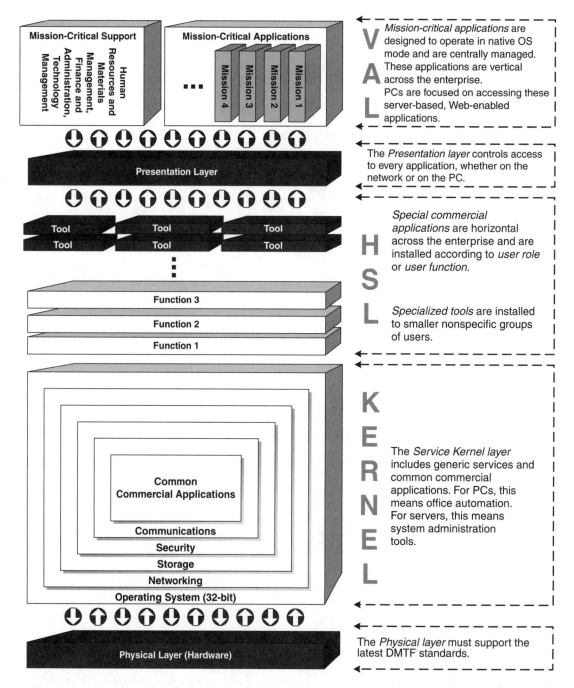

FIGURE 3.5 The IT Model for Service Points of Access. This image illustrates a complete model for the design of a SPA.

- *Common Commercial Applications:* These tools are mostly focused on office automation suites and any other common tool for which the corporation has a corporation-wide license or for which there is no fee.

- *IT Role Applications:* Instead of providing a set of tools to every corporate user, this section provides a set of common tools to a given *IT function* within the corporation. For PCs, these functions should include the following:[6]

  - Generic user[7]
  - Information worker
  - Management and management support
  - Professionals (financial, administrative, legal, and so on)
  - Application enhancer[8]
  - Web/intranet editor
  - System developer
  - Systems or security administrator
  - Systems and user support
  - The functional role is slightly different for servers. Here the functional role focuses more on the server's role than on the user role. As a result, for servers you will have roles that are defined by the type of software they run and the type of service they deliver. Two main categories are outlined here.
  - *Identity management servers:* These servers are the core identity managers for the system. They contain and maintain the entire corporate identity database for all users and user access. For Windows 2000, these would be servers running Active Directory Services. This function should not be shared with any other unless it is a core networking function, such as name resolution.

IT Function Definition

The IT functions included here are probably similar to, but not exactly representative of, the ones within your own corporation. IT functions are defined by business objectives. If you are in a service field, these functions may well be similar to those in your organization. Nevertheless, it is important for you to validate whether the IT functions within your organization are the ones listed here or if you need to make changes to the list.

---

6. A sublayer for mission-critical users is not defined here because it is addressed through the Corporate Applications layer.

7. No sublayer is given to generic users because the service kernel, which includes common commercial applications, covers their needs.

8. The role of the application enhancer is to automate processes within office automation suites as well as to develop localized database tools.

The Global Architecture

The Global Architecture designed in Chapter 2 will help you identify what you need to put into each one of the SPA Object model's layers.

- *Application servers:* These servers provide application services to the user community. Windows 2000 examples are Exchange Server, SQL Server, Commerce Server, and so on.

- *Specialized Commercial Applications:* The final sublayer of the Commercial Tool layer covers those applications in use by specialized groups within the organization. These applications simply do not fit within specific functions or they have a functional population that is simply too small to warrant the association of a functional group.

The model is left with five layers, some of which include sublayers:

- Physical

- Service Kernel

- Common and Specialized Commercial Applications (or the Horizontal Software layer)

- Presentation

- Corporate Tools (or the Vertical Applications layer)

At the core of this model is the concept of standardization, specifically within the Physical and Service Kernel layers. Remember, standardization does not mean reduction—it simply means doing everything in a single, unified manner. This alone can reduce costs in the IT enterprise.

For the model to be fully supported and accepted, it is important for the organization to precisely outline what standards are in fact to be supported, how each affects the various players within the IT environment, and what the impact of putting a standard in place is expected to be. This exercise is crucial to the EMF design.

The IT Model for Service Points of Access clearly displays the mechanisms you can use to construct either PCs or servers so long as standards are available to support all of the processes that it identifies (see Figure 3.5). It can also serve to help you identify the interactions you can expect to occur between servers and PCs (see Figure 3.6).

Defining IT Standards

You can find a list of standards that can be used in most IT organizations in Appendix B. It supports the elaboration of your own IT standards.

The Benefits of the IT Model for Service Points of Access

Using a single model for the outline of technical services provided by both PCs and servers has several major

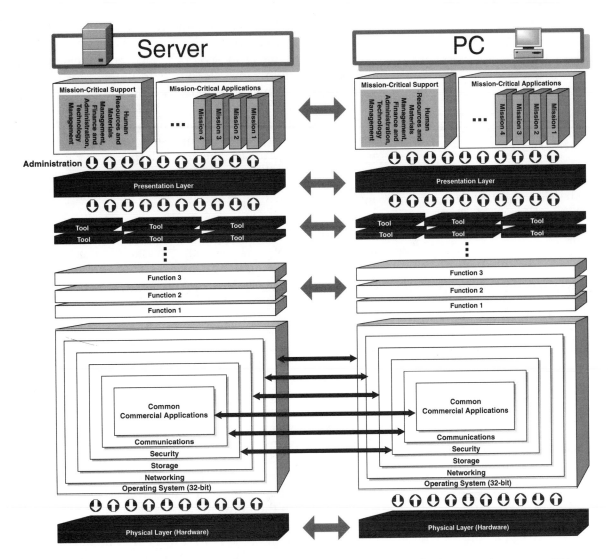

FIGURE 3.6 Interactions between Client and Server SPAs. By designing both PCs and servers as SPAs through a unified model, it is easy to see their levels of interaction.

advantages. First, by using layers and specifically including a Presentation layer, the model forms the framework for people, PCs, and process interactions within a Windows distributed environment. Second, the model outlines that there should be no difference in the approaches you use to manage and maintain SPAs (PCs or servers). Third, the model outlines how you can construct both servers and PCs. Finally, the model outlines a framework that will enable the systems to evolve with time.

In Chapter 1, we proposed that in an ever-changing world the only way to achieve stability is to prepare for change and manage change situations. The unified IT Model for Service Points of Access brings a degree of stability to IT services because it is ready for change at all times. In Chapter 4, we will outline the administrative approaches that must be put in place to manage both this model and standardization guidelines.

In addition, each of the five major layers of this model provides specific benefits.

Standardizing the Physical layer ensures that the organization has modern tools to perform its IT tasks. It also ensures the control of obsolescence within the organization. In addition, reducing the diversity of hardware within the organization reduces costs because fewer drivers need to be maintained for each type of peripheral.

The Service Kernel layer will save the corporation the most because it provides the framework for the integration of basic SPA services into a single unit. This means that the organization can devise the technical content of each of its sublayers, the rules and guidelines governing them, and their personalization or interaction with other sublayers. This information can then be used to interactively create model systems that will serve as sources of installation for all PCs and servers[9] in the network.

Using new disk imaging technologies, you can capture the complete Service Kernel layer into a single disk image.[10] You can then deploy this image to every single point of access within the network to provide a single standard.

Disk imaging technologies mostly focused on PCs in the past. Because corporations have massive numbers of PCs compared to the number of servers, they tended to install servers interactively (though some use automated setups, at least) and reserve disk imaging for PCs only. This worked well except for Windows NT. Because NT did not support *plug and play*—the ability to automatically detect and install new peripherals—it was important for the corporation

Specific Content for PCs and Servers

You can find a list of the actual technical contents of each layer for both PCs and servers in Appendix D. It supports the elaboration of your own service kernels.

Disk Images

A disk image is an exact copy of the contents of a hard disk. If you take a disk image of your system today, you would have a backup of your entire system because it copies every single sector of a hard disk in order to re-create it on any other disk (which must be at least close to the same size or bigger than the original hard disk).

Disk images are very practical for the massive or recurrent preparation of corporate computer systems. But beware: You must ensure that everything is just right *before* you take a snapshot of the system. Otherwise, you will end up with a massive distribution of problems.

Today, both Symantec's Ghost and PowerQuest's Drive Image Pro offer the capability to manage images through *deltas*—differential images that can be added onto an original. These programs greatly simplify the disk imaging process.

---

9. With Windows 2000, the creation of model systems can also be automated through scripting as mentioned previously.

10. Windows 2000 introduces a more powerful system preparation tool that can be used to prepare systems for disk imaging.

to create a disk image for each and every model of PC within the network. Standardization on PC brands and types was an important way to reduce costs.

With the coming of Windows 2000, IT departments can focus on the creation of a single disk image for all PCs because Windows 2000 supports plug and play. In addition, Windows 2000's System Preparation Tool for Disk Imaging can force every new system to automatically detect new hardware the first time it starts. Thus, a single disk image of a PC SPA based on Windows 2000 can seed every single PC model in the enterprise.[11]

In addition, Windows 2000 supports the disk imaging of server systems. With the movement toward Internet services, the appearance of Web farms and host Web services will quickly increase the number of servers within the corporation. Staging or preparing these servers interactively, even with a set of printed instructions, can never ensure the standardization of these systems. Windows 2000 supports either scripted or disk-imaged server preparation automation. For the EMF, staging servers *must* be automated.

But automation is not the only requirement. Planning is essential because the new system will be distributed to all users. Here the corporation will need to identify the specific content of each sublayer using the guidelines described previously. Only corporation-wide software components will be included into the Service Kernel layer. At this stage, it is also vital to properly preconfigure the Presentation layer for the model system that serves as the source device before imaging.

The Horizontal Software layer contains all commercial applications that do not have a mission-critical role. It benefits from application rationalization and thus provides a single application for any given IT task. This layer, especially the Specialized Commercial Applications sublayer, can save time and money because applications are grouped as functional families of products that provide specialized services. Deployment of these applications can be performed through the assignment of the family of applications to specific groups of users or servers within the corporation.

Here, it is important that the presentation of all applications is similar—that all menu shortcuts are coherently stored

---

11. This is true so long as the PC's hardware meets the requirements of the Physical layer.

Knowing the Philosophy of a Product

Every new technology brings new features, often at all levels of interaction with the technology. It is important—even crucial—to ensure that all of the new features are understood before their implementation. But it is also important, especially for workflow and enterprise architects, to understand the *philosophy* of the new product. The product's philosophy should be taken into consideration during the conception of the Presentation layer.

For Windows 2000, we recommend reading *Introduction to Windows 2000 Professional* by Jerry Honeycutt and *Introduction to Windows 2000 Server* by Anthony Northrup, both published by Microsoft Press.

in the Programs menu, that extraneous shortcuts are removed (you don't want users to go on the Web for promotional offers, do you?), that all programs are stored within a unified disk structure, and that all saving procedures use the same default folder. These four elements begin to form the standards for this layer.

Next is the Presentation layer. If IT is a service, then this is the most important layer of the entire model. It is the single aspect of the system that users will use and interact with on a daily basis. It is therefore crucial to ensure that this layer specifically includes defined zones for all aspects of network interaction. Ownership of each zone must be clear and precise so users know what belongs to them on their system (in other words, what they can personalize). But presentation does not stop at the desktop: Every element of what users can see on a system should be the same.

The corporation saves money through the definite reduction in retraining if all hard disks, all desktops, all menus, and all display features are standardized on all SPAs, because corporate users will always be able to perform work on any given tool within the network. The corporation can train newcomers on corporate systems, not on how to use basic Windows.

In the Introduction, we wondered why PCs couldn't be like cars—why they didn't provide a single, unified interface to users. The Presentation layer is the answer. It will not make the PC interface as widespread as the car's, but at least within your internal network, all PCs will be the same.

The final layer, the Vertical Application layer, focuses on mission-critical business roles. Once again, it is the guidelines of the Presentation layer that tie this application layer to the entire system. Application deployment costs are considerably reduced because once again, families of applications can be deployed to specific groups within the network. But if this model is to work, the corporate applications must be designed according to the standards set out in its underlying layers.

Defining Targets for the EMF

Given all of the information collected to date, you have probably begun to realize that the EMF is a must. Armed with the Global Architecture; the basic principles; the new IT Model for Service Points of Access; the driving forces of standardization, rationalization, and certification; and the

QUOTE System; your next step will be to move to the deployment of the Framework within your IT organization. To do so, you will need to define targets. *Targets* provide summaries that help direct you when you put the methodology in place. The definition of targets will simplify the roadmap to the EMF.

Targets should cover the breadth of the organization, and as a result they are divided into three categories: the client, the network, and the organization as a whole.

Targets for the Client

- Design and put in place a single IT Model for Service Points of Access for PCs and servers that covers all basic services required by the organization.
- Include all generic software in use by the organization in the Service Kernel.
- Use active technologies (such as Active Desktop) to differentiate user clienteles into groups and provide them with specific services.
- Use a horizontal approach for commercial software delivery on all clients using distribution groups based on IT roles.
- Use a vertical approach for corporate software access on all clients using distribution groups based on departmental regroupings.
- Use a scheduled delivery approach to maintain the SPA at all times in the network. This should be at a rate of three deliveries per year, if possible.

Targets for the Network

- Put in place an EMF based on industry standards and best practices that provides a single, unified approach for IT interactions inside and outside the organization.
- Use a centralized Web-based model for mission-critical applications and support to the mission applications developed in house. This model should be based on specific services provided by the Service Kernel.
- Implement an application rationalization program and maintain it through software lifecycle management practices.

- Standardize all products used within the network—focus on integration capabilities and knowledge reuse during the standardization.
- Implement network management technologies to ensure that the distributed environment is always under control.
- Integrate industry standards such as the Zero Administration for Windows (ZAW) and Distributed Management Task Force (DMTF) recommendations within the EMF.

Targets for the Organization

- Put in place a permanent communications program with the IT user base to enlist their support for the EMF. This communications program should support feedback mechanisms.
- Introduce new processes for the selection and acquisition of commercial applications in order to provide continued support for the EMF.
- Redefine the IT roles and interactions of IT, users, and the organization as a whole in order to support the EMF.
- Remove all blocks to departmental interaction during the design, the continued use, the administration, and the evolution of the EMF.

Case Study
Standardizing SPAs for the PC

Organization Type	Public Sector
Number of Users	2,000
Number of Computers	2,000
Project Focus	PC and Service Kernel Standardization
Project Duration	1 Year
Specific Project Focus	Standardizing PCs to Reduce Support Costs
Administrative Type	Centralized

This organization used PCs at all levels of its enterprise. Its needs had grown exponentially because it served a public need that required strict record-keeping and direct interaction with its customers (the public).

Before the standardization project began, the organization was living a nightmare in terms of PC support. In fact, each user recorded more than 15 level-two service calls per year.[12] The support group had almost given up on level-one calls because there were so many of them. This was the cost of supporting diversity.

The organization initiated a standardization project based on a single, standardized SPA IT model like the one described in this chapter. After deployment of the new unified standard, the organization saw its call levels completely change. Calls at the first level of interaction began to diminish and changed from system problems to usage questions. Level-two calls tapered off to less than 2.5 per user, a reduction of more than 600 percent.

Standardization provides a given level of stability within an ever-changing IT world.

Using the QUOTE System

Because you completed the Question Phase and now have a sound grasp of the Understand Phase through the various models you have designed, you can begin the Organize Phase. In this phase, you will outline the solutions you intend to apply to your environment. Of course, it will be essential for you to validate each of these solutions before proceeding to a total deployment.

Because the targets identified previously outline *how* you implement your EMF, you are now ready to more precisely define what is required in several aspects of this implementation.

- Support processes for administrative practices
  - Software lifecycle management
  - Software and hardware certification
  - Presentation layer definition
- Standardized management processes
  - Administration practices
  - Development guidelines
  - Support tools and techniques

---

12. Level-two calls involve, at the very least, a complete service interruption.

- Preparatory processes
  - Inventory procedures
  - Component certification
  - Machine staging
  - Application deployment approaches
  - Implementation approaches
- Project management structures
- Communications programs for all levels of the organization
- Training programs for all staff levels
- Principles required to support the evolution of the Framework
- Each process represents a stepping stone in a planned and structured deployment that will put your EMF in place.

CHAPTER ROADMAP

Use this flowchart as a guide to understand the concepts covered in this chapter.

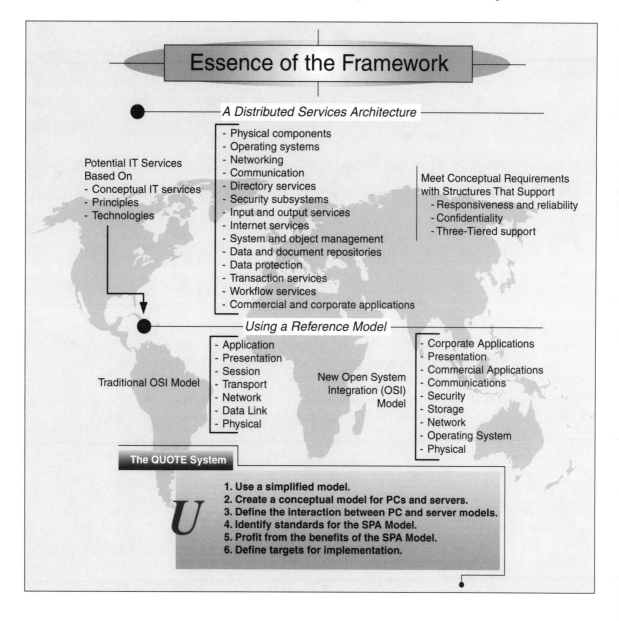

Essence of the Framework

A Distributed Services Architecture

Potential IT Services
Based On
- Conceptual IT services
- Principles
- Technologies

- Physical components
- Operating systems
- Networking
- Communication
- Directory services
- Security subsystems
- Input and output services
- Internet services
- System and object management
- Data and document repositories
- Data protection
- Transaction services
- Workflow services
- Commercial and corporate applications

Meet Conceptual Requirements
with Structures That Support
- Responsiveness and reliability
- Confidentiality
- Three-Tiered support

Using a Reference Model

Traditional OSI Model

- Application
- Presentation
- Session
- Transport
- Network
- Data Link
- Physical

New Open System
Integration (OSI)
Model

- Corporate Applications
- Presentation
- Commercial Applications
- Communications
- Security
- Storage
- Network
- Operating System
- Physical

The QUOTE System

U

1. **Use a simplified model.**
2. **Create a conceptual model for PCs and servers.**
3. **Define the interaction between PC and server models.**
4. **Identify standards for the SPA Model.**
5. **Profit from the benefits of the SPA Model.**
6. **Define targets for implementation.**

CHAPTER 4

Supporting Processes
Certification, Rationalization, and Presentation

The Cost of Saying "No"

One of the major IT issues in corporations today is the cost of saying no. Most organizations have designed their IT systems to respond to business and user needs. This is the right way to do it, but in an enterprise system, it is sometimes important to be able to say no to certain requests, especially if they seem unreasonable.

In determining the cost of saying no, you must review who has the right to deny requests. If this right is given to a technician within the corporation, does the proper level of authority come with it? When the technician says no, does the user accept this decision or does he or she "go up the ladder" until someone finally says yes and tells the technician to perform the work anyway?

The cost of saying no is evaluated by determining when the no is not accepted and how people try to countermand the decision. When putting in place an EMF, the entire enterprise must learn the value of no.

So far, several of the key processes required to put the EMF in place have already been introduced: standardization, rationalization, and certification. Standardization will be discussed in more detail in Chapter 5, because it covers the administrative processes required for the new IT environment.

This chapter focuses on the different solutions that are needed to support the EMF. If rationalization principles are not already in place in your organization, you're paying the cost of supporting diverse systems. But, before you can reap its benefits, you must understand why rationalization is required. For this, you need an understanding of software lifecycle management.

> ### The QUOTE System's Understand Phase
>
> We continue the Understand Phase with a look at the pillars supporting the EMF. The supporting processes we examine here will form the final elements of the initial solution we must put in place.

In addition, because we must all live with some degree of software diversity no matter how stringently we apply rationalization principles, you'll need a backup plan: the certification program. This is the program that will provide the most stability on all SPA objects.

And finally, because stability, reliability, performance, and productivity are the ultimate goal, we will cover the Presentation layer in more detail. This will help you understand how you can use active technologies to deliver and manage personalized environments on every SPA object. After all, meeting user needs to fulfill business goals is the first and foremost requirement of any IT system.

Rationalizing the Enterprise

Rationalization is the process of reducing diversity within the IT network. Because the purpose of an IT network is to provide an environment where users can collaborate on projects and share information, it is essential to ensure that information sharing is supported at every level of the enterprise.

Most organizations have already discovered the benefits of a single, unified office automation solution. Why? Because standard software tools can reduce costs dramatically while ensuring maximum content reuse.

Organizations that have standardized on Microsoft Office realize cost savings in automating setups, packaging, deployment, development and enhancements, training, and support. In many cases, organizations can build a single, automated setup file that can be personalized according to regional needs. In fact, with Office 2000 or XP, this is even easier to do than ever before because in these versions Office uses a deployment mode that supports a single source for setup that can be easily modified during installation by a transformation file. This transformation file includes anything that may be particular to a specific group within large organizations such as regional settings, localized dictionaries, group templates, and more.

The question becomes, "If you have standardized on office automation and probably on an operating system, why stop there?"

Software Rationalization

For an example of the rationale used during this process, see the Case Study on PC software rationalization at the end of Chapter 2.

Microsoft Office Retraining

Microsoft Office owes its success to its uniform look and feel. Because all Office applications use the same menus, the same interface, the same Help engine, and the same keyboard commands, user retraining for each of the applications is minimized. In fact, studies show that almost 40 percent of Office learning is reused when someone goes from Word to Excel or PowerPoint. The rest focuses on the particular features of the product itself. For Word, it is word processing; for Excel, it is calculations; and for PowerPoint, it is illustration and presentations.

With the inclusion of the Microsoft Management Console (MMC)—a unified administration console for all .NET Server products—in Windows 2000 and XP, Microsoft brings the retraining concept from Office to systems administration.

The Effectiveness of Rationalization

If you started using IT technology in the Windows 3.*x* days, you've amassed a plethora of different products within your network. Most organizations have. As people moved from Windows 3.*x* to Windows 9*x* to Windows NT, they often spent an enormous amount of energy making sure these products continued to work in their networks (especially with NT!). Does the corporation profit from the use of a multitude of often incompatible products? Does the cost of supporting often obsolete software warrant its use?

The requirement for older software products often comes from the user community. Because everyone fears change to some degree, people like to continue using the tools they're used to instead of learning new ones. But if the EMF is truly for the enterprise, *everything* must be standardized. Thus, organizations should perform a software rationalization to reduce operating costs. The cost savings inherent in a rationalization soon overcome the costs of replacing and upgrading products.

Following are a few tips for performing a rationalization.

- *Get rid of multiple versions of the same product.* Many organizations use several versions of the same product. Microsoft Office is an example. If you've invested heavily in application development with an earlier version of Office, or worse, if your users have developed their own tools with Office, you often don't consider changing these when upgrading to new versions. Some organizations even hold back Office upgrades because they fear the cost of redeveloping or converting existing applications.

- *Select products by function.* A single product should cover any given IT function. If you want to create technical artwork, use Visio. For illustrations, use CorelDraw or Adobe software. For development, use Visual Studio. Every IT function in your network should be provided by a single and unique product per function, unless a specific business requirement demands otherwise.

- *Provide conversion facilities.* If you are managing your IT investment by reducing diversity, you must provide your users with the ability to convert massive amounts of data.

- *Provide training.* One of the major advantages of rationalization is reduced training costs. By combining the

Standardizing Everything

In a .NET EMF, it is important to standardize as much as possible. .NET infrastructures by their very definition can support diversity within specific boundaries.

For a .NET Enterprise architecture to function at optimum capacity, you need to limit diversity as much as possible—not in the variety of your solutions, but in the tools you use to deliver them.

once diluted support budgets of multiple applications, you can finally provide standard training for non-traditional products.

- *Implement software lifecycle guidelines.* Software must be managed within the network. To do so, use the guidelines outlined in the following sections.

Rationalization Costs

There are costs associated with rationalization. When you convert from four or five drawing programs to a single program, you need to retrain users, convert their data, and acquire new licenses for the selected standard. Each incurs costs, but there are cost-reduction strategies.

- Most manufacturers offer competitive upgrade programs. These enable you to trade in your old product licenses to the new standard at a reduced price. In many cases, the cost savings for license acquisitions can range from 40 to 70 percent.

- Several firms market conversion tools. Most good ones include powerful conversion filters into their products. Two conversion strategies are possible: convert as you go or perform batch conversions. Both have their place, but the selection of one or the other depends on your needs.

- User training programs can be performed at reduced costs. Retraining for new products often implies learning how a particular product works rather than relearning everything about the function of the product. If your training programs are focused on the *difference* in the product interfaces, you can greatly reduce the amount of training required.

Software Lifecycle Management

All software has a lifecycle. It begins from the moment the software development project is initiated by a manufacturer until the moment the software is retired from the marketplace. For user organizations, the lifecycle focuses more on when it is acquired, when it is deployed, how it is maintained and supported, and when it is retired from the network. Figure 4.1 illustrates the industry adoption process for the manufacturer's product.

Batch File Conversion

Many organizations opt for batch conversions because in many cases it is impossible to search within other document formats. For example, if you convert from Micrografx Draw to Microsoft Visio, it is difficult to use Visio to search within Draw's document format.

If document reuse is a priority, you will need to perform batch conversions.

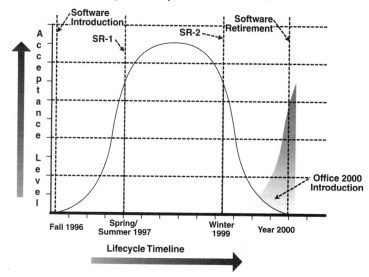

FIGURE 4.1 The Lifecycle of a Software Product. During the
lifecycle of a software product, the manufacturer releases several
corrective updates. Organizations that adhere to the product at
different times during its lifecycle must also manage these updates.
Then, once a new version is introduced, the manufacturer slowly
retires the product from the market. The corporation must do the
same within its own network.

During its lifecycle, most software will require corrections.
Manufacturers often call these *service packs* or *service releases*. If an organization adopts a software product before
these corrections are released, it will have to deploy the
service pack or service release in addition to the deployment
of the original product during that product's lifecycle. Figure
4.2 illustrates the corporate software lifecycle.

In addition, software, especially operating systems, tends
to be tightly bound to the capabilities of a hardware platform.
For example, if you use Windows NT and continue to buy
new systems today, you probably realize some of this operating system's limitations. Your new systems come with hot
new technologies such as USB or FireWire ports, but you
simply can't take advantage of them because NT can't. This
alone is a justification for a move to Windows 2000 or XP.

Software tends to grow with hardware capabilities. You
need to keep up if you want to make the most of your IT
investments.

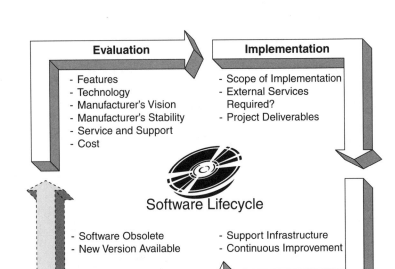

FIGURE 4.2 Corporate Software Lifecycle Management.
Corporations must manage an internal software lifecycle that
differs, but is related to, the software manufacturer's development
lifecycle.

Windows 3.*x*, Windows 9*x*, Windows NT, Windows 2000,
and Windows XP all include different capabilities in terms
of system integration. Software products built for these systems take advantage of these capabilities. This becomes
important when you discover that products designed for
Windows 2000/XP fully support the 32-bit capabilities of
advanced Pentium processors and can simply not be installed on any older version of Windows.[1] Lifecycles between operating systems and application software are closely
related. Figure 4.3 illustrates this relationship.

Defining Software Obsolescence

One major part of the software lifecycle is the definition of
its state of obsolescence. For corporations, *obsolescence*
should be defined as "a software product that is no longer
supported by the manufacturer, that is no longer available

---

1. Though most manufacturers create a single installation tool for multiple
operating systems, it is not the same product that is installed on NT, 95, or
2000.

on the market, and/or that is no longer required by corporate business processes."

In a Software Lifecycle Management Model, when a software product is obsolete, it must be either retired or upgraded. Upgrades can take the form of either the purchase of a new version of the same product or the deployment of a replacement product. As a result, an important part of the software management process is the software upgrade cycle.

To support the software upgrade cycle, you need additional processes and principles. You need to put in place standard methods that ensure you properly gauge value and benefits from a product upgrade versus its implementation costs. Cost/benefit analyses are crucial at this stage.

But these are not the only reasons to upgrade. User expectation is also a major factor. Software manufacturers do a good job of creating user desire through product advertising. IT managers are then faced with user requests for new versions of products. The Software Evaluation Model must also take these expectations into account.

The Cost of Obsolescence

Maintaining obsolescence bears its own costs. If an organization continues to use a product despite its obsolescence, it often faces hidden costs.

- Using a product for which the manufacturer has removed support means assuming these support costs internally.
- Older versions of software do not take advantage of newer operating system capabilities. If an organization decides to keep and maintain an older product, it is potentially limiting productivity.
- Older products lack functionality. They are often not integrated with newer companion products.
- Older versions can limit growth. If a corporate system is built around an obsolete product, the corporation can do little to improve its capabilities.

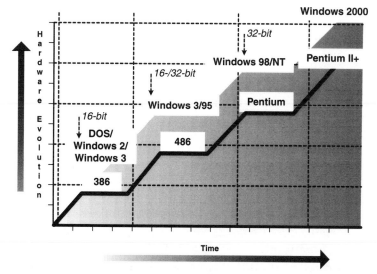

FIGURE 4.3 Hardware and Software Relationships. Software and operating system capabilities are closely related to hardware platforms.

Guidelines for Software Selection During Rationalization

Several factors influence the selection of software during a rationalization process, including

- *Purpose and scope:* What is the purpose of the product? Does it provide a unique functionality? How many users require the product?
- *Security and error protection:* How stable is the product? How secure is its data?
- *User-friendliness:* What is the product's learning curve? Does its interface operate like other products already in use? How much training is required?
- *Functionality:* What are the product's features? How easy are they to use? Do they respond to your functional needs?
- *Performance:* What is the speed of operation of the product? How realistic are the manufacturer's suggested minimum requirements?
- *Versatility:* How does the product compare to its competitors?
- *Compatibility:* How compatible is the product with older versions, with other products already in use, and with hardware platforms?
- *Installation:* How easy is the software installation process? Is it similar to other products in the network?

Positive response to all of these factors means that the product should be retained by the organization. Negative responses must be explained and documented.

Guidelines for Software Lifecycle Management

During the software lifecycle, four factors will initiate the software review process.

- *Software obsolescence:* The product is being retired by the manufacturer.
- *Projects:* A product is required to support business objectives and a project is launched to implement it.
- *New product versions:* New, feature-rich versions incite the organization to upgrade.
- *Corrective maintenance:* The current version has bugs that are repaired with a new version.

Given that these situations initiate a software upgrade, organizations should arm themselves with processes that

give them a measure of control over the software maintenance cycle.

Software Obsolescence Rules   The first thing to do
when implementing a software lifecycle management program (SLMP) is to outline the rules or guidelines that will
provide a framework for the program. These should include the following:

Rule 1: Coverage
Every software program that is in use in the network and
that has a clientele of more than ten users[2] should be covered by the software lifecycle.

Rule 2: Software Owners
Every software program in use should have a designated
software owner. This owner is responsible for managing
and maintaining the SLMP for the product.

Rule 3: Exceptions
Every software program that is included in the SPA kernel
is treated in an exceptional way because its evolution is
tied to the evolution of the entire kernel.

Rule 4: Obsolescence
Software obsolescence occurs when

- The manufacturer does not support the software any-
  more.
- Two newer versions than the one in use in your network are available on the market.
- The manufacturer announces that it is retiring a product
  from the marketplace.
- Upgrades for the SPA infrastructure require an upgrade
  of the product.
- The software product does not work on a new operating system.

The software upgrade cycle is mandatory for any software product that is deemed obsolete.

---

2. Ten users is the limit where cost exceeds benefits from the SLM program,
though some corporations opt to include *every* software product into the
program, no matter what the cost.

Rule 5: New Versions

Every new release of a product that fits within the guidelines of Rule 1 must undergo a software evaluation process. This process includes the following:

- Evaluation of software reviews published in IT industry publications
- Evaluation of the recommendations for use from consulting firms such as Giga Group, Gartner Group, and others
- Evaluation of the product's life expectancy predictions
- Preparation of an evaluation report recommending whether the software upgrade cycle should continue for this product

Rule 6: Software Update Request

Every software update request from any source must be accompanied by a valid justification for the business value of the move.

Managing Kernel Software   For the SPA kernel software, there are three additional rules.

Rule 7: Kernel Upgrades

Because the kernel is treated as a single, unified whole, upgrades or corrections for the kernel should be packaged together and released on a regular basis. The kernel deserves an approach that is different from other applications because it is critical to the business.

Rule 8: Corrective Maintenance

Because the kernel is critical to the operation of the network, service packs released for any product contained within the kernel *must* be applied. Before its application, though, the corporation should wait at least two months to ensure its stability as witnessed by the industry and through internal testing. If it is deemed satisfactory, this service pack should be included within the next kernel upgrade.

Rule 9: Software Interdependence

Every new software product released in the network must undergo a coherence evaluation. This ensures that the product is coherent with the components of the kernel and will not destabilize it.

Managing Nonkernel Software Three final rules apply to nonkernel software products.

Rule 10: Delivery Management

Because the introduction of a new product or a new version of a product affects the network, it should always be treated as a project with supporting budgets and processes.

Rule 11: Software Certification

Every software product that has a user base of greater than ten must undergo the software certification process. This process is described in the following section.

Rule 12: Software Lifecycle Management Program Evolution

The SLMP must be managed and periodically reviewed to ensure that its evolution keeps pace with software market trends.

Certification Processes

Now that you have reduced the diversity in your network, you must still arm yourself with processes that ensure stability. No matter how stringent your guidelines, you will always be faced with a certain amount of diversity. This is simply due to the breadth of functional requirements within any IT network. This is where the certification process comes into play.

The Evolution of Software

Software has changed over the years. In the days of DOS and Windows 3.*x*, software often consisted of a single, unified executable that simply required a copy from the installation disks to the hard drive.

Today, software is much more complex. Software manufacturers have changed their product design from single executables to the creation of *master programs* that orchestrate the operation of all of a product's components.

This evolution to master programs is an important development. In order to manage memory more effectively, software manufacturers have divided their products into a series of subcomponents loaded into memory only when users require it, which frees up memory for important tasks.

For example, when you're working with a word processing program, printing is not required all the time. So

---

Software Certification

For an example of the benefits reaped from the software certification process, see the Case Study at the end of Chapter 3.

Remember DOS?

DOS was a very limited OS. People who produced software for DOS had to worry about every single component of the computer—keyboard drivers, screen drivers, mouse drivers, and so on. This was because DOS provided very limited services to manage the PC. Software manufacturers had to provide every function if they wanted their product to work.

Windows changed all of this (though it wasn't the first program to do this on the PC—remember GEM?) by providing a single, unified environment to manage all of a PC's processes. With Windows, software manufacturers only had to ensure their programs worked with Windows interfaces. This enabled them to concentrate on their product's features.

Unfortunately, this caused another problem: DLL hell.

the printing module (often called a *dynamic link library,* or *DLL)* is only loaded when you want to print. Then, when printing is complete, the DLL is removed from memory to clear it up for more important functions.

In addition, because the OS provides most functions, software applications must often call upon system functions to work. Printing, for example, is provided by the OS, whereas the product only needs to know how to call upon the function (see Figure 4.4).

Facing DLL Hell

The problem with the DLL[3] approach is that it is now very difficult for software manufacturers to ensure that all the components that ship with a product are up-to-date. When software is installed on a system, the components it includes often replace existing components that may be more recent. This causes instability within the system.

For example, say Company A decides in 1998 to develop a new product. The product development cycle will take two years to complete before the product reaches the market. They ensure that in 1998 they have the latest and greatest systems and that every OS component is up-to-date.

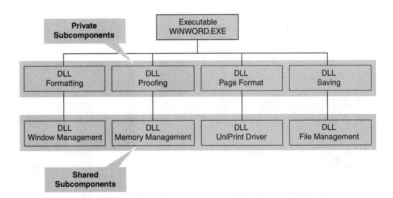

FIGURE 4.4   The Heart of an Executable. Software programs today include a master program component that calls upon either private or shared subcomponents as required during operation. Figure 4.5 illustrates how this interacts with the PC memory management process.

---

3. DLLs are not the only components that may cause conflicts and instability, but they are the most well known. Conflict resolution tools can identify all of the other types of components.

The problem arises when, while Company A is in development, operating systems continue to evolve. In 1998, Company A may have been using Windows NT with Service Pack 4. Meanwhile, Microsoft released Service Packs 5, 6, and 6a along with numerous hot fixes.[4] In February 2000, Microsoft released Windows 2000. In June 2000, Microsoft released Service Pack 1 for Windows 2000.

If Company A does not ensure that it keeps all of its systems up-to-date and does not perform compatibility testing of its product when it does upgrade, the product that hits the marketplace in July 2000 will definitely include components that are older than those that may exist on your system. This process is illustrated in Figure 4.6.

The software industry has taken steps to reduce the impact of this problem. For one thing, many manufacturers ensure that all new versions of a DLL support all of the functions of all of the older versions. So even if a product thinks it requires version 1, it will still work with version 2 because the new version supports all of version 1's functions—it is *backward compatible*.

Unfortunately, this does not work with every product. Some manufacturers do not provide backward compatibility for their components. If you want to run two conflicting products on the same operating system, you must figure out a way to make two versions of the same component work on the same system, otherwise known as *side-by-side operation*.

Table 4.1 describes the differences between backward compatibility and side-by-side operation.

As you can see, the DLL problem can become a major headache. It is often this very problem that causes instability in Windows systems.

Windows 2000 and DLL Hell

Microsoft is conscious of the DLL problem because they have received numerous support calls relating directly to it. This is why Windows 2000 includes for the very first time several technologies designed to avoid DLL hell, and Windows XP expands on these technologies.

The Fear of the Unknown

Like most of us, software manufacturers fear the unknown. Because they know their product works with version 1 of DLL A, they will tend to include this DLL in the installation routine of their product.

You *always* face a problem when you have already upgraded your systems to use version 2 of DLL A because during installation their product will replace your version of the DLL with their own.

It gets worse. Given that every product has dependencies on system components, you may have one product that requires version 2 of a DLL and a "new" product that requires version 1. What can you do?

---

4. A *hot fix* is a software correction that focuses on a single problem. A *service pack* is a collection of software corrections packaged into a single installation file.

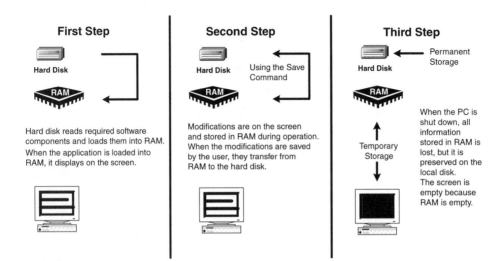

FIGURE 4.5   The PC Memory Management Process. Most users have difficulty understanding how rapid access memory (RAM) is related to permanent storage on the hard disk. Note that software developers use the DLL approach to reduce RAM usage.

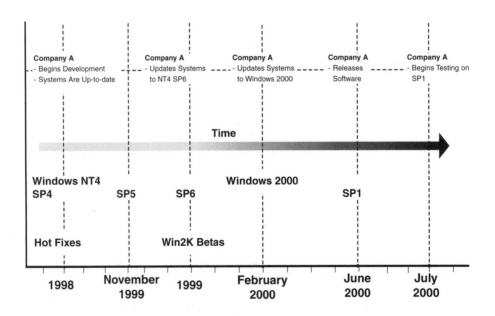

FIGURE 4.6   Development and OS Timelines. Software Company A begins its development cycle with updated systems. As time passes, the company updates its systems, but it is difficult to keep up. One of the ways Software Company A can keep up-to-date is to use beta versions of upcoming systems to test the compatibility of its solution.

TABLE 4.1 Backward Compatibility versus Side-by-Side Operation

Backward Compatibility	Side-by-Side Operation
Requires consistency of behavior and interface over time.	Interface and behavior change over time.
All versions can and must share state.	Requires isolation of state by version.
All applications use the "latest version" of the component.	Applications all use their own version of the component.
Applications support the activation of the component by its absolute name.	Applications call specific component names.
Service is straightforward.	Service is complex because care must be taken when changing system components.

System Security

Like Windows NT, Windows 2000 uses a 32-bit file system called NTFS. The advantage of this system over its predecessors is that every object stored in the system includes *attributes*. These attributes can contain security features—security features that are different for users, power users, and administrators. The greatest limitations are applied to users. Because users only operate the system, they only need read and execution permissions for every system component. In this way, NTFS "protects" system and application files by restricting access to those files.

In Windows NT, users were given too much leeway because software integration was not controlled effectively. Many software products would install into and require constant read and write use of the system directories. Giving users these rights would open the system to potential damage.

Realizing this, Microsoft released the Zero Administration Kit for Windows NT. This kit provided corporations with the tools to increase system lockdown to further limit user access. But this system was complex to use, and organizations often had to invest in its management.

With Windows 2000, Microsoft changed the nature of the NTFS system lockdown. They added further restrictions

Blocking Software Installations by Users

The security features of NTFS enable administrators to block users from installing software. Many users see this as a limitation of their "rights" on a PC. But this is not the case. Because a PC is a corporate asset that provides support for business processes, it must be stable. If a corporation puts in place a strategy for managing software stability within its network, it must restrict users from installing uncontrolled components on their PCs. This is simply because these uncontrolled components will most likely damage critical system components and destabilize PCs.

Conversely, users must have the right to choose the products they need for their job functions. By providing a self-serve center for approved and controlled products, the corporation meets both user needs and the corporate software management strategy.

In Windows 2000/XP, the user profile includes every element that is modifiable by the user.

Windows XP and DLL Hell

With Windows XP, Microsoft enhances the DLL hell management process with a new folder to store side-by-side DLLs and virtual DLL redirection. DLLs no longer need to register within the Windows Registry. Applications designed for Windows XP now include descriptive files that are read by XP's DLL Loader before loading the application. This means that in a pure XP environment, DLL hell may become a ghost of the past, but it will be some time before organizations can move to pure XP environments.

In addition, because it is no longer based on DOS, XP includes new virtual Windows and DOS compatibility environments, supporting even more applications than Windows 2000.

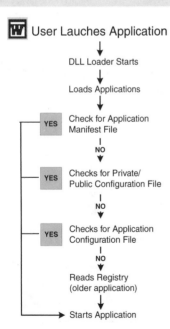

Windows XP goes beyond the capabilities of Windows 2000 to manage the DLL process as is demonstrated in this flowchart.

to users and changed the way applications worked with the OS. As a comparison, users in Windows NT have the same rights that power users do in Windows 2000. Today, users have significant restrictions within the operating system directories and within application directories.

Software that is designed for Windows 2000/XP does not install any component in the system directories. All of its components go into its own application directory. In addition, every component that is modifiable by a user (configuration settings, user preferences, and so on) is stored within the directories containing the user profile. Here users rule and can read and write to their heart's content. Moving modifiable components to the user profile is a good strategy because critical system and application files are protected for all users. If users damage something within their own profile, it simply needs to be erased and re-created.[5]

Side-by-Side DLL Management

In addition, Windows 2000 and Windows XP include side-by-side DLL management. This means that if two applications require the use at the same time of two different versions of the same DLL, Windows 2000/XP can load both into memory but into separate memory spaces. Side-by-side DLL management avoids conflict and relieves organizations from having to manage this process.

Windows System File Protection

Windows 2000 also includes System File Protection (SFP). This feature stores a backup copy of critical system files (within the DLL Cache subdirectory). A special agent is constantly watching the system directories. If, during the installation of a new application, a critical system DLL is replaced and the original system DLL is crushed, this agent automatically replaces the new file with the original and proper file.

In addition, SFP enables only the OS to update files within these directories.

Windows Installer

For software applications, Microsoft introduced the Windows Installer service.[6] This system service is designed to

---

5. Care must be taken during this operation because the profile also stores user preferences. These must be recovered after the profile has been re-created.

6. This service was first delivered with Office 2000, but it was refined with Windows 2000 and later, Windows XP.

assist in the control and management of the software lifecycle on Windows 2000/XP systems. For stability purposes, Windows Installer has the capability to provide the same type of protection to application files that the SFP provides for system directories.

Applications whose installation is integrated with Windows Installer include an installation database. This database is stored on the system during installation. Then, every time an application is launched, Windows Installer verifies its consistency based on the database settings. If everything is okay, the application starts normally. But if critical components are missing or damaged, Windows Installer searches the database for the location of the original installation file and repairs or replaces the component, and then launches the application normally. This process is called *self-healing*.

Windows Installer is not perfect, but it does provide some measure of protection for applications. But beware: For self-healing to work, installation files must *always* be available to the Windows Installer service. This means that installation sources must permanently remain available in the network.

Certified for Windows 2000/XP

With all of these changes, Microsoft has implemented a new approach for software manufacturers to integrate their products with Windows 2000/XP: the Certified for Windows 2000/XP initiative. A product that is certified for Windows 2000/XP supports the following features:

- Its DLLs are designed to be backward compatible.
- All of its operation files are stored within an application directory in the Program Files folder.
- Its installation process is integrated with Windows Installer (the extension of the installation file is then .MSI).
- It can be delivered to SPA objects (PCs or servers) through Windows 2000/XP's Active Directory service.
- All user-modifiable files are stored in the user's profile directories (within the Documents and Settings folder).

In fact, when a product is certified for Windows 2000/XP, the product will provide as much stability as is available from the OS.[7]

Viewing System File Protection at Work

To view the System File Protection (SFP) feature at work, log on to Windows 2000 as an administrator. Navigate to the WINNT\SYSTEM32 directory. Locate CALC.EXE (the calculator) and delete it. Empty the Recycle Bin.

SFP should replace it within seconds.

Windows Installer

Windows Installer does much more than just provide self-healing capabilities. It is a complete system designed to manage software on a SPA object. It can provide deployment through Active Directory, Windows 2000's central system and user management service. It can personalize installation settings through transformation files applied during setup. It can provide clean uninstallation of a software product. It can support the application of corrective maintenance (service packs) during the product's lifecycle.

---

7. "Certified for Windows 2000" means much more than just the features outlined here. For a complete description of the requirements, go to http://msdn.microsoft.com/certification/appspec.asp.

Hardware Certification

Windows 2000/XP includes a hardware certification program. You can find most of the products that have been certified for Windows 2000 in the HCL available at http://www.microsoft. com/windows2000/server/howtobuy/upgrading/compat/search/devices.asp. If the product you want is not on this list, ensure that the manufacturer provides a Windows 2000 driver for the product; otherwise, you may destabilize your systems.

Running Pre-Windows 2000 Software

Pre-Windows 2000 software works on Windows 2000. But, because of the changes in NTFS security and because these applications have a tendency to store components within system directories, you will need to "loosen" system security. Otherwise, users will not have the ability to execute these applications, because in Windows 2000, they do not have write access to these directories.

To run most pre-Windows 2000 applications with user accounts, you must apply the Compatibility Security Kit to your systems. To do so, run the following command:

secedit /configure /cfg ↵
  compatws.inf /db ↵
  compatws.sdb

This command will modify the security level of Windows 2000 to make it operate like Windows NT.[8]

Stabilizing Windows Technologies

The problem is that not all applications on the market today comply with Windows 2000/XP standards. Until they do, you will need to have pre-Windows 2000 applications coexisting with Windows 2000/XP–certified applications.

This may be cause for concern, but not if you apply a software management strategy within your network. Because the problem has been defined, you now know where to look for application and system instability issues.

Certifying Software: Managing DLL Conflicts

To face the DLL problem, you can implement a software certification process within your corporation. This process is based on the identification of all of the components you install on your systems and the repair of damaging applications. If an application includes a DLL that is older than the one stored in the system, you can take the following actions.

- Upgrade the DLL during the installation of the product. This works if the DLL is backward compatible.

- Move the DLL to another directory. This will take advantage of Windows 2000's side-by-side operational capabilities.

Other conflicts can arise, but their impact is not critical. They can be repaired on an as-needed basis. The entire DLL management process is outlined in Figure 4.7. Wise Solutions, Inc.,[9] a software manufacturer specializing in software delivery technologies, was the first to formalize this process.

Because the SLMP requires all products that have a user base larger than ten to be managed centrally, corporations must use automated techniques for installation. Installation automation is required because the corporation does not want users to be faced with configuration decisions during installation. Most products aimed at the corporate marketplace include technologies that enable preconfiguration of installation parameters. Windows 2000/XP applications au-

---

8. The ↵ symbol represents word wrap on the command.

9. You can find more information on Wise Solutions at http://www. wisesolutions.com/.

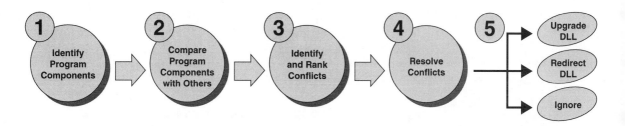

FIGURE 4.7 The DLL Conflict Management Process. Managing DLLs involves identifying conflicts and taking proper action.

tomatically include such a system because it is one of the functions of the Windows Installer.

In some cases, corporations will need to deploy and manage software that does not include automated setup technology. This is generally referred to as *software repackaging*. Software repackaging consists of taking a "snapshot" of the system before installation, performing and customizing the installation, and taking a snapshot after installation. A software-repackaging program records all of the changes and inserts them into an executable that automates setup.

These tools are useful, especially when the corporation needs to deploy internally developed software.

It is during repackaging that conflict detection can occur. Here the packaging tool inventories all of the packaged components. This inventory is stored in a database containing all of a system's components. The database is then checked for conflicts. If conflicts are detected, action can be taken to repair damaging components.

Proactive and Reactive Conflict Management Strategies

It is clear that with its new features, Windows 2000/XP improves stability. But for applications, it does so only for those that are certified for Windows 2000/XP. Older applications are not integrated with Windows Installer because their setup is not integrated into this service.

It is possible, though, to integrate older applications into the Windows Installer service at the repackaging phase. Every application that is repackaged using a Windows Installer–compatible packager will gain some, but not all, of the features of a Windows 2000–ready product. It will, for example, have self-healing, but it will not operate with simple user rights. It will also take advantage of Windows

Wise Solutions' Conflict Manager

Wise Solutions, Inc., offers a product called InstallManager. This product is designed to perform installation automation. Within InstallManager is a module called Conflict Manager. Conflict Manager uses a database to store all component information and also provides a Conflict Resolution Wizard to repair damaging components.

Lanovation Prism Pack Enterprise Edition

Lanovation was the first to introduce a single, integrated product that managed both DLL conflicts and created Windows Installer (MSI) installation files. Their product is very simple to use. There is very little training required, so long as technicians understand the concepts of DLL management and Windows Installer integration.

This product is definitely a boon to the software lifecycle and certification processes. More information is available at http://www.lanovation .com.

Managing Older Applications

Most organizations moving to Windows 2000/XP today will need to live with three types of applications.

- 8- and 16-bit applications from DOS and Windows 3.*x*
- 32-bit applications that are not ready for Windows 2000/XP
- Windows 2000/XP–certified applications

The latter are by far the most stable, but you need to wait for manufacturers to update their products.

In order to properly manage these applications in the network, use the following three installation directories:

- APPS16 (for DOS and Windows 3.*x*)
- PreWin2K (for older, 32-bit software)
- Program Files (for certified products)

Then migrate applications from the two first directories as you update them. You will be able to destroy these directories when they are empty.

Veritas WinInstall LE

WinInstall LE is located on the Windows 2000 Professional installation CD. It comes with a 60-day trial license.

Component Inventories

Eventually, all applications that want to make it in the Windows market will be designed for Windows 2000/XP. As a result, repackaging may no longer be necessary. But it will always be vital for organizations to inventory components. Nothing is better than knowing exactly what is out there. Then, if problems arise, you will at least know what you have.

Installer's reactive DLL management techniques (if the DLL is the same as another already loaded, load this one into a different memory space).

Several software manufacturers offer repackaging tools—for example, Wise for Windows Installer from Wise Solutions, Inc.; WinInstall LE or WinInstall 2000 from Veritas, Inc.; InstallShield for Windows Installer from InstallShield Corporation; and Prism Pack from Lanovation, Inc.

Using both repackaging for Windows Installer and repackaging conflict detection techniques enables corporations to be both proactive and reactive when designing Windows 2000/XP networks. These techniques proactively repair applications *before* they are deployed in the network. And, if some conflicts are missed and deployed anyway, they reactively support conflicts *after* deployment through the Windows Installer service.

A Certification Approach: Complete DLL Management

Introducing a certification process is not much more costly than managing software in traditional ways. Most medium- to large-sized organizations already have software repackaging facilities because they want to take advantage of central deployment strategies.

Identifying and correcting DLL conflicts while packaging means adding two additional processes to the traditional software repackaging approaches.

- Inventory components to identify conflicts
- Repair damaging components

These two processes fit very well into most packaging methodologies because testing is already covered (if a software is repackaged, its installation must always be tested before deployment). With conflict detection, testing changes slightly to verify if either the backward compatible or the side-by-side strategy is required. Figure 4.8 illustrates this process.

Using a Certification Center

In this process, the software repackaging center becomes a certification center. Its nature is permanent and must be staffed as such. Certification activities will include kernel

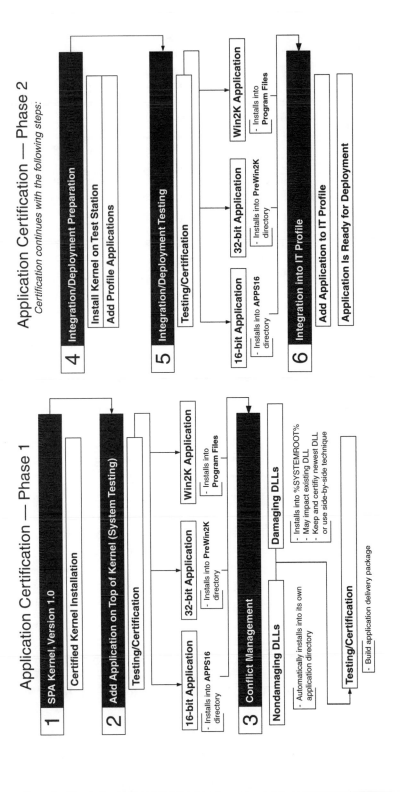

FIGURE 4.8 The Software Certification Process. The application certification process involves six major steps.

Deploying MSI Software in the Enterprise

Software deployment in a large enterprise is difficult because of all the different source locations you need to manage. It becomes even more difficult when you include self-healing capabilities. Self-healing means that the source of the installation must always be available. Each different site must have a different source address. This may be simple for SPA objects that are always linked to the network, but it is more complex for portables because they must carry the source files with them.

One of the best methods is to use a variable on the SPA object. Here's how it works:

1. Prepare all of your installation packages using a variable such as %Source%.
2. On the preparation systems, define this variable as the source of the installation (Set SOURCE=\\Server\Folder).
3. Define a variable on the SPA object. This variable can map to different locations on different SPA objects, but your installation packages all point to the same destination: %Source%.

For example, on a portable this variable can be set to a local, hidden partition on the hard disk; in a region, it can be a local server; in the certification lab, it can be the staging server; and at headquarters, it can be a central server.

However, if you are using Windows XP, all you need to do is redirect the software source URL.

management and software lifecycle management. Every software addition into the network must pass through this center. No deviation is allowed. The return on investment for the certification center is provided by the increased stability of software in the network. Payback is also evident in a significant decrease of support calls related to nonfunctioning software.

Certification Center Processes

Several processes support the certification center. The first is the software certification process. It includes the following steps:

1. *System testing:* Prepare the application for automated installation.
   a. Perform software configuration and installation process validation to determine if the installation fits within standards.
   b. Perform repackaging or package analysis. If the application is packaged to Windows 2000/XP standards, proceed with component inventory and conflict detection and resolution. If the application is not ready for Windows 2000/XP, repackage it, inventory components, and perform conflict detection and resolution.
   c. Finalize the package.
   d. Move on to system testing.
   e. Perform system tests.
   f. Document the installation.
2. *Integration/deployment preparation:* Prepare and test the remote installation of the application.
   a. Update the deployment mechanisms.
   b. Deploy on test systems along with profile contents.
   c. Update the documentation.
3. *Integration testing:* Test application cohabitation.
   a. Test the operation of the application within a complete user profile.
   b. Update the documentation and have it approved by the software owner.
4. The application is ready for deployment.[10]

---

10. There is an additional acceptance testing phase that will be covered later.

The next process is the kernel update process. This process singles out the kernel from any other software that is in use within the network. This is because the kernel is the only globally used component in the network. Because every user requires the kernel, its level of stability must go beyond that of other applications.

This means that the kernel must be updated on a constant basis. Because there are a number of different products covered, a change request and evaluation process must be put in place. This change request process uses the rationalization guidelines outlined previously to evaluate the validity of the request. If approved, the change is delivered in the next kernel update.

Given the rate of change in the software industry and the number of different software components that often reside in the kernel, it is essential to manage this process on a four-month basis at the very most. Waiting longer for update collection creates packages that are very unruly. Deploying more frequently is too expensive.

Figure 4.9 illustrates the kernel update process.

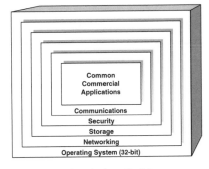

The kernel includes all of the components required for the operation of a basic SPA object. It is discussed in more detail in Chapter 5.

Rate of Updates

Three updates a year has proven to be optimal for the kernel in all of the organizations using this process to date.

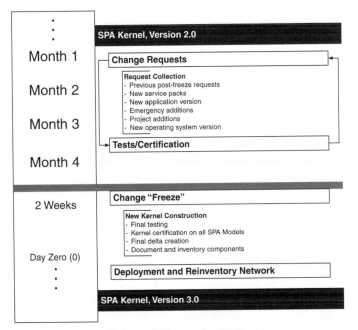

FIGURE 4.9 The Kernel Update Process. The SPA kernel update process should occur every four months. One month before release, a freeze is applied to change requests in order to allow update preparation.

Certification by Profile

Even with rationalization practices, organizations often have several hundred software products to support and manage in the network. Therefore, it is important to regroup applications by user type. These IT profiles[11] will include every application that is common to a group of users performing the same type of task. This regrouping by IT role or function simplifies certification testing (only those applications most likely to cohabit on a system will be tested) and deployment (applications are automatically deployed to users that fit the IT profile).

In addition to kernel updates, the certification center is responsible for software update validation and preparation. This means applying the same processes used with the kernel to every managed software product.

Though 90 percent of applications are managed because they have a population greater than ten users, it is also necessary to put in place standard procedures for the other 10 percent. Applications with less than ten users do not warrant certification because if they have conflicts, they do not impact many people. In addition, so long as they are designed to work with Windows 2000/XP, corporations can use the reactive approach to DLL management. Their installation can be manual, but it should be structured. Specific procedures for manual software installations should be put in place and monitored by the certification center. This is called the "less than ten" management process.

Finally, the certification process must support two additional situations: emergency updates and project requests. Both situations require a shorter timeline for deployment. If a fatal bug has been missed during testing and has been deployed by mistake, it is vital to perform an emergency update deployment. This deployment must have a very short timeframe because vital operations are nonfunctional.

In addition, when projects are launched, they often require newer versions of components or components that are not already in use in the network. This situation also requires a shorter timeframe. Figure 4.10 displays these processes.

All of the processes in the certification center help maintain stability within your network. These and the software rationalization processes must become part of your everyday operations if you want to profit from their benefits.

Certification and Consultant PCs

One of the questions you will be faced with when you implement your certification program is "What do you do with systems that operate in your network but don't belong to you?"

Continued next page

---

11. In some cases, user application profiles are called *software configurations* or *software configuration management*.

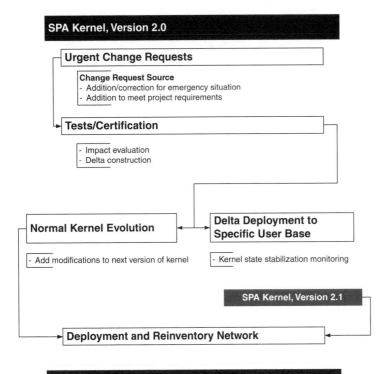

FIGURE 4.10 Emergency or Project Certification. The emergency or project deployment leads to incremental version updates of the kernel.

Concluded

It all depends. If the system belongs to a consultant and is used only as a productivity tool, the issue has less importance. If consultants want to manage their own PCs without certification, that is their issue and not yours.

But if the computer is connected to the network, you have some degree of control. The least you can ask for is that the computer use a secure OS that conforms to your corporate security guidelines.

The certification problem is compounded when consultants use their own systems to perform development for your network. If this is the case, these consultants are in a situation where they introduce components into your network. As such, their systems should conform *completely* to your certification standards.

Presentation Layer Management

The third supporting process is the Presentation layer management process. Because improved user experience is one of the goals of the IT Model for Service Points of Access, it is important to identify the technologies and systems that define the Presentation layer.

Defining the Presentation Layer

Recall that the Presentation layer is the interface layer; for users, it most often means the desktop. For IT, it means the administrative interfaces for all PCs, servers, and services.

Desktop layer ownership focuses on three owners: users, IT, and the corporation. This means that the desktop must be divided into specific areas, or *zones of ownership.* But before these zones can be designed, several principles must be defined.

Principle 1: Default Corporate Desktop

The default corporate desktop should offer a single, unified interface to all users. This desktop should be the default desktop created at any new logon—when new users first log on to their PCs, or when current users use another PC, they should be presented with a desktop that meets every basic requirement and that provides access to all of the productivity components[12] of the SPA kernel.

Windows 2000/XP has the capability to store an editable default desktop and generate it for every new user. Corporations should update this default desktop with their own customized versions before deployment.

Principle 2: Personal versus Corporate Zones

Because the PC is a corporate asset, it belongs to the corporation. The corporation needs to keep a measure of control over it. But because users are people and people have a sense of propriety toward their tools, users also need to have control over some portions of the desktop. Negotiations for this shared ownership are performed through extensive communications programs outlining the reasons for this division of responsibilities.

Reduced Training Costs

Providing a common desktop for all PCs uses the same principle that made Microsoft Office so popular. If the basic desktop interface is exactly the same for all users, retraining costs as users move from position to position within the corporation are greatly reduced.

Windows XP brings the power of desktop design to bear with a new interface that is completely customizable to organizational needs.

Communications Program

Chapter 8 discusses the specifics of a communications program.

---

12. For administrators, these should be all the administrative components of the kernel in addition to the productivity components.

Principle 3: Virtual Desktop

Using Windows 2000/XP's Active Desktop technology,[13] corporations can create and present *virtual* desktops to their users. In addition to conventional components on the desktop (icons, tool bars, menus), users can have direct access to intranet components based on who they are, which department they belong to, and which IT role they occupy.

Every department in the corporation can design a standard desktop page that includes tools, news, information access, and more, and have it directly displayed on each user's desktop when he or she logs on to his or her system. The desktop is deemed virtual because the content of these pages can change at a moment's notice and be automatically updated on all targeted desktops at the next automatic refresh sequence.

Now that you have the basic principles in place, you can begin the desktop zone design process. This process should aim to cover the following requirements:

- *Corporate tools zone:* The desktop should not be cluttered. Because Windows 2000/XP includes other, more practical areas for the location of shortcuts, only the most basic shortcuts should be on the desktop. These should include My Documents, My Computer, My Network Places, and Recycle Bin.

- *Personal tools zone:* Users should have the right to place additional shortcuts on the desktop because these are stored within their own profiles and do not affect others. But they should not be able to destroy any of the corporate items placed on the default desktop.

- *Common application access menus:* The Programs menu in the Start menu should be as clean as possible. Software tools should be grouped into types, and shortcut folders should be redirected during installation to these tool-type menus. All extraneous shortcuts, such as Uninstall or Register Now, should be removed. The menu should be clean because its role is to give quick access to common tools and stored access to utilities.

- *Quick Launch area:* Next to the Start menu, Windows 2000/XP offers the Quick Launch area. This area pro-

An example of the corporate tools zone.

An example of a corporate Programs menu.

---

13. Active Desktop displays Web content on the desktop. In addition, it enables users to display many more image types on the desktop, something all users appreciate.

Tool Groupings

Chapter 6 covers the methods used to identify tool ranking in your corporation.

The Screensaver Craze

People have always enjoyed using screensavers and wallpaper on their desktop. The advent of the Internet has made a wide variety of screensavers available. The problem is that because the most sophisticated screensavers require additional software to run, some of the products downloaded from the Internet need to install components before they can run. These components are renowned for damaging systems.

In certified environments, corporations cannot allow users to install these faulty products, especially when they require the deactivation of critical components such as virus scanning to work properly. Unfortunately, there are many such screensavers on the market.

Corporations should provide banks of approved screensavers for users to install. This lets users have their fun and maintains system stability.

vides one-click access to the tools for which it stores shortcuts. In addition, because this area is stored within the Windows taskbar, it is always available. This should be the preferred method of access for all the tools located on the system. For users, the Quick Launch area should include access to productivity tools. For IT staff, it should provide access to administrative tools.

As you can see in Figure 4.11, tools located in the Quick Launch area are grouped according to usage. First come the desktop, exploration, browsing, and research tools; then come office automation tools in order of usage; and finally come productivity tools that are required infrequently.

- *Wallpaper and screensavers:* Wallpaper is an area in which there is a lot of contention between corporate standards and personal taste. Dozens of companies have built their success on the production of wallpaper and screensavers for all tastes, good and bad. Corporations should provide some leeway for users here. Wallpaper and screensavers are something that users like to personalize, sometimes every day. But they are also something that the corporation needs to control in a certified network if PCs are to remain stable. A central bank of approved (for stability purposes) screensavers and wallpaper should be made available to all users.

- *Departmental Web zone:* This is an active zone. It can display the message of the day and provide access to mission-critical virtual[14] tools. This zone is controlled through an intranet Web page managed at the departmental level. Departmental zones vary on the desktop because they are displayed according to the department to which a user belongs.

- *Corporate Web zone:* The corporate Web zone includes global messages and access to corporate systems such

FIGURE 4.11   A productivity Quick Launch area

---

14. Virtual tools are Internet-enabled tools. They are deemed virtual because they often do no require the installation of local components to work. If local component installation is required, the intranet Web server can install them automatically on the client.

as human resources, automated document templates, and global intranet research tools. This zone is displayed on all desktops. The Web content of this zone is controlled by IT for the corporation.

- *Project Web zone:* Project teams have special requirements. With new intranet-based project management technologies, such as those of Microsoft Project with Project Central, the inclusion of a project Web zone on the desktop provides support for personnel belonging to project teams. The project team is responsible for the management of this Web zone.

- *IT Web zone:* The last zone on the desktop is the IT zone. This zone can include several IT-related components such as help desk access, productivity support sections such as FAQs, tools and tips, training program booking, and emergency messages about the system. This Web zone is controlled by IT.

With Windows 2000,[15] your corporate desktop can become a very powerful tool if managed properly. The inclusion of Web zones on the desktop is a boon to productivity. With Web technologies, corporations can manage content in real time, and through central policy management technologies, they can choose to activate them at will. Figure 4.12 illustrates a sample desktop design.

Group Customization of the Presentation Layer

Every single network needs to categorize its users. Most do it for reasons of security. Managing access rights within the network is much simpler if all users requiring the same access are grouped within some type of container. These containers have in the past been limited to user groups, but Windows 2000/XP introduces the notion of organizational units as well. Whichever method is used—and in most cases, organizations will choose to use both—it is important that corporations take aspects other than security into consideration when designing user groupings today.

Microsoft has integrated this notion into Windows 2000 as *distribution groups*. These special groups are separate

---

15. Windows 2000 is not the first technology to support Web content on the desktop, but it is the first to provide an integrated management approach to all desktop content.

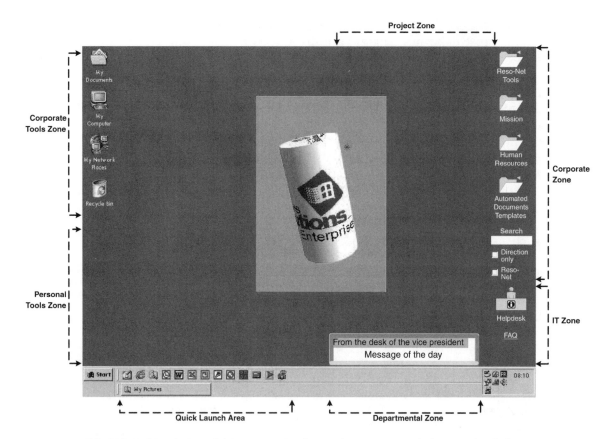

FIGURE 4.12   A Sample Corporate Desktop. The corporate desktop is divided into zones. Ownership of each zone is clearly defined. For users, the Active Desktop offers sophisticated wallpaper and screensaver images.

from security groups and are used for distribution purposes only. With these types of groupings, organizations can ensure that their central systems deliver specific content to specific groups of users.

With technologies such as Windows 2000, this means that corporations can deploy information to users—information that can take the shape of software products, software upgrades, documents, system updates, and Web content.

When designing the corporate desktop, organizations must take into account the granularity they want for specific content delivery. By determining how finely you want to detail your distribution points, you can determine how many levels are required in your distribution groups.

For example, several corporations have opted to divide their groups of users based on three major guidelines:

Microsoft offers free Web channels. This is an example of the Microsoft Finance channel. It is used to display stock information in real time on the Active Desktop.

- *Department minus 1:* Users are grouped by department and by division. Smaller groupings are not determined. This allows for distribution of line-of-business information and toolsets.
- *IT function:* Users are grouped by user role within the IT framework. This allows for the delivery of the software tools required to support the function.
- *Project groups:* Groups are created for project teams to support their specific requirements.

Remember, groups can be either organizational units or user groups. Use both judiciously. Organizational units are ideal for the department minus 1 guideline because groupings are vertical. User groups are the best for IT function and project groups because both cover the horizontal breadth of the enterprise—both cut across departments.

Managing Web Content on the Desktop

Web content must be managed, so it requires a supporting process. Because Web zone owners are responsible for their content, this process needs to be simple and straightforward. It must also be widely communicated to responsible groups.

An organization that has an intranet has usually provided some form of Web control to each of the responsible groups identified previously. Managing Web content is simply creating and maintaining a special type of Web page: the Web channel. Channels are stored as Channel Definition Format (CDF) files and are displayed within a special frame on the desktop.

On the creation side, a channel is just another Web page. Applying the channel to a desktop is done through a group policy in Windows 2000. This means that a policy enforcing the activation of the channel on given desktops is applied to the group container within Active Directory, Windows 2000/XP's central identity administration environment. Group policies are applied and refreshed on SPA objects (servers or PCs) on a regular basis that can be modified to suit your requirements. (The default is 90 minutes.)

Managing the Web content for the Presentation layer (see Figure 4.13) involves the following steps.

1. Prepare channel content.
2. Create or modify target groups.
3. Target specific groups with a group policy within Active Directory to activate the zone. The zone displays on the desktop.
4. Perform recurrent administration of the zone.

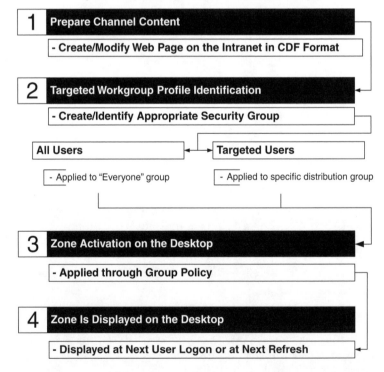

FIGURE 4.13 Presentation Layer Management. Active Desktop zones are managed as Web pages and are applied to workgroups through group policies.

Using the QUOTE System

We have now covered all of the supporting processes required to put in place the EMF. You are now well on your way through the Organize Phase. You know how rationalization, certification, and Presentation layer management work. Before you finish this phase, you need to identify how management and administration of the EMF differs from traditional IT management.

In the next chapter, we will outline traditional IT administrative roles and describe the additional roles required to support the new processes introduced by the EMF.

Then you will be ready to move on to the Transfer Phase, the phase where you can put the new Framework in place.

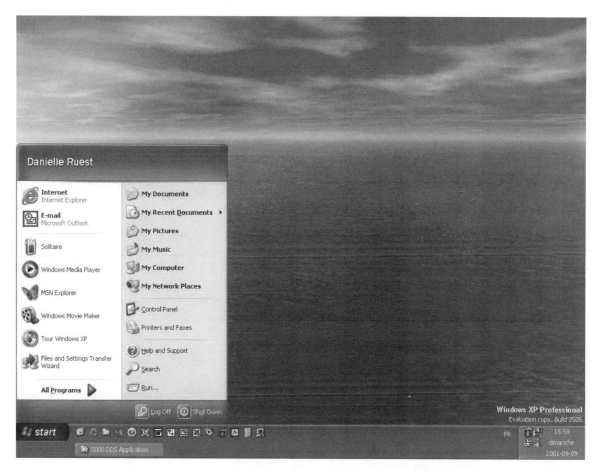

FIGURE 4.14 Windows XP's "Luna" interface supports richer content on the desktop.

CHAPTER ROADMAP

Use this flowchart as a guide to understand the concepts covered in this chapter.

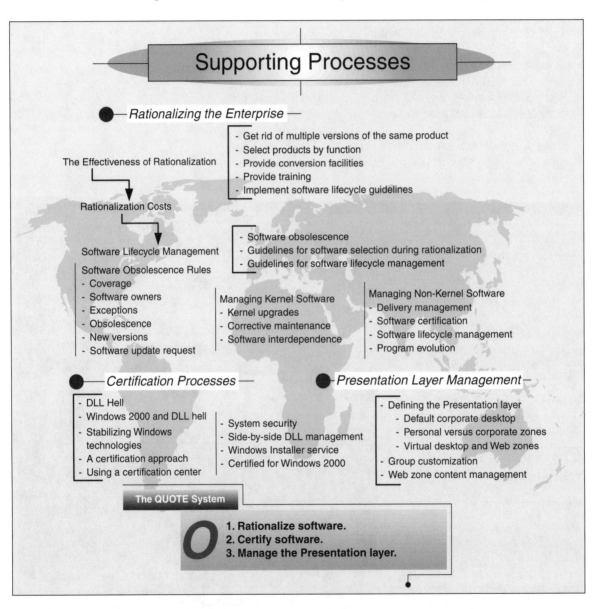

CHAPTER 5

Standardization Management Processes
Managing the Enterprise Management Framework

In the world of mainframes, standardization is a must. When all of the processing power of your corporation is located within a single object and when the entire corporation shares the same logical space, you cannot afford to let anything disrupt it. No IT manager would ever consider allowing a single user to install a noncorporate application and possibly disrupt the mainframe's operation. In this environment, standardization is a must.

But in a distributed environment, it is more difficult to enforce standards. Why? Because every SPA object is deemed to be independent. Every PC and every server can appear to be an island within the network. In the case of servers, standardization is simpler because people share components on the server; if the server goes down, other people are impacted. But on the PC, it is very hard because people tend to think of the corporate PC as their own.

The EMF compares the entire network of SPA objects to a single, unified mainframe. Just as in Microsoft's .NET architecture, every object is an integral component of the infrastructure. No object is isolated so long as it is tied to the network in some way. Every object is a point of access for the network and as a result, every object must be protected, secured, and controlled. Every uncontrolled object immediately becomes a security risk.

Drawing from mainframe practices around the world, you can begin to form the list of services required to manage and support your standardized EMF. These include

> **The QUOTE System's Organize Phase**
>
> We continue the Organize Phase with a look at the IT management infrastructure required to support the EMF.

A Standard Environment

Providing a standard environment to users should not be considered restrictive. It is simply a matter of answering decentralized demands with centralized responses. These responses must first consider the request, map it to network standards, and then provide the appropriate response. The response should meet the requirements of the demand while maintaining corporate standards.

- *Standards management:* Enforcing standards, authorizing new standards, retiring obsolete standards
- *SPA object kernel management:* Watching for new versions of kernel components, updating kernel components as needed
- *Secure component access control management:* Managing how groups of users are allowed to interact with the kernel and other components that are available on either servers or PCs
- *Deployment management:* Software delivery on servers or PCs for update and recurring purposes
- *Desktop active component management:* Managing distribution groups to ensure each group has access to required Web content
- *EMF evolution management:* Maintaining an industry and internal watch to ensure the flexibility and the evolution of the Framework

These management areas are identified because they cover processes that are not traditionally included in the IT management structure.

Traditional IT Service Structures

Traditional IT service models abound in the industry. Microsoft published an IT Service Lifecycle Management Model in its "Planning, Deploying and Managing Highly Available Solutions"[1] white paper, which was released in 2000.

This model identifies four phases of service lifecycle management:

- *Planning:* Identifying and preparing solutions for deployment
- *Deployment:* Acquiring, packaging, configuring, installing and testing deployment strategies
- *Production:* Problem, change, optimization, and administration management within the production network
- *Retirement:* Replacement/upgrade planning and removal of obsolete technologies and processes

---

1. This document is available at http://www.microsoft.com/technet/analpln/availsol.asp.

This model is illustrated in Figure 5.1.

To support this service structure, organizations need to include the following staff within the IT department:

- Managers and support staff
- Problem management and support personnel
- System developers
- System administrators
- Security administrators
- Security officers
- Trainers

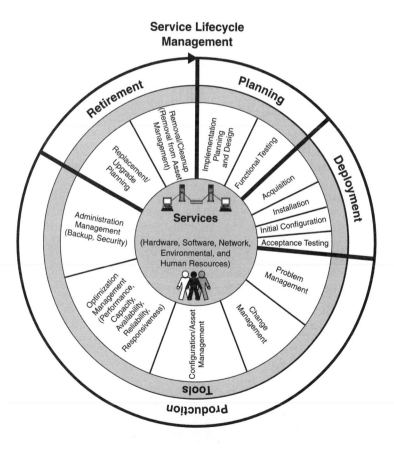

FIGURE 5.1 Microsoft's Service Lifecycle Management Model. The Microsoft Service Lifecycle Management Model covers the elements of traditional IT service delivery.

Using Windows Technologies

Technical training is a major issue for corporations. One of the advantages of standardizing on Windows technologies at the PC and server levels is reduced training costs. Because Windows operates with a single, unified user interface, there is little retraining required when technicians and administrators move from one tool to another. Once they understand the basic concepts of the interface, the only thing they need to concentrate on is the actual tool function.

It is often for this reason alone that corporations standardize on these technologies even though they may not be the best-of-breed solutions at all levels.

Other organizations prefer to use mixed and matched technologies: Novell for one function, UNIX for another, Windows for a third, and so on. While these systems may offer benefits over a unified Windows system, the cost of personnel training is often much more significant because none of the interfaces are the same.

In an enterprise system, organizations must weigh the cost of retraining versus the perceived benefits of a heterogeneous system.

- Integrators and technicians
- Data administrator[2]
- Planners
- Architects
- Analysts
- Performance and optimization administrators
- Software owners
- Asset manager
- Inventory administrators
- Output and printing administrators
- System preparation and installation technicians
- Communication system administrators
- Network change management administrators
- User service representatives
- Intranet administrators
- Information depot administrators

The previous list is not exhaustive, but it is representative. Certain specialized businesses will have roles that are not identified here. In addition, staffing levels will depend on the size of the organization. Small organizations may have several roles played by the same personnel. And organizations supporting diverse technologies must have more personnel because of the different interface standards that must be supported.

In addition, the following IT functions are provided by other departments:

- Web/intranet editor
- Application enhancer
- Office automation experts
- Software owners

All of these departmental functions are discussed later in this chapter. For now, it is important to focus on more centralized IT services and, more specifically, on their relationship to the EMF.

---

2. This includes database and transactional service management along with data depot management.

A .NET Framework Management Structure

Before we outline the additional roles required to support the new Framework, we must review the basic concepts of the models upon which the Framework is based.

The IT Model for Service Points of Access includes the following principles.

- The hardware for each PC or server in the network may not necessarily be the same, but it must be based on a minimum capacity[3] that is revised annually.
- The SPA kernel includes everything that is required to support the basic functions of either PCs or servers.
- The kernel can support any locally installed application, commercial or otherwise.
- The kernel can support any mission-support application, either remotely or in client/server mode. These applications should be designed to take advantage of the operating system's native mode of operation; that is, if it is a 32-bit OS, applications should be conceived in 32-bit mode.
- The kernel is designed to support the concept of personalization—it uses Active Desktop technologies to provide personalized toolsets (in the form of Web elements on the desktop) based on the groups to which a user belongs.
- The kernel is designed to support all security and access policies within the network.
- The kernel is designed to support the protection of critical operational components from unauthorized tampering because all components are certified.
- The kernel is designed for centralized management.

Thus your new IT service model must support the core components of every SPA object, maintain remote management technologies, update and administer the SPA object, and support the EMF itself and the standards upon which it is based.

Supporting Technologies

Several technologies are required to remotely support the IT Model for Service Points of Access. For most organiza-

The SPA Object

The SPA object is either a PC or a server. As a single point of access, it acts as a unique "object" within the framework of the network.

---

3. This minimum capacity is different for servers and PCs.

tions that aim for standardization, today's basis for all platforms should be Microsoft Windows 2000 or XP in all its versions. It should also include technologies from Microsoft's .NET Enterprise Servers.

These technologies are described in Table 5.1. This table includes three columns.

- *Technology:* This column lists the required management technology.
- *Component:* This column identifies the component required within the IT Model for Service Points of Access to support management.
- *Service:* The final column lists the services that are managed by the technology through its SPA component.

Each of the technologies in Table 5.1 has an impact on the kernel. This is why they must also have an impact on the management of the SPA object. Individual SPA objects are not "islands" in the network, but rather integrated components that interact through the network.

Your service model for IT should aim to manage and administer the rules and guidelines that make up your EMF. Figure 5.2 illustrates how these technologies are related to the SPA object and the kernel in particular.

Designing a Service Model for IT

The breadth of technologies required to manage, maintain, and interact with the SPA shows how closely related these technologies are. With this in mind, you will be able to prepare it, put it in place, and support it. But, before you can put it in place, you will need to define the new roles IT needs to fulfill in order to administer the IT Model for Service Points of Access. For this, you need to identify new tasks, new roles to fulfill them, and staff them appropriately. In many cases, change takes place only in the processes covered by existing roles. All roles will need to be aware of and understand the new standardization principles of the EMF.

The new roles have been defined by the different topics covered in previous chapters: Global Architecture, EMF, conceptual and technical IT service lists, and principles and standards. Your new service model will, in fact, combine the old with the new.

TABLE 5.1 .NET Management Technologies

Technology	Component	Service
Microsoft Windows 2000 Server	Operating system • Windows 2000 Professional[4] for PCs • Windows 2000[5] Server, Advanced Server, or Datacenter Server for servers • Active Directory • Microsoft Index Server • Windows Terminal Services	• Authentication services • Security service for kernel protection • Unified scripting facilities • File and print-sharing services • TCP/IP protocol management services (address allocation, name resolution, and so on) • Content indexing • Identification services (Active Directory maintains user identities) • Server remote control functions • Event management • Remote operating system installation • Limited software or update delivery
Active technologies: • Microsoft Internet Information Server (IIS) • Internet Security and Acceleration Server (ISA)	Web browser • Internet Explorer • Active Desktop • Internet Security and Acceleration Server client	• Presentation layer management • Web component management • Active application management • Intranet content management • Internet security control • Internet usage optimization • Spam and unauthorized Web content filtering
Microsoft Systems Management Server (SMS)	SMS client	• Inventory control (software and hardware) • Software and software update delivery • Software metering • Remote control for PCs • Network monitoring • Limited server health monitoring
Antivirus technology[6]	Virus control client	• Antivirus client management on the SPA object • Antivirus signature update deliveries
Microsoft Host Integration Server (HIS)	HIS client	• Mainframe computer access management • Single sign-on for MS networks and mainframes
Microsoft Application Center Server (ACS)	ACS client (servers only)	• Application component management • Web farm fault tolerance

---

4. You may decide to replace this with Windows XP Professional.

5. You may decide to replace this with Windows .NET Server.

6. Microsoft does not offer an antivirus product, but several are available. Though this is not a .NET product, it is still essential in any network.

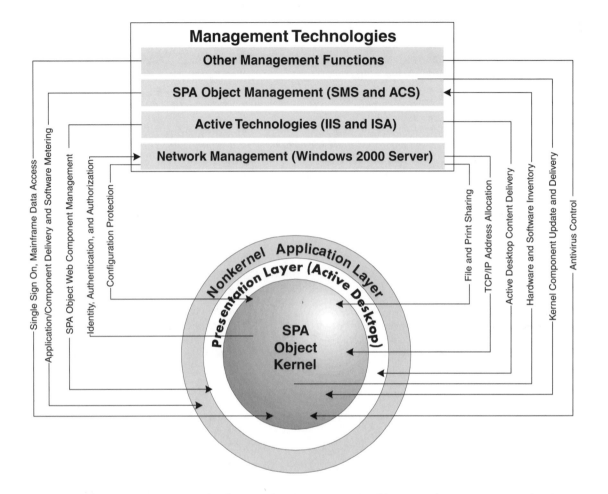

FIGURE 5.2 Management Technologies. The EMF is supported by several management technologies, though not all are illustrated here. The information flow goes from the SPA object to the management technology and vice versa.

Managing Standard IT Environments

Several new processes are required to manage standard IT environments.

- Standards management
- Kernel management
- Component access management
- Software lifecycle management
- Certification management

- Web content management
- EMF management

The responsibilities of each of these processes are described in the sections that follow.

Standards Management
Standards management focuses on four specific processes.

- *Standards monitoring:* Identify when and how a standard has been implemented in the network and/or why it was not implemented and determine the appropriate actions to take.
- *Standards approval:* Manage the standards approval process for the addition/retirement of standards with the appropriate personnel. This should include a committee of all interested parties, developers, administrators, and planners.
- *Standards communication:* Broadcast information about new standards, how they are applied, what benefits they bring, and what changes may be required by users to conform to them.
- *Standards evolution and retirement:* Regularly review all standards, introduce new standards as required by technological changes, and retire obsolete standards.

These processes can be managed by two IT roles:

- *Standards manager:* Part of the IT planning processes, this function covers standards implementation and evolution in collaboration with representative members of the enterprise.
- *Standards framework operator:* This role administers the day-to-day implementation of standards.

Both roles are governed by four simple rules:

- *Scope of the standards implementation:* Standards are applied without exception throughout the network.
- *Industry monitoring:* The standards officers are required to monitor the industry for significant technological changes. They must monitor the Desktop Management Task Force (DMTF), for example, to keep abreast of new remote management standards and updated hardware platform descriptions.

- *Communications plan:* Standards officers are responsible for the standards communications plan. The user community should be aware of the reasons for standards as well as the contents of any given standard.
- *Standards responsiveness:* Standards must be defined with collaboration and business requirements in mind. They must fit within the processes defined in the EMF while responding to user and business demands.

Kernel Management

Kernel management focuses on several processes.

- *Kernel content monitoring:* Monitor the content of the kernel and ensure its viability.
- *Kernel update production:* Collect change requests and integrate approved changes into the next version of the kernel, including two deliverables: change deltas for existing systems and new installations for new systems. Kernel updates must all undergo rigorous testing before deployment.
- *Kernel certification:* All kernel updates must be certified before release.
- *Kernel update deployment:* Updates are delivered into the network on regular schedules as discussed in Chapter 4.
- *Emergency situation or project delivery affecting the kernel:* The kernel management staff must be ready and able to deploy corrections or updates to targeted user bases. This process is described in Chapter 4.

Kernel management processes can be handled by the following IT roles:

- *Kernel operations manager:* This role manages kernel update operations.
- *Kernel change request administrator:* This role administers all kernel change requests, follows up on their integration into the next version, and freezes change requests periodically before update deployment.
- *Kernel component owners:* Software components within the kernel require owners just as does any other corporate software product.

Delta Management

How many deltas are required before a new version must be created? Often the process of creating a new version depends on the hardware evolution cycle. If you change or update hardware on a yearly basis, new installations should be created on a yearly basis. Deltas should be created during the year.

- *Kernel change operators:*[7] Integrators package, certify, and deploy kernel changes. This role is divided into two groups: one for servers and one for PCs.

These roles are governed by the following simple rules:

- *Kernel updates:* These updates are treated as whole units despite the number of different products updated within the version release.
- *Update delivery schedule:* Three updates must be sent to every SPA object every year. This rate is sufficient to keep systems up-to-date, reduce costs, and keep system updates relatively small.
- *Delivery methods:* Update deliveries are treated as deltas until a total of three deltas has been reached. At that point, a new installation is produced.[8]
- *Emergency or project updates:* If updates are required for emergency situations or project teams, they must be deployed in a timely manner, and updates must be included in the next revision cycle.

Component Access Management

Component access is controlled through the security features of platforms such as Windows 2000 or XP for reasons of stability and confidentiality. Users are grouped into profiles. Security and standard configuration settings are controlled through centralized group policies. Component access control includes

- *Group management:* Maintenance of lists of users within specific security and distribution groups
- *Profile content management:* Definition of the actual content that is controlled through group policy and preparation of the group policy
- *Group policy application:* Deployment of new policies and maintenance of existing policies

---

7. Organizations often choose to create two groups for this role: one for PCs and one for servers.

8. New systems are installed with the original kernel and existing deltas until a new installation is created.

Local Distribution

Many organizations keep distribution at the central level, but this can cause problems. Local administrators often tend to be more aware of local business issues and requirements than central administrators. As a result, local administrators are often better informed of when a package distribution or security modification will least affect business operations.

Creating packages centrally and distributing them to local distribution points, and then allowing local administrators to activate the package are often the best operational methods.

Windows 2000 and Software Delivery

One of the great advantages of Windows 2000/XP is that it is an evolved OS. As such, it has the ability to truly perform several tasks at the same time. In addition, it can use different security contexts to perform these tasks. When a software product is deployed to a local PC, it can be installed in a different process than the user's with a security level that has more rights than the user's.

This means that you can deploy software from a central location in a process that is transparent to the user.

These processes can be managed by three IT roles:

- *Security officer:* This role administers and deploys policies affecting security issues and manages security groups.
- *Distribution officer:* This role administers and deploys policies affecting nonsecurity issues and manages distribution groups.
- *Policy architects:* Architects plan and develop new policies and troubleshoot policies at a high level.

All three roles are governed by the following simple rules:

- *Profile limitation:* Authenticated users are automatically given generic user rights. Management must approve all requests for rights elevation.
- *Group inclusion:* Requests for inclusion into groups must be approved and authorized.
- *Group policy management:* Wherever possible, use enterprise-level policies to apply basic security settings. Then use local policies to provide further granularity.
- *Local Distribution:* Wherever possible, give distribution rights at the departmental level.

Software Lifecycle Management

Software lifecycle management is focused on managing software products within the enterprise. It is closely tied to rationalization principles.

Software lifecycle management processes are similar to those of component access management. These processes include

- *Group management:* Maintaining lists of users within specific distribution groups
- *Profile content management:* Definition of the software products that are controlled through policy management and preparation of the software product (including certification of the product)
- *Software product deployment:* Deployment of new policies and maintenance of existing policies
- *Software product maintenance:* Preparation and delivery of required updates
- *Software upgrades:* Selection and preparation of approved upgrades

- *Software retirement:* Removal of obsolete software products from the network

These processes are managed by the following IT roles:

- *Software product owners:* Owners are responsible for the evolution and use of the product within the network. They select and recommend upgrades, accept repacked products during setup preparation, and ensure that products meet certification guidelines. Owners are required for both commercial software and corporate applications. This role may be decentralized.
- *Software lifecycle manager:* This role manages lifecycle operations.
- *Program component administrators:* PCAs administer specific application components for distributed Web-based applications. In Windows 2000/XP, PCAs use Microsoft Application Center Server to manage and distribute load balancing of COM+ programming components.
- *Operations administrator:* This role administers and monitors network operations, checks event logs for errors, and manages and responds to the problem alert system.
- *Change management committees:* These committees debate and approve changes to the network infrastructure.
- *Software profile administrator:* This role manages and administers software profile content, updates and maintains profile content lists, and retires components from the profile as required.
- *Software delivery system operators:* Operators prepare software packages for deployment, deploy software, and manage distribution lists.

These roles are governed by simple rules:

- *Application rationalization:* Whenever possible, a single and unique product should be used for any given IT function. Selection should be performed according to rationalization criteria.
- *Software certification:* All products with a user base greater than ten must be certified. Figure 5.3 illustrates this decision-making process.

The Software Evaluation Process

Software evaluation includes eight steps:

1. Needs analysis: Is the software or software update required? Will it benefit the organization?
2. Function comparison: Does the product fit within standard guidelines? Does it duplicate existing functions?
3. Software selection: If the product passes the first two steps, approve initial testing.
4. Kernel test: Test the product on the basic kernel for viability.
5. Hardware impacts: Are there any hardware impacts (more power, more RAM, and so on)?
6. Quality evaluation: Does the product provide advertised functionalities?
7. Product approval: If the product passes all initial tests, approve the product for certification and inclusion into a software profile.
8. Deployment analysis: Prepare for product deployment, analyze costs, and initiate a project.

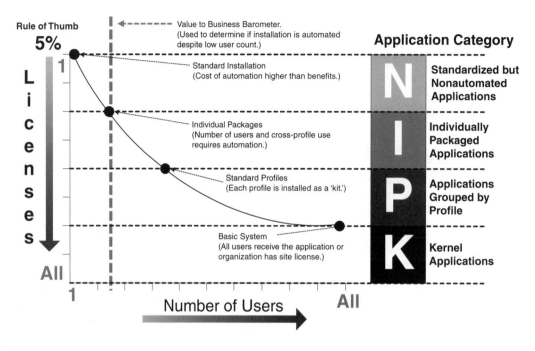

FIGURE 5.3   The Installation Automation Decision Process. In some cases, applications are automated even though they have small user bases because they are valuable to the organization. About 5 percent of software does not require an automated installation.

Change Management Committees

In a Standardized Enterprise Framework, it is essential to put in place approval committees for significant change requests.

For example, in a Windows 2000/XP network, it is important to have a *schema change management committee*. Because Active Directory is at the core of your network infrastructure, a change to the basic structure of the Active Directory database—the Active Directory schema—must be evaluated and approved before the change takes place because it may impact every single user in your network.

- *Service Level Agreement[9] (SLA) update:* If new products are introduced into the network, the corresponding SLAs must be modified.

- *Software directory:* Every managed application must be added to the corporate software directory in order to ensure its full integration into existing processes.

- *Change management:* Change to the network infrastructure must be managed and controlled. The impact of every change request should be evaluated before approval.

- *Training and support:* Software owners must plan for both training and support of all products introduced into the network.

- *Software profile limitation:* The number of software profiles or configurations within an organization should be as limited as possible. More profiles mean more management and administration and higher costs.

9. See Chapter 2 for an example of a Service Level Agreement.

Certification Management

The component certification process provides stability in the network. Every single component that is introduced into the network is catalogued and identified. Corrections are implemented if possible. Its processes include

- *Certification center management:* Because the certification center is permanent, it must be set up as a proper business unit.

- *Certification center coordination:* Because all network components must undergo certification, testing and operations coordination is crucial. Coordination also provides quality assurance checks.

- *Certification testing:* Every certified product must undergo thorough testing. Certification testing includes three test levels: system, integration, and acceptance.

The process begins with initial application installation, update of the conflict database, and initial application packaging. For Windows 2000/XP, the latter is created using Windows Installer Integrated Packages or MSIs.

The first test, *system testing,* consists of testing the application on the kernel. This verifies the application's compatibility with kernel elements.

Integration and deployment testing focuses on testing the viability of the package with other elements contained in the software profile. This is also where delivery and administration of the software package will be tested. If problems arise, the package must be corrected. If not, it is ready for acceptance.

Acceptance testing focuses on presenting the packaged application to the software product owner for acceptance. Here, functional testing will identify if the product operates in the proper manner. After this test, the product is ready for deployment. Packages are documented at every stage of the testing process.

Figure 5.4 illustrates the testing process.

These processes can be fulfilled by the following IT roles:

- *Certification center manager:* This role manages the operations of the certification center.

- *Certification center coordinator:* This role administers and coordinates the activities within the certification center, schedules tests and manages deliverables,

Lanovation Prism Pack Enterprise Edition

Lanovation (http://www. lanovation.com/) offers the only product to date that includes both the ability to detect conflicts and the ability to create a Windows Installer software installation.

Lanovation also offers PrismXL, a complete suite of application lifecycle management tools.

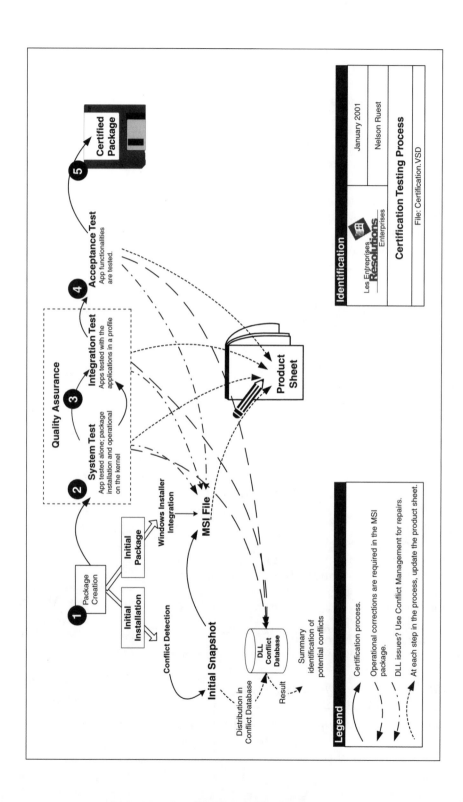

FIGURE 5.4 The Certification Testing Process. The proactive certification blueprint includes five testing phases.

administers conflict management databases, and enforces certification guidelines.

- *Certification center integrators:* Integrators prepare packaged and certified components for both the kernel and nonkernel applications, prepare and test kernel deltas, prepare staging for new systems, update installation and deployment kits, and document all configurations and conflict management approaches.

- *Software product owners:* Responsible software product owners must accept all hardware and software installations that are delivered by the certification center.

These roles are governed by the following simple rules:

- *Certification inclusion:* All products that will affect a user base of greater than ten must be certified. This includes both hardware and software.

- *Hardware certification:* For Windows 2000/XP, all hardware products must either be listed on the HCL or include a Windows 2000/XP certified driver. Drivers should be digitally signed by the manufacturer.

- *Software certification:* Components of software products must be inventoried prior to network introduction. DLLs must be checked for conflicts. Side-by-side DLL installation should only be used as a last resort.

Web Content Management

Web content management is mostly a decentralized function because departments are responsible for their content, though some administrative operations are centralized.

- *Zone maintenance:* This process involves the maintenance and administration of Web zones on the desktop and the update of all content as required.

- *Zone approval:* Departments must approve zone content at the local level, and a content authority must approve it at the central level. Central zone approval can be delegated if the delegation process is clearly defined.

- *Zone activation:* Individual Web zones are activated on the desktop through the component access management processes identified previously.

These processes can be managed by the following three IT roles:

Driver Digital Signing

Windows 2000/XP supports digital driver signing. This means that an identification certificate is included within the driver itself. Windows 2000 recognizes this certificate when the driver is installed and authorizes the installation.

When driver signing is enabled on Windows 2000, only tested and approved drivers can be installed. This ensures that your PCs remain stable.

- *Zone content editor:* This operator is at the departmental level. Because this role focuses on intranet content management, it can be assumed by existing Web editors.

- *SPA Web content authority:* Part of the standards management group, the Web content authority provides global Web zone standards and is responsible for the global Web content approval.

- *Active zone manager:* This manager is at the departmental level. This role focuses on departmental content approval.

These roles are governed by the following simple rules:

- *Zone usage:* By default, Web zones are not activated on the desktop. Activation is performed only when required. And if the requirement is temporary, the zone must be deactivated when its function is complete. (For example, if the zone is used to send a temporary message, it should be closed after the message has been sent.)

- *Zone ownership:* Individual departments are responsible for the content of their zones. This role must be part of regular departmental operations. Departments must approve all content before deployment.

- *Global zone ownership:* IT is responsible for enforcing standards in terms of Web zone content and format.

IT roles span the enterprise. In Figure 5.5, new .NET IT roles are located in a gray box.

.NET Enterprise Framework Management

The EMF is a series of processes and standard operating procedures that ensure the viability of the corporate network. The processes supporting this Framework are often based on the capabilities of the technologies that are in place within the network. It is important that as new technologies are introduced into the network, Framework processes and procedures are updated as required. This means managing the Framework's evolution.

The evolution of the Framework is in the hands of the standards management group. Their role is to ensure the following:

- Standards are in place and are maintained.

- Existing standards continue to meet corporate operational requirements.

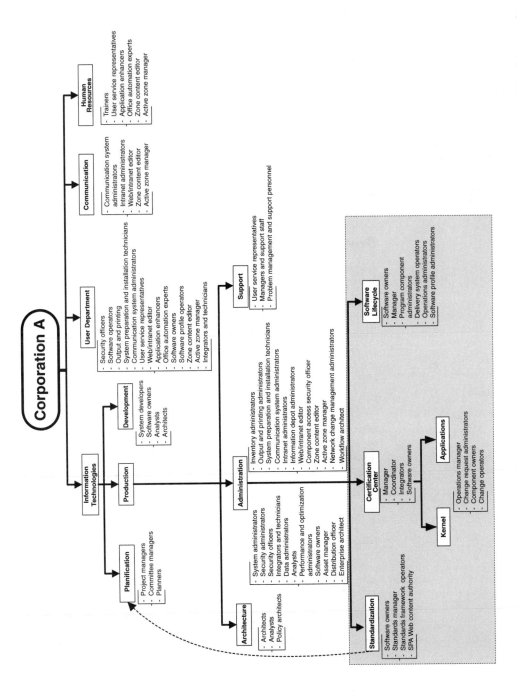

FIGURE 5.5 The New IT. The entire bottom section of the organization chart is specific to the EMF. Most of these roles existed before the EMF and have only been restructured to support the Framework's processes[10].

10. This is a decentralized model. For smaller organizations, this defines the roles that should be covered, not the people you need. One person can play several roles.

- New standards fit within the standardization scheme.
- Standards are retired as technology evolves.

Moving to the EMF

The EMF brings change to the organization. But this change has a definite payback because it enables IT to move from an architecture focused on individual requirements to one that covers the entire enterprise.

Two more processes must be examined: development within a .NET Framework and support for the .NET Framework. Both of these also require change to properly fit within the global aspects of the EMF.

Developing for the EMF

As described in Chapter 4, the major problem causing instability on SPA objects comes from development platforms that are not up-to-date. It is therefore crucial for the EMF to ensure that all development platforms are more up-to-date than the systems currently in use within the enterprise.

Because timelines are the issue, corporate development should always provide project timelines to ensure that the standards and certification groups can determine which updates are required when by the development team.

For example, if a project will last two years, the standards and certification groups must ensure that during the two years, the development platform will be updated at regular intervals so that at project completion, the development platform meets or exceeds current operational environments.

If the project has a shorter timeline, its environment issues are not as significant and can be maintained through normal kernel update programs, especially the project update process.

Centralized versus Decentralized Development

Corporations perform two types of development:

- *Centralized:* Corporate line-of-business applications are developed centrally with fully supported development teams.

Single Point of Failure

In the EMF, there is no such thing as a single point of failure. Consider this when you assign IT responsibilities. Always ensure that there are at least two people responsible for any single task no matter what the size of your organization is.

- *Decentralized:* User departments perform both application enhancement and local system development. These are distributed development teams.

Both groups have different requirements within the EMF.

Centralized Development Strategies

The elaboration of centralized development strategies must begin with a look at the changes to development practices brought on by the implementation of a standard IT environment. But it must also take into account the particular needs of centralized developers.

Developing in a Standard Environment

The centralized development team must produce applications that are standardized like all other software within the organization. This means that they must follow certification procedures and must adhere to integration guidelines for interaction with the kernel.

In addition, organizations adopting Windows 2000/XP should ensure that all corporate products are Windows 2000/XP–compatible and follow Windows 2000/XP certification guidelines. Microsoft's MSDN Internet Web site (http://msdn.microsoft.com/) lists all of the information required to modify current development approaches to meet these standards.

Developer "Freedom"

It is also important for central developers to perform exploratory work. For example, if a new corporate product will modify basic network infrastructures, it is important for IT to provide an exploratory testing environment that is in no way tied to production environments. This ensures that exploration can continue without affecting production.

Finally, products like Windows 2000 provide "locked" software environments. Because developers are constantly adding and modifying components as their development progresses, they must have more local rights than a normal user. Windows 2000 includes the Power Users security group to allow specific users more leeway when operating their system. But this does not grant enough rights to developers.

The Developer .NET Framework

Much can be said about the .NET Framework for centralized developers—and much has been said, in fact. Microsoft provides extensive documentation on standardized development practices for .NET Frameworks through its Solutions Framework Processes. You can find more information on Solution Framework Processes at http://www.microsoft.com/msf.

Development Is a Service

Corporate developers provide a critical service to an organization. Their customers are the corporation itself, the line of business for which they develop, and the corporate user. In a world of service, development needs to meet high quality standards. The best way to do this is to develop internally as if you were going to sell your product on the open market.

IT Is a Service

In a world of service, IT also needs to consider the level of service it offers developers. Developers are customers too.

Developers must be local system administrators if they are to perform their tasks properly. This local administration right must be used according to strict guidelines.

In addition, corporate developers must sometimes modify network environments as they work to continue the development process. In a global network, it is often best to give them an environment that is separate from production and that allows them more freedom if at all possible. Figure 5.6 illustrates this type of environment within a Windows 2000 Active Directory.

Decentralized Development Strategies (DDS)

Decentralized development often focuses on product enhancements. These can include word processing macros and templates, automated spreadsheets, and local database systems.

Because the EMF is a standard and locked environment, it is important to ensure that it will continue to support local development because most local developers will *not* have installation rights.

DDS Code Signing

Corporations using Windows 2000/XP should implement code signing. This means that a valid code signing digital certificate is provided by IT to DDS developers. Developers can then include this certificate with their applications. When the new component is installed, Windows 2000/XP will authorize the installation because it contains the proper signature.

The advantages are clear. You can control which macros and automations can be installed safely within your corporation and provide protection from macro viruses because Windows 2000/XP will not allow macros to run if they are not properly signed.

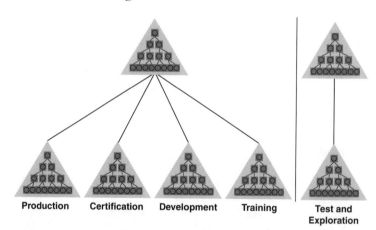

| Production | Certification | Development | Training | Test and Exploration |

FIGURE 5.6 Active Directory Development Domains. Active Directory for your organization could include two forests: one for production and one for exploration. In the production forest, you can have independent security zones for production, development, certification, and training. You could use organizational units (OUs) to achieve the same goal, but OUs do not provide security boundaries, as do domains. The exploratory forest is the same, but it is unrelated to your production environments. Thus, if mishaps occur there is no impact on productivity.

DDS Standards

DDS applications consist mostly of the following:

- Word processing macros
- Automated word processing templates
- Automated spreadsheet tools
- Localized database applications
- Localized Web content development
- Localized Visual Basic applications

Local development roles include the following:

- *Application enhancer:* This role focuses on enhancing office automation products by personalizing templates and creating macros. It also includes local database application development.
- *Web/intranet editor:* This role focuses on departmental intranet content administration and creation. It also includes Web zone content administration and creation.
- *Software owners:* Software owners are not developers, but rather application experts. Because commercial applications cover the organization in a horizontal manner, these roles are often distributed across departments. They can also be local roles.

Application Processes

The problem with localized applications is application deployment and installation. Because most deployment infrastructures are centrally controlled and are often not accessible to local developers, decentralized deployment strategies must be put in place.

In addition, because the kernel is locked, installation of local application enhancements is not allowed by default. The EMF must make allowances for decentralized installation of products that conform to standards.

Both of these processes are described in the sections that follow.

DDS System Processes

The best way to ensure the viability and stability of the production kernel is to ensure that no one has the right to disrupt it. For this reason, most organizations do not want to allow local developers installation rights.

It is for this reason that the core components of the kernel include *distributed application support*. Each corporation-wide development tool should include a *runtime* version, meaning that all of the program components that are required to execute a program written by the development tool can be separated from the program and installed independently. These components require installation rights on a Windows 2000/XP system because they must be integrated and registered in the system. These components can be included in the kernel, thus eliminating the need for decentralized installation. Files created for application enhancement can be copied to the system instead of installed on the system. And because all users have file-copy rights to specific folders, decentralized applications can easily be installed without actually giving installation rights to developers.

For example, Microsoft Access and Microsoft Visual Basic for Applications both include runtime editions. These runtime versions must be included in the kernel. Like all other kernel components, they must be managed and updated as required. When developers create applications, they must ensure that they are designed to run with runtime components instead of requiring Access or Visual Basic to run. When developers must "install" their application, all they need to do is copy the files to appropriate locations because the runtime is already included in the kernel (see Figure 5.7). They do not need to have elevated rights to do this.

The Microsoft .NET Framework

The basic concept of the .NET Framework is the same as the concept for DDS system processes. Microsoft has created the CLR, a common language runtime, which will be included into each system. Applications are designed to run with this runtime. Thus, applications will no longer need to be "installed."

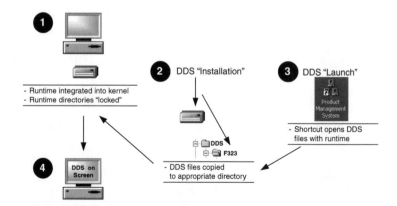

FIGURE 5.7 DDS Application "Installation" Process. Because core DDS components are already in the kernel, the DDS installation process is a simple file copy.

Thus the kernel must make allowances for these types of applications. By including runtime versions in the kernel, the issue of installation is resolved. The inclusion of runtime components must be complemented with special DDS folders within the kernel. These folders give copy and edit rights to both users and local developers.

In addition, local developers must be able to deploy their applications. Because they do not have access to traditional deployment tools and because they do not want to go from desk to desk to manually install their tools, they must use other means—means that fit within the EMF.

Most organizations do not have complete inventories of their decentralized applications. Local developers may say that their department is special and has needs that are not required by others. Developers like their own approaches instead of others'. For this reason, many organizations have four or five timesheets, four or five corporate letter templates, and four or five expense sheets. This occurs because the corporation overlooks two processes: inventory and communication. If there is no inventory, it is hard for the corporation to identify and manage its assets. It is also hard for the corporation to communicate to decentralized developers all of the products that it owns.

Decentralized developers are a part of every network. They should be organized as a team that provides the same type of function at local levels. This team should be structured through standards and processes just like every other part of the EMF. These processes should include centralized systems for decentralized development support.

The centralized system should consist of an application depot that includes all of the elements required to make the application work properly. This depot should include a master directory for the application that is named after the application asset number (four digits is usually sufficient). Subdirectories should include

- *Clients:* All client components that must be copied to a PC.
- *Documents:* All product documentation or links to user documentation on the intranet.
- *Icons:* The application's icon on the desktop.
- *Shortcut:* The program's shortcut.
- *Source data:* If the application requires shared data, it should be located here.

The Cost of Decentralized Applications

Many organizations allow and profit from decentralized development. Many also have a tendency to provide these applications within the tool used to develop the application. For example, if the application is developed in Microsoft Access, they install Access on the PC along with the application.

Modifying applications to run with runtime versions for users means not having to pay for Access on each user's PC. That's right—runtime versions are free of charge!

DDS Depot Structure

The DDS depot should be structured in the following manner:

Each folder always contains the same subfolders. Shared databases are stored centrally. Updates are applied centrally and downloaded to desktops automatically by the shortcut.

- *User groups:* This folder contains the list of authorized users.

Users should be allowed read and execute rights on this depot. Developers should be allowed read, write, and execute rights to their own particular application directories. New application directories should be created centrally through the inventory and asset management process. This process should automatically publish information on the application to the central Intranet Application Inventory page.[11]

An additional tool—a code-signed Visual Basic script that replaces the normal application shortcut on the desktop—supplements the central application depot. This script performs the following steps:

1. *Shortcut launch.* Instead of launching the application, the VBS shortcut begins the authorization and update/installation process.
2. *Authorize users.* Is the user authorized?
   a. The VBS shortcut reads the file GROUPS.TXT within the USERGROUPS subfolder to determine if the user is authorized. If Yes, it moves to the next step.
   b. If No, it stops operation and displays an Unauthorized User message.
3. *Install/update verification.* Is the application on the user's PC?
   a. If Yes, is there a new version of the application? If No, behave as a normal shortcut and launch the application.
   b. The shortcut copies itself to the PC and then proceeds with the next step.
4. *Install/update/launch.* Does the application include local or updated local components?
   a. If Yes, copy the contents of the CLIENTS subfolder to the local PC, and then launch the application.
   b. If No, launch the remote application.

This simple program serves several purposes.

- It automatically updates local components if local components are required.
- It validates user authorizations.

---

11. Developers can use this page to search for existing applications.

- It automatically installs local components if local components are required.
- It automatically performs an application validity check at start-up.

Decentralized developers can use the VBS shortcut to manage all of their updates and installations. By properly placing all of their applications within the structure of the DDS depot, they can facilitate their application management process. They can use the VBS shortcut to automatically install applications on user systems through a simple e-mail message to the user. Before doing so, the developer must ensure that the user's name is included into the GROUPS.TXT file on the server. When a user receives the e-mail message, all he or she has to do is launch the shortcut and the VBS program will automatically install and then manage the application through its lifecycle.

A single VBS shortcut program can manage all of the decentralized applications within a corporate network. The only object developers need to modify on the VBS shortcut is its properties. This must be done to ensure that it points to the appropriate application directory on the server. Figure 5.8 illustrates this modification.

An Example of a VBS Shortcut

While the icon appears to be an application, it is in fact a shortcut to the VBS program.

FIGURE 5.8 Modifying the VBS Shortcut Properties. The DDS developer must tell the VBS shortcut which application folder to start in. This folder bears the application's asset number.

Several other technologies can be integrated to this process as technology changes within the network. For example, the VBS shortcut could verify actual user groups within the security database instead of user lists in text files. But this change would require central administrators to give DDS developers rights to manage their own distribution groups within the security database. This is not a very likely scenario today because delegated management of distribution groups is a new concept brought about by Directory-Enabled Networks (DEN), such as Windows 2000 or Windows .NET Server.

Decentralized Application Deployment Process

Thus the decentralized application deployment process includes the following steps:

- Inventory all decentralized applications
- Create centralized or localized application depots on system servers
- Implement a strict directory structure for application storage
- Create a code-signed Visual Basic script to replace the application's normal shortcut
- Distribute the application shortcut through e-mail or deposit the shortcut on the departmental intranet page
- Communicate with and train to users
- Communicate with and train to DDS developers
- Provide centralized DDS development guidelines and support
- Provide centralized DDS depot administration

Case Study
DDS Deployment and Update System

Organization Type	Public
Number of Users	3,500
Number of Computers	3,500
Project Focus	Standardization
Project Duration	1.5 Years
Specific Project Focus	Standardize the Network and Lock Down All Systems
Administrative Type	Decentralized

This organization implemented a system as described in the preceding pages for DDS deployment. At first, decentralized developers were uncooperative, but their attitude changed as they discovered the advantages such a system would offer them. In the end, the system was implemented to deploy and manage over 350 decentralized applications.

In turn, the organization gained

- A central, documented application depot
- A system automatically updating all DDS clients in real time, without much overhead (if any)
- A low-cost deployment tool through either e-mail or the local intranet page
- Centralized backup and recovery of all decentralized applications
- Complete freedom for DDS developers with their applications so long as they remained within published guidelines
- Awareness for DDS developers of other applications that are available within the organization
- Stable SPA kernels
- The creation of a support group for DDS developers

A .NET Development Support Program

By addressing issues for both centralized and decentralized development, the EMF ensures the viability of both processes and ensures the continued stability of the SPA object. This support program is essential even if you haven't fully decided to implement the EMF.

Strife between developers and systems administrators has arisen with the ability to centrally lock down distributed systems. Every organization that has not dealt with development issues but has implemented controlled environments with Windows NT or Windows 2000 has experienced this strife to some degree.

Supporting the EMF

Support and help desk operations are in and of themselves the subject of another book. Suffice it to say that today most organizations have moved from user support to problem management. This approach serves to more precisely target the ongoing issues within the network. Unfortunately, this approach also serves to remove existing services from the network.

When user support becomes problem management, user support itself disappears. The original name of support services was "Help Desk." By focusing on problems, organizations tend to forget user assistance issues.

As such, most organizations today provide only problem management and no longer provide end-user assistance with difficult operations. This has the effect of reducing productivity.

With the implementation of the EMF and especially its certification and standardization guidelines, organizations will find that their problem management processes will change.

Supporting a stable network is not the same as supporting diversity. Diversity leads to instability. In these types of logical networks, problem management becomes a full-time job. With stable networks, organizations have seen a major decrease in low-level problems. Applications no longer fail as often[12] and systems always work.

In one case, problem reporting was reduced from 15 per user per year to less than two! This reduction enabled the organization to free its support resources from first-level problem management to other duties such as certification and standardization support.

Usage and Productivity Support

But having a stable system is not the only element required to improve productivity. While it is true that users of an EMF will have improved productivity because systems are always up, there is one element that will always remain an issue: user knowledge.

It is also true that most organizations have tried to relieve the problem by providing user training along with intranet sites oriented toward application usage. Tips and tricks documents, FAQs, and training manuals are now available on many corporate intranets. But studies[13] show that when faced with a productivity problem, most users tend

---

12. Unfortunately, even certification procedures cannot guarantee that any given software product will work as advertised or that other specific components will not fail.

13. Studies performed by Resolutions Enterprises at various client sites.

to turn to a local person who has demonstrated knowledge of the application.

This, in fact, is one of the hidden costs of TCO: Not only is the first user nonproductive, but he or she also disrupts the work of others. The question becomes the following: "If this is the default behavior of any given user, why not formalize the process?"

Local Productivity Support Teams

Organizations that formalize this process within their IT framework soon reap its benefits. By identifying key advanced or "power" users within the organization, the corporation can use them in local productivity support teams. These people can be formally identified and supported by IT. They should be the first to be trained whenever a new technology is made available to the corporate network. As a result, when users need help, they will know exactly where to turn. And in doing so, they will not disrupt both their operations and their colleagues'; they use the appropriate process to increase productivity.

Support teams should include enough members to provide an adequate ratio of team members to individual users. One team member per 25 users is usually an appropriate ratio. In addition, you must remember that these team members will tend to have limited scope. That is, they will tend to be experts in only a few applications—some will support Microsoft Word while others will focus on Microsoft Excel. The limited scope combines with the number of team members to provide a support ratio of approximately 1 to 50.

Users will appreciate the local productivity support team program more than any other within the EMF because it is something from which they can directly benefit.

The corporation also benefits because, after all, corporate IT networks are only tools that are put to use by users. The EMF puts people, PCs, and processes together to improve productivity and stability within the organization. This final process is worth its weight in gold simply because it is near and dear to the entire user base.

Managing User Change Requests

Many organizations have made of the support center as the single interface for user change requests within the organization. This means that one of the support center's respon-

First Point of Contact

Local productivity support teams are useful in problem management. Because they are more knowledgeable about the systems, they can act as the first point of contact for system support. In this way, they can communicate problems in a more technical way to problem support personnel and reduce problem resolution time. Figure 5.9 illustrates this concept.

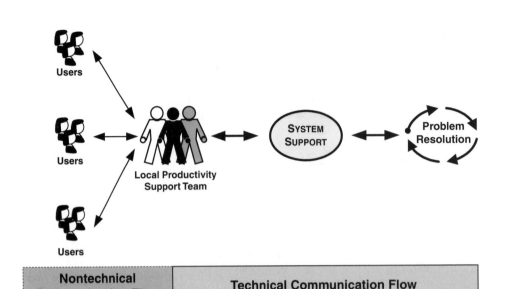

FIGURE 5.9   The Chain of Support. The local productivity support team serves as the first point of contact during problem resolution.

sibilities is to respond to user requests for new products, new systems, and/or product updates on existing systems.

In an EMF, the user change management process needs to be defined and needs to focus not only on product delivery, but also on user productivity.

Product delivery is simple in a standardized network. Because all products are certified, the support engineer only needs to locate the product, target the user's PC, and deploy it. In fine-tuned environments, this can take as little as a few minutes.

What is more difficult is ensuring and guaranteeing that user productivity will be a factor that is included in the process. Training requirements must be taken into consideration. This should come from a global corporate user knowledge-level database, which should be directly linked to the support engineer's desktop. In this way, the engineer can determine if delivery of the product should be tied to a training program, and the engineer can sometimes delay the delivery to ensure that training is received. After training is received, the user's record in the database should be updated.

This system should be closely tied to existing inventories and should automatically update these every time a change is made. One of the cornerstones of the EMF is knowledge of what you have in your network at all times. For this, inventory systems must operate in real time. Figure 5.10 illustrates the user change request management process.

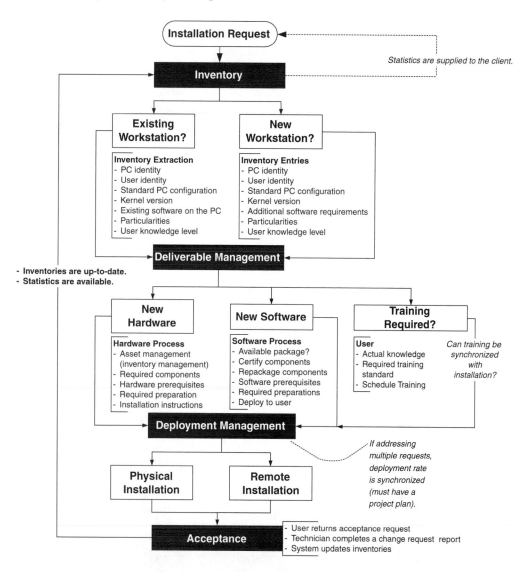

FIGURE 5.10 User Change Request Management. Change request management must be an integrated process. Its goals should include increased productivity as well as knowledge and understanding of internal assets.

Using the QUOTE System

You have now completed the Organize Phase. You have learned how traditional IT administrative roles are changed by the EMF. (This change is illustrated in Figure 5.5.) You should also understand how these changes help you support your new Framework.

Now you are ready to move on to the Transfer Phase, the phase in which you put your new Framework in place.

Case Study
Local Productivity Support Teams

Organization Type	Public Sector
Number of Users	10,000
Number of Computers	10,000
Project Focus	Windows 2000 Deployment
Project Duration	2 Years
Specific Project Focus	Increase Local Productivity Support
Administrative Type	Decentralized

This organization migrated from an obsolete network OS to Windows 2000 in the course of two years. Because of the scope of the change and the number of users undergoing it, the organization decided to use a "fast-track" end-user training program. Users attended a half-day presentation focusing on the differences between the old system and the new. At the end of this presentation, they were given a training guide outlining the procedures that would change.

At the same time, the organization selected key personnel to become local productivity support team members. The ratio used was 1 to 25. The goal was to put these 400 people through a special training program that would show them all of the differences between the old and new OS and train them on all new products. In addition, the organization published lists of these team members on the company intranet, letting end users know exactly where to turn when they needed help with the new system.

By giving a five-day training program to a select group of advanced users and identifying them to the user base, the corporation was able to cut training costs significantly and put in place a new user support infrastructure at the same time.

Now, local productivity support teams are part and parcel of the corporation's internal culture.

CHAPTER ROADMAP

Use this flowchart as a guide to understand the concepts covered in this chapter.

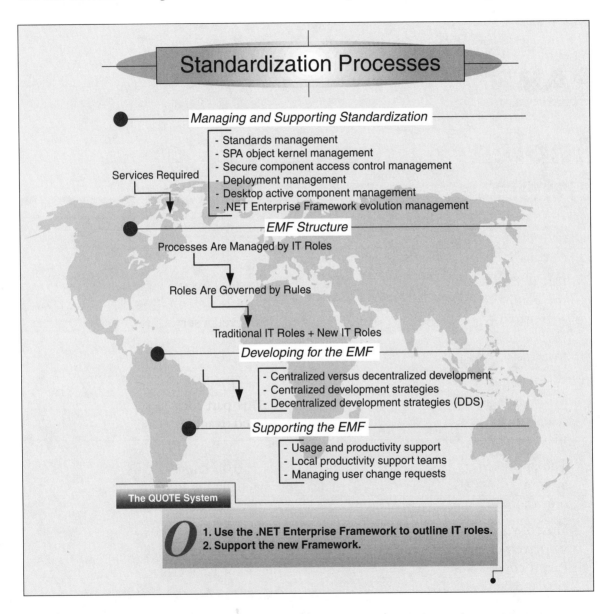

Standardization Processes

Managing and Supporting Standardization

Services Required
- Standards management
- SPA object kernel management
- Secure component access control management
- Deployment management
- Desktop active component management
- .NET Enterprise Framework evolution management

EMF Structure

Processes Are Managed by IT Roles

Roles Are Governed by Rules

Traditional IT Roles + New IT Roles

Developing for the EMF
- Centralized versus decentralized development
- Centralized development strategies
- Decentralized development strategies (DDS)

Supporting the EMF
- Usage and productivity support
- Local productivity support teams
- Managing user change requests

The QUOTE System

1. Use the .NET Enterprise Framework to outline IT roles.
2. Support the new Framework.

PART II

Implementing .NET Enterprise Technologies

Part I: The Roadmap to .NET Enterprise Technologies covered all of the components required to understand how you can move from a segregated IT service model to a unified enterprise level of service. No part of the IT environment is an island. All parts integrate together to form a single, complete whole.

Part II begins to look at all of the elements required to put the Enterprise Management Framework (EMF) in place. This part focuses on deployment projects and how they can be organized to achieve complete success in any implementation.

The approach used in Part II is the same as in Part I. The QUOTE System continues to form the basis of this approach. But, as in Part I, only those elements that are truly different will be covered.

Most of you have already experienced several deployment projects, so we have not covered basic project structures and processes. Rather, Part II covers the factors that can make the difference between success and failure in deployment projects.

This focus is the basis of the EMF implementation.

CHAPTER 6

Putting the Enterprise Management Framework in Place

Gartner Group, a high-level consultancy, claims that the vast majority of IT projects are failures—failures in terms of cost overruns, missed deadlines, nonimplementation of required services, inability to profit from new benefits, and inappropriate project structure.

Why is this the case? Do the organizations that Gartner mentions think their projects were failures? Surely not. In fact, actual failures where projects need to be abandoned or where technology utterly fails to meet objectives are quite rare. But it is true that though a project does implement new technology and is deemed a success internally, it may not measure up to Gartner's standards.

This "failure" is often a result of improper scoping of the project and lack of preparation. Preparing for a project means preparing for every situation that can occur in the project. It is an exercise in imagination—trying to imagine everything that could go wrong and preparing for it, trying to imagine everything that needs to be done and preparing for it, and trying to identify all of the potential costs and budgeting for them.

Then, once you've imagined and identified all of this information, you have to test it. Review it with your peers, both inside and outside your workgroup, and make appropriate changes.

Preparing for a project involves planning, budgeting, organization, and risk management.

> **The QUOTE System's Transfer Phase**
>
> We begin the Transfer Phase with a look at the processes required to implement the EMF. We need to be prepared, monitor the progress of the implementation, and proceed with caution.

Managing IT Change

Preparing for an IT project involves preparing to manage IT change within the organization. Chapter 1 described the nature of change and how people react to it. One of the key factors of a change situation is the emotional cycle people undergo when they are faced with change. Whether you agree or not with the coming change, you and your peers *will* undergo a period of pessimism or negation.

Part of managing a major IT change project is preparing to help people face this change. Doing this while minimizing negative impacts on business operations is quite a challenge.

But there are ways to minimize the risks. When faced with change, IT or otherwise, people will resist to some degree. When faced with a change that has the breadth of the EMF implementation, resistance may be greater—not because people don't welcome the change, but because it affects almost everyone in the organization. It may rock some people to their very foundation. To keep the change as smooth as possible, you will need to pay particular attention to known pitfalls and be prepared for the unknown.

Some of the common risks people face when implementing change include

- *Lack of communication:* "Because I think of it, everyone will think of it." Communication is one of the cornerstones of change management.
- *Rational viewpoints:* "Because this change is logical, everyone will want to do it." Standardizing the EMF is very logical, but it does not mean that everyone will accept it without resistance. The implementation will have to focus on the *benefits* of the project.
- *Closed leadership:* Implementing major changes involves discussion and negotiation. The leaders of the change must be available as much as possible. Leaders who are not available will not be able to garner support for the change.
- *Support concepts instead of the implementation:* The concept of the EMF is easy to adopt; it is learning to live with it that is harder when you've never done it before.
- *Rigid plans:* The nature of change is that it occurs constantly. Putting in place rigid plans that do not "go with the flow" can be a risk. Your plan will need to be able to adapt as needed. That's why you build in contingencies.

The Cyclical Nature of IT Change

One of the constants of IT is that technologies are always updated. This is one of the basic precepts of the EMF. By putting the EMF in place, you can master IT change and integrate it into your everyday processes. All of its processes are oriented toward facilitating IT change management.

- You know to use software subscriptions instead of purchases. This way, you don't have to allocate special budgets to acquire new technology. It is part of the subscription price.
- You know how to manage kernel changes, so integrating new versions of the OS to your SPA objects should not be a major undertaking.
- And, if you've moved to Windows 2000, you know that Microsoft won't make any major changes to the core features of its operating systems for a few years. Windows 2000 is revolutionary compared to Windows NT, and major software revolutions don't occur in short time spans; they occur regularly over longer periods of time. Because Windows 2000 is still new, its basic structure will not change for a few years. And when this change comes, the EMF you put in place will probably be capable of integrating it into normal operations.

Moving to the EMF

But before you can take advantage of your new IT structure, you'll need to move to the EMF itself. If you haven't implemented Windows 2000 yet, you're lucky because the best time to integrate the .NET model is when you are implementing major infrastructure changes.

When organizations implement new technology, they have to undergo an entire series of preparatory phases to get ready to deploy the change. For example, moving to Windows 2000 would most likely involve testing and repackaging all of your existing applications to make sure that they operate with and are ready for this new OS. It would also involve preparing your Active Directory and integrating your application management strategy to this directory.

This is the ideal moment to include deployment of the EMF. The cost of implementing the .NET model by itself is quite significant. But the cost of implementing it along with

Windows XP

While Windows 2000 was four years in the making, Windows XP, its successor, was only two. Why? Because the revolutionary changes occurred in Windows 2000. Windows XP is the refinement of those changes. If Windows 2000 was version 5.0, Windows XP is version 5.1.

Using the kernel update process, you should be able to move quite easily from Windows 2000 to Windows XP without having to undergo a new massive deployment project.

Implementing the EMF

If you do not have a technological project that can bear the implementation of the EMF model along with it, you can minimize costs by implementing the model one piece at a time. This will greatly reduce costs and allow for better integration in the organization because people will have time to adapt to the change.

Using Internal Personnel on the Project

One of the new trends in IT today is the use of internal personnel for project implementations and technological migrations. Organizations create working teams mostly composed of internal personnel along with consultants in key positions.

This is an excellent idea because it is one of the best ways for your personnel to live through the change. In addition, by putting them on the front line of the project, they have to master the technology. Finally, using subject matter experts in key positions and placing them with your personnel means they are in an excellent position to profit from knowledge transfer.

There is one caveat: Personnel must understand what "project mode" means.

Organizational personnel are used to working in *recurrent mode,* meaning that they perform work for which there may not be a deliverable. In *project mode,* deliverables are essential. They come with due dates and dependencies.

When people participate in a project without an understanding of project mode, they put the project at risk. Remember, a short course on project participation is a boon to such a project.

a migration to a new technology is much less because most of it is borne by the technological project itself. Whether or not you include the .NET model, the technology migration will require a significant budget. Including the EMF adds to this budget, but not as significantly as if it was implemented on its own.

Mapping the Project through Deliverables

One of the best ways to manage deployment projects is to identify the deliverables of such a project. Mapping project activities to deliverables makes sense. People know what they have to do. Tasks are divided into subcategories and are more readily identifiable.

Figure 6.1 illustrates how this could work. It integrates the EMF implementation along with a migration to Windows 2000 on both servers and PCs. Its objectives are to demonstrate activities through deliverables.

This graphical representation of the activities required to deploy technology makes it easy for everyone to see how important each task is and how other tasks will suffer if the previous tasks are not completed in time.

Two key factors of any project are *dependencies* and *deadlines*. The first factor is outlined by an illustration, such as the map in Figure 6.1. The second factor is outlined by the project plan. This plan lists start dates, deadlines, milestones, and critical activities. It outlines who does what and when. This plan forms the core of the project itself, and it needs to be structured in order to be effective. This is where the QUOTE System comes into play.

Using a Structured Project Approach

Chapter 1 introduced the QUOTE System as a structured approach for change management. This system includes five phases: Question, Understand, Organize, Transfer, and Evaluate. In fact, this system defines the structure of this book. It begins by identifying the problem, viewing potential solutions, testing retained solutions, deploying the solutions, and reviewing the results. This system forms a structure that is similar to that of a project.

The QUOTE System is ideal for the preparation and review of deployment projects. In this instance, each stage focuses on the following activities:

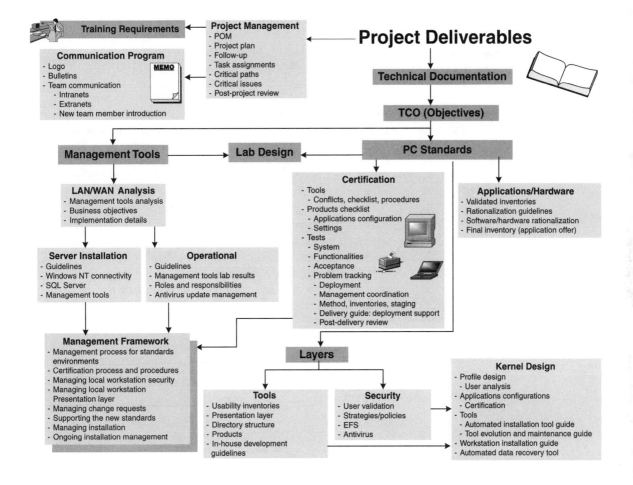

FIGURE 6.1 A .NET Deliverables Map. Mapping project deliverables clearly demonstrates deliverable dependencies. It also illustrates how all of the pieces of a .NET puzzle fit together during implementation.

- Identification of the problem and inventory of the organization (Question)
- Identification of potential solutions (Understand)
- Validation of the selected solutions and definition of a technology transfer methodology (Organize)
- Deployment and activation (Transfer)
- Project finalization and preparation for the support and evolution of the solution (Evaluate)

Why the Word "QUOTE"

Our change management strategy is called a "QUOTE" because a quote has the same characteristics as a project:

- It defines the *scope* of work.
- It identifies a *budget* for the work.
- It outlines objectives that *qualify* the work.

The QUOTE Cycle

What's important to note here is that the QUOTE System is a cycle. The last phase of the QUOTE System, Evaluate, is the starting point for the next phase, Question. Once new technologies are implemented, you begin to see new possibilities.

For example, organizations that implement a technology such as Windows 2000/XP will do so in stages. Because Windows 2000/XP includes so many new capabilities compared to older versions, most organizations want to proceed with care. To do so, they categorize Windows 2000/XP's features into short-, medium-, and long-term implementation stages. This is a very good idea. The organization cannot face too much change at once. Dividing it into smaller pieces makes it more manageable.

But this division also means that the organization requires a three-phased project to implement the new technology. If they use a system such as the QUOTE System, they will tend to reinitiate the QUOTE System as soon as the first project is finished. The cyclical nature of the QUOTE System is illustrated in Figure 6.2.

The EMF is designed to help you cope with constant IT change while providing a stable environment. The cyclical QUOTE System is one of the cornerstones of this model.

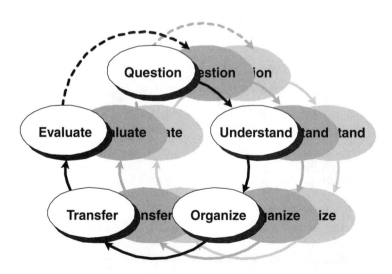

FIGURE 6.2   The QUOTE Cycle. The QUOTE System forms a cycle that is in continuous motion.

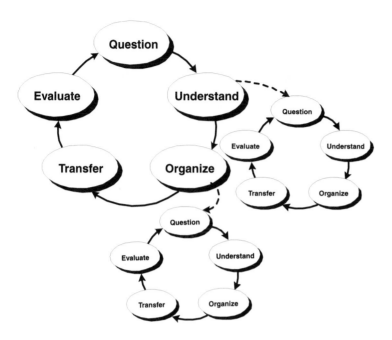

FIGURE 6.3   QUOTEs within QUOTEs. Each phase of the QUOTE System can include the complete cycle if required. This is the case for the Transfer Phase section of this book.

QUOTEs within QUOTEs

The first five chapters of this book stepped through the initial three phases of the QUOTE System. These phases have helped define the problem, identify potential solutions, and structure the processes that are required prior to deployment.

This chapter begins the fourth phase: Transfer. The Transfer Phase involves the actual deployment of the EMF. But even though the Transfer Phase concentrates on actual deployment, it still requires preparation. As a result, you need to identify which elements you want to put into place, integrate the elements into your existing processes, and then test them before deployment.

In fact, you will find yourself performing a QUOTE within a QUOTE. This is another aspect of this system: *Each phase can include the complete cycle.* Figure 6.3 illustrates this concept.

Case Study
Applying the QUOTE System to a Large Deployment Project

Organization Type	Private Sector
Number of Users	20,000
Number of Computers	20,000
Project Focus	Migration to Windows 2000
Project Duration	1 Year
Specific Project Focus	Increase Stability for PCs
Administrative Type	Decentralized

Like many global corporations, this organization managed growth through acquisitions. As such, the company was not a single organism, but rather a collection of loosely tied divisions, each having its own IT system and its own internal culture. With the move to Windows 2000, this organization chose to implement the EMF because the Framework would begin to tie each of the separate divisions together and integrate them into a single, unified team.

In the past during major deployments, each division would put in place and manage its own project. The only activity that occurred at the enterprise level was the decision to migrate. This was the case for projects such as migration to Windows 95 or the Y2K bug. In addition, each division used diverse networking technology.

The Windows 2000 project was the first project whose specific goal was to bring every IT group together and make them work and operate as a single unit. The challenge was daunting, but with the use of the processes inherent in the EMF and its change management techniques, cohesion began to form between the groups.

Each group discovered that most of the other groups used processes that were similar to theirs. Each also discovered that despite the fact that their decisions on technologies did not produce the same results, their decision-making processes were very similar. Bonds were created and teams began to work together smoothly.

This process did not complete with the Windows 2000 migration. It is still going on today, though the technological migration project proved to be the right vehicle for the implementation of the EMF.

Deploying the EMF

As mentioned earlier, this chapter begins the Transfer Phase of the EMF, the actual deployment of the processes and systems that make up the Framework. But because the purpose of the Framework is to bring people, PCs, and processes together, and because its objectives are to increase productivity with as little disruption to business operations as possible, it is important to ensure that you are completely ready *before* you initiate this deployment.

Though this is the Transfer Phase for the book, it still requires a review of how the systems will be put in place—it requires a QUOTE within a QUOTE.

Preparatory Activities for Delivery

Several activities are required before the actual deployment can begin. So far, you've identified the problem and seen ways in which it can be solved, but the generic processes covered here must be adapted to your own environment. For this, you need a clear and complete understanding of your organization. You'll also need to look at deployment techniques that will disrupt operations as little as possible. These latter methods assume that the EMF is being deployed along with a new OS such as Windows 2000 or Windows XP.

Specific Inventories

Inventories are at the core of any new technology implementation. If you are going to replace the OS on every system in your organization, you *must* know exactly what is available on that system.

There are several types of inventories. If your asset management system is truly up-to-date, you can use it to create a detailed inventory of the components on each system. But in most cases, this is not sufficient.

Take, for example, a user's PC. The asset management system details what brand of PC it is, how much disk space it contains, how much RAM it includes, and what software is installed. But the asset management system will not tell you if all of the RAM slots are full in the machine. It will not tell you if all of the applications located on the system are actually required by the user. It will not tell you what it might have missed.

As a result, you need to ensure that your inventories are up-to-date. You'll also want to make sure that the person

---

Personnel Mobility and Asset Management

There is a lot of personnel mobility within organizations. When a person moves from one position to another within the same department or even across departments, it often means that he or she will "inherit" the previous person's PC.

In an ideal situation, this PC would have the data backed up, the hard disk erased, and a new system installed. But this is rarely the case today. People tend to just pick up where their predecessor left off.

As a result, when you perform inventories, it is important to ensure that each person (or each person's boss) validates every single tool on the PC.

You will be surprised at how many products are installed in your network without any real reason for them.

who is responsible for the machine validates the particular inventory for a PC or for a server. For PCs, this is validation by the principal user; for a server, this is validation by its administrator.

User Needs Assessment

The purpose of the EMF is to increase productivity and reduce TCO. One of the best ways to increase productivity and reduce TCO is to ensure that the systems you put in place respond to specific user needs. To do this, you need to inventory user requirements.

This doesn't mean that you have to inventory the entire user base. Using statistical techniques, you need only identify and inventory a significant sample of the user base. The significant sample depends on the size of the organization. The ideal is 10 percent, but for organizations with several thousand employees, this amount becomes unwieldy. In this case, "significant" means representative. For example, if you sample only 4 percent of the user base, make sure that your sample includes 4 percent of every significant role within your organization: 4 percent of managers, 4 percent of administrative staff, 4 percent of technicians, and so on. Representation is often more important than numbers.

Now you'll have to decide what to analyze. The purpose of this inventory is to identify the following:

- Usage patterns for existing software
- Current problems faced by users
- Workflow patterns
- Communication patterns
- Repetitive tasks
- User mobility and accessibility requirements
- Information repositories in use
- Support patterns and problem resolution techniques
- User knowledge level

Identifying this information will help you plan your .NET implementation and enable you to identify how your Presentation layer should be configured. It should also help show you some of the hidden TCO costs within your own organization (how people use and get support and assistance, the level of knowledge of your personnel, and so

---

User Needs Assessment

More on the user needs assessment is covered in Chapter 8.

on). This should enable you to identify potential cost reductions for the project. Finally, it will greatly assist in the
preparation of the training program for the deployment
project.

Additional Activities

Another activity is related to the methodology used for deployment. Several activities are required to identify this
methodology, especially if one of the objectives is to disrupt business operations as little as possible.

For example, if an organization has several thousand
PCs to deploy, it might consider several different technologies, especially remote technologies. But if the organization is migrating from an environment that does not support
system locking (such as Windows 95), it may well prefer to
erase[1] everything that is on a PC and replace it with a managed kernel.

Few systems can remotely erase a PC and put in place a
new OS. Most are oriented toward an upgrade. Thus, the
organization will have to review the methods it intends to
use to prepare PCs with little or no business operations
disruption.

You need to devise a system that will enable you to
replace PCs without bothering users. This system requires
the following preparatory activities:

- Application packaging/component certification
- Machine prestaging
- User data/profile recovery
- Synchronized training and deployment

You must put all of these activities in place before you
can begin to deploy. The first three activities are covered in
this chapter. The fourth, synchronized training and deployment, is covered in Chapter 9. For now, it is only important
to note that you may want to have training occur at exactly
the same time you deploy because it removes users from
their desks and enables technicians to perform whatever
work is required free of user interventions.

---

1. There are several issues related to upgrading an OS, especially from an
uncontrolled environment. Most technologists say that upgrading an
uncontrolled system means upgrading the "garbage."

Application Packaging/Component Certification

The first activity is application packaging. Because you intend to deploy the new system as smoothly and as efficiently as possible, all applications must be packaged for deployment. This way, they will install automatically without user or technical intervention.

Application packaging and conflict detection are covered in Chapter 4. You need to put this strategy in place and prepackage everything that you will retain in the organization in terms of software. The best cost-reduction technique for this activity is the rationalization process, which is also covered in Chapter 4.

Machine Prestaging

Because you need to replace the entire OS—in fact, you'll erase the entire hard disk—you need to put in place a strategy that will enable you to do so with a minimum of effort. The best way to achieve this is to use a machine prestaging strategy.

Machine prestaging involves using a staging area to prepare machines before they are put in place within the network. You can apply this process to both servers and PCs.

For servers, this process makes complete sense. By preparing a server ahead of time, you can minimize the impact of its replacement by changing it overnight. The next morning, users log on to the new server without knowing that it has been changed. But prestaging user PCs is the most rewarding.

For PCs, it makes more sense to prepare the machines beforehand than to prepare the machines while at users' desks. Imagine a technician having to prepare 50 or 100 machines per day at users' desks. You would need to have dozens of technicians! But if you gather the machines beforehand, bring them to a staging area, mount the system on them all at once, and simply deliver them to users' desks, you minimize the impact of system replacement on business productivity and user effectiveness.

How can you remove a user's PC without completely disabling the user?

To do this, you need a PC rotation program. When organizations migrate to a new OS, they inevitably have to replace some systems. New operating systems are more demanding and require more powerful machines. Thus, organizations have to replace portions of their PC network

How Many Machines per Day?

When migrating operating systems on user PCs, you need to determine how many machines per day you will migrate. Several factors will influence your decision, including the size of your organization, the physical location of the PCs, and the method used for PC preparation.

We have discovered that with a staging area and custom staging tools, you can easily expect a single technician to prepare up to 35 PCs per half-day.

because the machines are not powerful enough to run the new OS.

By purchasing these new machines ahead of time, the deployment project can use them as a bank of machines that can be staged beforehand and deployed to both replace older systems and to provide a source for PC rotation.

The offer made to users is simple: Users will gain machines of the *same or greater capability* as the ones they had before. This offer forms the core of the PC rotation program. Of course, this program requires a lot of coordination—machines have to be prepared before delivery, machines have to be recovered in time to meet demand, and machines have to be cleaned[2] during the rotation process. This process is illustrated in Figure 6.4.

PC Cascades

One of the major issues that organizations must deal with when managing PCs is the rotation of systems. In an IT corporation, it makes sense that people who have the most demanding IT job functions get the most powerful PCs. The problem with this concept is that because organizations upgrade PCs regularly, they need to constantly change everyone's PC every time new systems are introduced into the network. This is the *PC cascade process*.

There is no doubt that the cascade process is a good idea. Illustrators, engineers, and developers should all get the latest and greatest machines. It doesn't make sense to have an administrative assistant with a Pentium II 850MHz machine while a developer is struggling with a Pentium 120MHz.

The EMF, with its IT profile management strategies and its standard approach to SPA objects, can truly facilitate this process.

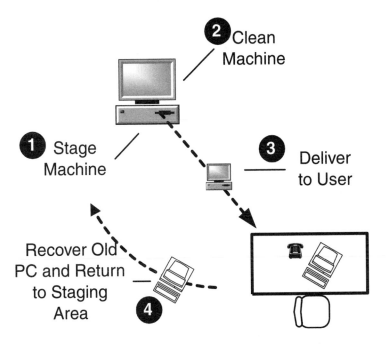

FIGURE 6.4 Machine Preparation and Delivery Procedure. Machine preparation is a cycle that includes four basic steps: stage the machine, clean the machine (it then appears to be new), deliver the machine to the user, and recover the "old" PC and return it to the staging area.

---

2. Cleaning the machines is considered a hassle by technicians but a boon by users. Receiving a clean machine, even if it is used, makes all the difference in a rotation program as far as users are concerned.

Staging Proof of Concept

Disk imaging for staging is a great technology. Technologies such as Symantec's Ghost, PowerQuest's Drive Image Pro, and Altiris' RapiDeploy can capture the image of a hard disk and replicate it on hundreds of machines.

In fact, the best performance we have seen to date was the staging of 35 machines linked at 100Mb. Using multicast technologies (the message was sent only once on the network), the entire kernel image was installed on all 35 PCs within 5 minutes!

One advantage to this process is that only the actual PC box needs replacement. Keyboards, monitors, and mice can all remain the same because these tend to be standard and will work with almost any box.

There are issues with this procedure, though, having mostly to do with logistics and departmental budgets. But machine rotation is a must if you want to be able to take advantage of machine staging.

Staging and Application Deployment Approaches

Staging is an important factor in quality of service during deployment. Using a special mounting area, organizations can prepare dozens of PCs at the same time. To do this, they need to have a staging technology. Several products are available on the marketplace, but custom solutions are often best.

Staging takes advantage of the preparatory work done in previous phases, especially application packaging. It also takes advantage of disk imaging technologies. One of the great advantages of the IT Model for Service Points of Access is that the kernel includes everything that a user may require to operate within the network. And, as was discussed in Chapter 5, the entire kernel can be captured with disk imaging technology. As a result, the basic installation of a PC is taken care of with disk imaging. In many cases, this is the only preparation required because the user requires only the kernel.

If more preparation is required, the staging process moves on to the user IT profile installation. This installation involves adding all of the applications included in a given IT profile or configuration. Profiles can be delivered to the PC through system management tools, but performance is better when the applications within the profile are installed through a *pull* mechanism.

System management tools *push* applications to PCs. This process always includes an uncontrollable delay because the system has to locate the target PC, determine when the PC can accept the applications, and then initiate delivery.

Using SysPrep

If you use disk imaging to deploy Windows 2000 or XP, you will need to modify your original image with Microsoft's SysPrep utility. This utility ensures that the original image is depersonalized and will work with every PC model.

Pulling is more appropriate when staging PCs because the technician is in control of the entire operation. Pulling occurs immediately and is thus more practical at this stage. The advantage of all of the application packages (remember the certification process?) created through the EMF is that they can be delivered with either push or pull mechanisms. Figure 6.5 illustrates the machine staging process.

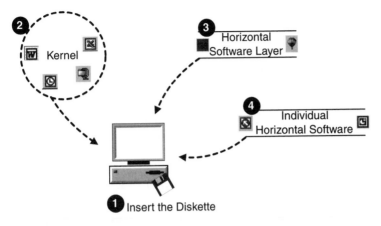

FIGURE 6.5 The Machine Staging Process. Machine staging involves installing the kernel, adding the user's application profile, and then finalizing with individual software components if required. Everything begins with a personalized staging diskette.

Data Recovery Strategies

One of the great advantages of PC staging is that there is very little time spent at the user's desk. When the installation technician arrives, all that is required is the removal of the old machine and its replacement with the new machine. Ideally, it is as simple as that, but usually it's not. Why? Because when you replace a machine, you need to recover user information and restore it to the new machine.

Users will invariably store corporate information or personal environmental information locally on their machines, so a data recovery tool is required. Ideally for users, the migration experience should be completely transparent. In fact, they should find their personal shortcuts, their Favorites, and so on just the way they were on their old system.

The data recovery tool (DRT) should take into account not only the protection of information, but also the replacement of that information in the proper format and in the proper place on the new SPA system.

The DRT should protect and restore the following information:

- Web or intranet Favorites
- Data files (Word, Excel, PowerPoint, Access, Outlook, and so on)

Prestaging at Purchase

Many PC manufacturers now stage PCs before delivery. This means that you can prepare your standard PC image and deliver a copy to your vendor. The vendor will prestage the PC for you (at an additional cost, of course). For smaller organizations, this makes more sense than having a staging area.

Inventory Data Sheet

For an example of an inventory data sheet, see Appendix C. This inventory is the basis for the DRT process.

The DRT Tool and Windows XP

Windows XP has a built-in DRT-like tool called the User State Migration Tool (USMT). It migrates user information from Windows 95, 98, NT, and 2000 to Windows XP.

Other commercial tools may be more powerful than the USMT.

- Desktop elements (including shortcuts)
- My Documents folders on local drives
- Custom data such as Word templates, personal dictionaries, AutoCorrection files, and so on
- Any personalized initialization files

You can purchase the DRT from a series of manufacturers—more and more data recovery tools are available on the marketplace. But because the DRT will mostly be used for the migration and later for ongoing machine replacement, it may be easiest for organizations to write their own. A simple DOS batch file can perform all of these actions.

Now that you have all of the tools you need, you're ready to move on to the actual deployment project itself.

Delivery Support Tools

As a final preparation, you'll need to set up teams to support the deployment. For this, you'll have to review and prepare the following three crucial activities:

- Project management
- Communication
- Training

These activities are covered in the final chapters of this book.

Using the QUOTE System

You have now begun the Transfer Phase. You are in the process of preparing the .NET deployment. The next chapters examine three crucial deployment elements: project management, communications, and training.

Case Study
PC Deployment Program

Organization Type	Public Sector
Number of Users	5,000
Number of Computers	4,500

Project Focus	Deployment of a Standard Kernel on PCs
Project Duration	6 Months
Specific Project Focus	Standardize the Entire Network
Administrative Type	Centralized

This organization used a staging and PC rotation program to deploy a new standardized kernel on all of their PCs. The list of activities they used to perform the actual positioning of the machines was as follows:

1. *Specific PC inventory:* The organization used a variety of means to identify every single software component on each user's PC. These included Microsoft Systems Management Server inventories, login script routines, and asset management databases. All were combined to get a precise picture of each PC. In addition to software, this inventory included personal items such as shortcuts, Internet and intranet Favorites, personal dictionaries, local documents, macros, templates, and so on. This complete inventory was deemed essential because everything on the hard disk was to be erased at the installation of the new system.

2. *Identification of items to recover:* To facilitate the recovery process, the project clearly identified the recovery offer that was to be made to users. This offer listed everything that the project would protect during migration. In some cases, it meant that users would have to perform preparatory work to clean up or reorganize their information on their PCs. Even though the organization published a specific list of directories that would be recovered, the DRT performed a final global search on the PC for any of the items that required recovery, just in case.

3. *Rationalized software offer:* Because the organization performed a software rationalization, it was important for the project to clearly identify to users what would be available on the new PC. When software was retired, this offer listed the replacement product, including conversion facilities and training programs if required.

4. *User representatives:* All direct communication to users was performed through an intermediary: the user representative. Each representative was responsible for at least 100 users. These representatives were the people

who interacted directly with users and reported information back to the project team.

5. *User validation of the inventory:* User representatives met with each user to validate that the user actually required all of the software on his or her current system and to assist the user in the preparation of his or her PC. This validation served two purposes. The first was to reduce software usage as much as possible.[3] The second was to create a contract between the project and the user. This contract indicated both the user's and the project's responsibilities.

6. *User Inventory database:* User inventories were integrated into a database that was finalized once the user contract was received. This database served as the source database for what needed to be installed on the "new" PC.

7. *Package Source database:* Every rationalized software product was packaged for automated installation. All information about these packages (source file for installation, command parameters, source directory, and documentation on the installation) was stored in the Package Source database. This database was linked to the User Inventory database.

8. *PC staging:* All PCs were prepared in a staging area. A third database was used for preparing the staging information for every PC. This database identified the new PC, linked to the User Inventory database to identify all of the software to be installed, and then called upon the Package Source database to identify the command lines required to install each software package. The final result was a special staging diskette for each PC. This diskette included the start-up program required to name the PC, copy the kernel to the PC, and then automatically pull every other software product in the PC's profile. At this stage, the PC was ready for delivery.

9. *Mandatory training:* A special half-day training program was put in place for all users. This program was mandatory. For installation purposes, this training served to remove users from their desks during PC delivery.

10. *PC delivery and replacement:* A technician delivered the PC to the user's desk while the user was at the

---

3. Remember, users often inherit PCs with existing software on them even though they will never use it.

training session. Before the removal of the old PC, the technician launched the DRT to recover the user's existing data. This tool performed an automated search on the PC to copy all user information to a transition server on the network. Once this was complete, the technician removed the old PC (just the box—the screen, keyboard, mouse, and so on all remained in place).

11. *Data retention period:* Recovered data was kept online for a period of two weeks, giving users time to validate that they had everything. After two weeks, the data was archived on tape backup. These tape backups were kept for a period of three months. All user data was compressed into Zip files to conserve space.

12. *Installation of the new PC:* The technician put the new PC in place, plugged everything in, booted the PC, and performed a data recovery. This first live boot of the PC also served as a quality control measure to ensure the PC was functioning properly on delivery. Data was recovered to a recovery directory because the user had not accessed the PC yet.

13. *First user login:* When the user returned from the training session, the user performed his or her initial login. This action created the user's personal profile on the PC. The DRT automatically placed recovered items in appropriate locations within the newly created Windows NT profile. The user was responsible for the validation of his or her information on the PC.

14. *User coaching:* Even though users received special training and automated procedures were used to recover data to appropriate areas on the PC, users were given special coaching. This coaching took two different forms. Headquarters and large offices had special personnel for coaching, and remote offices used remote control technology to assist users during their initial login and PC validation processes.

15. *Special support services:* The problems that may occur during a massive migration program are not the same as those that occur during recurring use of a network. As such, a special support task force was put in place to provide support to users of the new PCs. The mission for this support group was to deliver and repair problems as quickly as possible. For example, if users claimed they were missing software components, they were delivered without any questions asked. Once

users were operational, only then did the group worry about asset management issues.

16. *Optional training:* The mandatory training program covered only the essentials required to get users up and running. An optional training program was made available to users who wanted more in-depth training on specific tools. This program was available to users after they had been migrated.

Though this entire process required a lot of coordination and several migration resources, the organization deemed the project a complete success. Ninety-nine percent of users were satisfied with the strategies used for migration. Less than 10 percent of users claimed that software programs or data was missing from their new systems. Every user was satisfied because each had the feeling that he or she had received a brand-new PC.

CHAPTER ROADMAP

Use this flowchart as a guide to understand the concepts covered in this chapter.

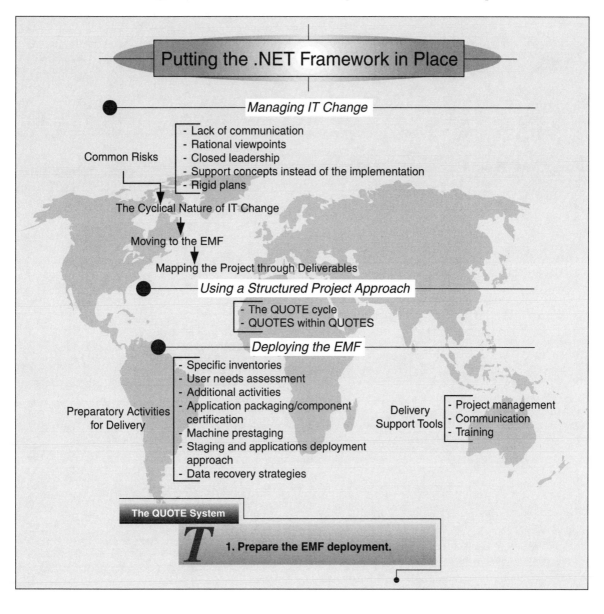

CHAPTER 7

Project Management
Building Teams for Result-Oriented Projects

In 1994, hockey fans everywhere were very surprised to see the Vancouver Canucks, a little-known team with no star players, rise to the Stanley Cup Finals.

What was even more surprising was that during their hockey season, the Canucks had undergone several major setbacks. Despite these setbacks, the entire team managed to rally supporters and investors alike to go for the Cup.

For once, hockey saw what a team of "nobodies" could do when they put their hearts into it. The Canucks beat the odds and managed to end up in the finals against the New York Rangers—the league's champions and a team made up mostly of individual star players. At this stage most fans thought the game was up. The Rangers would eat the Canucks alive. But once again, the Canucks surprised everyone by staying on top of the game and drawing the finals to a seventh game.

Their success was due to the fact that this group of players played like a team. Each player knew his role and each played to support the others on and off the ice. Their supporters also rallied to the call. Vancouverites and hockey fans everywhere were on their side. Everybody loves an underdog.

Perhaps you remember the 1994 Stanley Cup Finals, perhaps you don't, but one thing is sure: If you want to understand what a team is and how every member fits into a tightly integrated pattern supporting group objectives, watch the replays. It's history in the making.

What the Vancouver Canucks understood and demonstrated was that you don't need individual stars to achieve

The QUOTE System's Transfer Phase

The Transfer Phase continues with a look at how to structure deployments through project management techniques. Here you'll examine the structure required to ensure that your deployment of the EMF will be a complete success by embodying the very principles of the Framework itself.

Working as a Team

Teams can form tightly woven groups that work toward common goals.

Migratory birds are great team players.

greatness.[1] What you need is a group of individuals working toward a common goal and sharing a common vision. When you understand that each and every member of the team plays a critical role that fits within the group like a cog in a machine, you'll be able to build teams that can focus on success.

In a team, individual roles don't matter. What is important is that each member understands his or her relationship to the group and has a clear definition of his or her tasks within the group. It is also important for leaders to understand the value of each member no matter what the individual's level of expertise or the complexity of that person's tasks. In addition, each and every member must have a forum to express his or her opinion. Leaders should let team members know that their opinions count.

Migratory birds fly in a V formation because it is aerodynamic. The fact that they relieve each other at the head of the V gives each of the team members 70 percent more reach in a single flight. Strong teams can achieve similar results.

When people bind together as a team they can achieve much more than a group of individuals.

The Golden Rules of Deployment Projects

The *Concise Oxford Dictionary* defines a project as "a planned undertaking . . . for presentation of results at a specified time."

Projects are about teams working together to achieve common objectives in a defined period of time. Projects must always meet deadlines. Projects are defined by their deliverables. Projects are managed through dependencies.

In an EMF, projects must meet quality of service standards. It is often the teams that are put together to provide the service that define the quality of the service to be delivered. For projects, the *right* team is crucial.

Deployment Project Truisms

The starting point for any project is its objectives. Deployment projects in particular are initiated by the arrival of a

---

1. Unfortunately, the Canucks didn't win that last game, but they sure gave it a good try. As for the Rangers, it had been 54 years since they'd won the Cup!

new technology. With Windows 2000 on the market, Windows XP out, and Microsoft already working hard at developing Longhorn and Blackcomb, IT organizations adopting the Windows standard will have ample opportunity for deployment projects caused by the arrival of new technologies. Because these new technologies are all operating systems, deployment projects will be significant in proportion.

For instance, look at the rate of adoption of Windows 2000. People are impressed by its new features, but they soon realize that implementing Windows 2000 is nothing like implementing Windows NT. With Windows 2000, organizations must take a long, hard look at how people, PCs, and processes will interact together in the virtual environment created by their new network. Active Directory alone is something that makes organizations think twice before taking the Windows 2000 plunge. And they're right to do so: Their entire virtual environment is based on how they design their Active Directory and what they put into it, so organizations must learn to understand themselves before they are able to benefit from Windows 2000. In addition, Active Directory will be the basis of the entire .NET Enterprise System.

But the arrival of a new technology is not an objective in and of itself. It can be a cause, but it is not an objective.

First and foremost, the objective of any deployment project is to "put in place, as a minimum, the same capacities as the current system." Of course, new technologies bring with them new capacities and inherent improvements. If the project's objective is to replace an existing technology at the existing level of capacity, it must at least add a second objective: "Include in the first delivery all of the improvements that are inherent in the new technology while still meeting current capacities." For example, if you need to reactivate a shared folder under the new system, use its publication in the directory service as a tool for improved service delivery.

If your organization is preparing to replace Windows NT, Banyan Vines, or Novell NetWare with Windows 2000, you must at the very least collect and identify all of the problems and issues existing in the current network and try to identify which ones can be immediately resolved through the inherent features of the new system.

> **"Longhorn"**
>
> Microsoft is preparing significant changes in the upcoming Windows version, "Blackcomb." As such, it has decided to release an interim version first, code-named "Longhorn."

> **Future Windows Upgrades**
>
> Organizations migrating to Windows 2000 would do well to take this opportunity to put in place the EMF. Its principles and standards can prepare organizations for the arrival of and a smooth integration to systems such as Windows XP, Windows .NET Server, Longhorn, and Blackcomb.

Windows 2000 Features

Windows 2000 included over 100
improvements or new features
compared to Windows NT. These
ranged from features that were
simple to absorb into the organization, such as a more robust OS, to
more complex capabilities that
challenged how organizations work
with technologies, such as Active
Directory.

For example, with Windows NT Workstation, identifying new and improved features is easy. Anyone who has
used NT on a portable and then worked with Windows
2000 even for a short time will immediately tell you that by
simply installing Windows 2000 on the portable, he or she
has vastly improved his or her daily life with its power
management features.

It is with Active Directory that things begin to become
more complex. Active Directory or any Directory-Enabled
Network requires serious reflection by the organization
before it can be fully leveraged because the concepts it
brings are completely new.

One of the best approaches to implement Active Directory is to create a basic directory structure that is comfortable and stable. This structure can resemble current Windows
NT environments. Then, as time passes, you can make it
evolve as necessary because once your users, servers, and
PCs are within Active Directory boundaries, you can ma-
nipulate them at will.

When replacing any technology, the organization should
begin with a thorough examination of that technology's
capabilities and determine which will be included in the
initial deployment. Proceeding otherwise can only lead to
"mega-projects" that can't end. Thus, another objective of
projects is to have *realistic goals*.

These realistic goals often include

- System improvements
- Service-level improvements
- Increased productivity
- Increased return on investment
- TCO reductions
- Review and revision of existing processes

The objectives help define the project's *vision*. This vision is necessary to help bind the project team together. A
clear description of the vision helps everyone know where
he or she is going.

Both the vision and the project objectives should be
thoroughly communicated to all project team members as
well as to the user base that is the focus of the project.

Regarding the latter, letting them know that the project's main objective remains the replacement of existing functionalities with as little disruption to everyday work as possible is crucial.

Working SMART

Microsoft offers a simple approach to the definition of the project's vision and objectives through its Solutions Framework. When defining the vision, Microsoft uses the SMART approach. SMART is an acronym for Specific, Measurable, Attainable, Result-oriented, and Timing. In addition, the vision you define should include a statement about service delivery, usually to users.

The Microsoft Solutions Framework (MSF) uses the SMART approach for vision and objective definition.

If you ensure that your vision includes all of these elements, you'll be right on the mark.

Here's an example of a vision: "Design and deploy a structured technological solution based on Windows 2000's inherent capabilities to improve our capacity to meet business and user needs, and complete the project within the next year."

This vision includes all of the elements described previously. In addition, it is short, easy to understand, easy to remember, and easy to rally to.

The best way to define a project's objectives and its vision is to hold group meetings where everyone is allowed to express his or her opinion. In fact, the object of these types of meetings is to obtain everyone's opinion on the matter. These brainstorming sessions release a lot of steam and help you identify just where your efforts should be placed to improve the quality of service of your technological solution.

Preparing the Project

Once you've defined the vision and identified a *scope*—the extent of the change you intend to carry out—within this vision, your next step is to prepare the project itself. Here you'll have to create the project team, define the rules that will govern interactions within the team, define the processes that will control the activities of the project, and put in place a series of project management and tracking tools. Then you'll be ready to begin the project activities.

The Project Team

The success of a deployment or migration[2] project is dependent on the team that supports it. One of the first dangers to avoid is an incomplete team. Every team member must be given a specific role within the team. Each member must also be made conscious of the responsibilities and tasks tied to his or her role and accept them. And each member must be available for the entire length of the project. Changing team members halfway through the project can be a significant risk. Your best bet is to avoid it right at the start.

Put together the best team possible. Mix and match various combinations of internal and external personnel until you get the fit that is right for you.

In terms of personnel, project teams should always include

- A team sponsor
- A project director
- A project manager
- An enterprise architect
- A workflow architect
- A communications agent
- Technical staff
- Training staff
- Committees representing critical levels of the organization: users, training groups, human resources, managers, regional groups, and technicians

Each role is reviewed in the sections that follow. An organizational chart illustrating the team's structure is displayed in Figure 7.1.

Project Sponsor   The project sponsor is the person who supports the project within the organization. During a project, sponsors use their influence within the organization to help the project go forward. The sponsor provides a direct link to management and high-level decision making affecting both the project and the organization. The sponsor must be someone with decision-making power at a strategic level within the organization.

---

2. Deployment projects are often called "migrations" because they migrate from one technology to another.

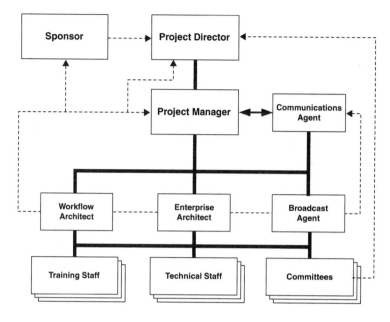

FIGURE 7.1 A Project Team Organizational Chart. The structure of the project team identifies the relationships between each team member.

Project Director

The project director is the person in charge of decision making for the project. This director watches the project team in its activities and ensures that deadlines are met. This person must be made aware of all of the milestones that have been achieved by the project and of any significant problems that arise. In addition, the project director approves all deliverables with the support of the technical members of the project team.

The project director must be a member of the IT group and must have a significant level of decision-making power within this group.

Project Manager

The project manager coordinates all of the activities of the project. These activities include human and technical resource allocation and management. The project manager uses project management techniques to achieve project objectives, follow project deadlines, and respect budget allocations to the satisfaction of the project director and the organization as a whole. These responsibilities form the basis of the contract between the project and its director.

Illustration Legend

Many of the illustrations in Chapters 7, 8, and 9 include both solid and dotted lines.

Solid lines illustrate a constant relationship.

Dotted lines illustrate a recurring relationship that occurs at specific times during a process.

The project director should be well versed in project management strategies and be very familiar with project management tools, such as Microsoft Project.

Enterprise and Workflow Architects   As mentioned in Chapter 2, two new architecture roles are required. Both roles bring new approaches to technology implementations. The enterprise architect's role is to assist in the elaboration of all of the technological decisions for the project. The workflow architect's role is to understand the workings of the organization and adapt technological solutions to ensure maximum integration into the organization's operations. Both roles are as crucial to the success of the project as the project manager's.

The enterprise architect is the resource person for the technical, development, and support teams. This architect's responsibility is to follow the *technical* activities of the project and report on activity progress to the project manager. The enterprise architect is responsible for finding and identifying technical solutions to problem situations.

The workflow architect is the resource person for the communications, training, and solution-support teams. This architect's responsibility is to follow the *human* activities of the project and report on activity progress to the project manager. The workflow architect is responsible for finding and identifying human solutions to problem situations.

Both architects must have a sound understanding of the goals of the organization in light of the implementation of new technologies. Both must achieve this insight at the earliest stages of the project in order to properly direct organizational decisions in regard to the project and provide the soundest technological solutions to the project's objectives.

If either role is provided through external resources, they have to be matched with internal representatives at the same level in order to ensure that a transfer of knowledge to the organization is ongoing and that organizational particularities are integrated into the project's solutions. A good mix is to use external help for the enterprise architect because consulting firms have a sound grasp of new technologies and an internal resource for the workflow architect.

Communications Agent   The communications agent's role is critical, especially in the case of a migration to technologies such as Windows 2000/XP because the breadth of its penetration into the IT infrastructure of the organization touches absolutely everyone. In order to minimize the impact of this change, it is important to include this team member at the earliest stages of the project.

The first task of the communications agent is to put in place a project-driven communications program for the following individuals and groups within the organization:

- Upper management
- The project sponsor
- The project director
- Project teams
- The entire IT department
- The entire user base
- In some cases, the organization's partners and clients

This communications program should include the communications methods, the general content of each message and its intended audience, and the message delivery timeline. And, if the project has a significant timeline (such as one or two years), the program should include an introductory project manual for new team members. Chapter 8 provides more information on the communications program.

Other Team Members   The project team should also include several other members: integrators, administrators, support personnel, developers, and users. The selection of the right team members for each team function is a difficult process. The project manager should perform the selection with the help of the enterprise and workflow architects.

The team should be composed of nine different groups.

- *Project management:* This group includes the sponsor, project director, project manager, and administrative staff.
- *Communications:* This group consists of the communications agent and communicators.
- *Training:* This group includes technical and user training as well as project training.
- *Solution design:* This group focuses on the enterprise and workflow architects as well as internal architects if external resources are part of the project team.
- *Solution development:* This group performs required customization and/or development.

The Communications Agent

You'll learn more about the role of the communications agent in Chapter 8.

Team Members

Technological projects should include team members from every level of the organization that plays an IT role, including personnel from IT, development, the user base, human resources, communications, and client departments.

Training Types

Chapter 9 provides more information on training types.

- *Solution integration:* This group designs the tools and techniques used to deploy the solution.
- *Solution acceptance:* This group consists of targeted users represented in the project to provide acceptance of the solution.
- *Delivery management:* This group includes project administrators and coordinators.
- *Solution support:* This is a special team that supports the deployment.

Figure 7.2 illustrates project team interactions.

In a project with the breadth of an OS migration, team members should come from every level of the organization. As such, they will have time to absorb the change and will act as informal communications agents to the rest of the organization.

Putting Tools and Processes in Place

Once the team is identified, it requires structure in the form of project processes. These processes are in turn supported by project tools.

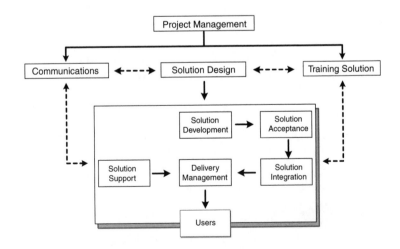

FIGURE 7.2   Project Team Interactions. Project teams interact according to set parameters.

Team Interaction Rules

Project processes include regular activity follow-up meetings, clear and precise task definitions and task dependencies, problem escalation mechanisms, structured problem resolution strategies, and more.

Each team member must understand the objectives of his or her own position and the relationship of his or her role to other roles in the group. The definition of these roles should be performed in a brainstorming session including all team members. This meeting enables each member to clearly see the interactions his or her role has with other roles and it also begins the bonding process for the team. The result should be an organizational chart that identifies members and their roles and responsibilities. This kind of chart helps everyone visually identify team dependencies.

One of the major challenges of deployment projects, especially projects including technologies such as Active Directory, is the integration of technical and nontechnical staff. Your personnel will have to learn to work together and respect each other's opinions if the project is to be a success.[3]

Preparing the Project Team

Because deployment projects always deal with technology that is new to the organization, it is vital to ensure that all project members undergo some form of technical training at the very beginning of the project in order to introduce them to the new technology. Projects deploying Windows 2000/XP, for example, require information programs for managers, technical training programs for technicians and support personnel, development training programs for developers, and end-user programs for everyone. With the assistance of Internet-based information sources, these programs provide information that can greatly assist the project team in defining technical solutions during the implementation.

External Resources

External resources are often change agents hired by the organization to affect and assist in the change. It is important to remember that they will leave once the project is done. It is crucial to ensure that everything they have done is fully documented before they leave.

Deployment Training Programs

Chapter 9 offers more detail on deployment training programs.

---

3. This will be most difficult for technicians because they are very familiar with their technical world. They will have to learn a new nontechnical language if they are to communicate effectively with nontechnical personnel.

Team Tools

It is necessary for the project to select a single set of support tools. Each team member should use the same tools for word processing, project management, presentations, budget calculations, and so on.

Project Management Tools

Following the progress of a project is quite complex, and it is important to put in place appropriate tools for project management. In this case, the right tool for the job is a computerized tool.

Microsoft Project 2000 is by no means an easy tool to use, but anyone with an understanding of project management should be able to quickly use this tool to integrate activities, team communications, and project budgets. In addition, if your deployment aims to include Microsoft technologies such as Windows 2000 or Windows XP, you'll find that Project includes project management templates for deployments of all sizes. And for novices, Project includes detailed project creation and management assistance.

In addition to traditional project management and tracking functionalities, Project 2000 comes with Microsoft Project Central, an integrated Web site enabling the exchange of information between team members and updated project status information for the entire project team. Because Project Central uses a Web-based interface, team members do not require any other tool than a Web browser and/or Microsoft Outlook to participate. Putting Microsoft Project Central on your intranet enables team members to follow specific and global activities through simple tools such as a Web browser or Microsoft Outlook. Figure 7.3 and Figure 7.4 illustrate some of the views that are available with Project Central.

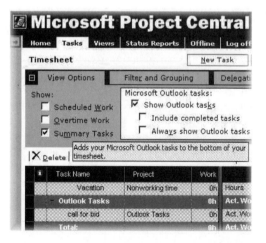

FIGURE 7.3 Microsoft Project Central's Tasks view

FIGURE 7.4 Microsoft Project Central's Status Reports view

Project 2000 uses object linking and embedding (OLE) technology to directly link to a team member's task management tool (in this case, Microsoft Outlook), giving the team member a specific view of his or her own activities and deadlines. When the team member completes a task, he or she simply updates it within Outlook to automatically update the task status in Project Central.

Designing your own internal Project Central site can be one of the success factors of your deployment project.

Continuous Project Evaluation

A technology project requires an evaluation plan. This plan should be applied consistently for the duration of the project. It should focus on activity follow-ups, deadline revisions as required, and communication of major milestones achieved by the project.

The project management team should regularly ask the following questions:

- Does our approach meet with required objectives?
- Are we still on track?
- Are projected budgets still valid and deadlines still realistic?

If at any time the answer to any of these questions is negative, the project manager should immediately initiate a project review.

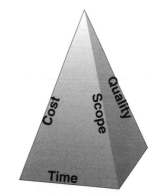

Project Control Factors

There are four factors that control a project: scope, cost, time, and quality. Risk management means affecting one or more of these factors according to the realities of project delivery.

Case Study
Managing Project Meetings

Organization Type	Private Sector
Number of Users	5,000
Number of Computers	6,000
Project Focus	Migration from Windows 95 to Windows 2000
Project Duration	1 1/2 Years
Specific Project Focus	Moving to an EMF
Administrative Type	Decentralized

This organization decided to use internal staff for delivery of the project. They hired outside consultants for specific project roles. The team mix was designed to provide key support to internal personnel. Problems began to arise when outside consultants found that internal personnel were not structured during project meetings.

The consultants identified that internal personnel were not in project mode. For the internal personnel, the project was just another activity within their routine tasks. Given this approach, internal staff would not take notes or minutes during meetings and did not learn to prioritize project activities. In response, the consultants proposed to organize the meetings. They provided the following structure for each meeting:

- Each meeting was assigned a meeting owner. This person was in charge of the meeting and was responsible for the management of follow-up activities.
- A meeting secretary was assigned. This person's responsibility was to take notes and produce the minutes of each meeting, clearly identify follow-up activities, and then send the minutes and follow-up activities to meeting attendees for validation and acceptance.
- Agendas were prepared for each meeting. The meeting's first objective was to accept the agenda and include any last-minute additions.
- Follow-up activities were identified during the meeting. These were assigned specific delivery dates. Activity owners were also identified to assign activity responsibility.

The result was a major increase in efficiency. In fact, the number of meetings was cut in half.

Creating the Project Plan

The core of any project is its plan. Once again, the QUOTE System can help. Deployment projects are about change and the QUOTE System is about structured change management—the two go hand in hand.

Remember, the QUOTE System includes five phases for change management (see Figure 7.5).

- *Question:* This is the phase that helps identify existing issues or the emergence of new technologies. The focus of this phase is both internal to the organization and external in the marketplace.

- *Understand:* This phase focuses on the initial solution design—marrying solutions based on the capabilities of new technologies to existing internal problems. This stage may include a *proof of concept,* a working mock-up of the solution in place. This phase identifies the scope of the project and its structure.

- *Organize:* This is the preparation phase. It includes everything from a detailed conception of the solution to a pilot project—testing all of the facets of the solution to ensure quality of service within the next phase.

- *Transfer:* This is the deployment phase. All systems are go, and a production environment is used to deploy the solution on a massive scale.

- *Evaluate:* This is the project finalization phase. The project's performance is evaluated against objectives. Rules are learned for future projects, and adjustments are made to future approaches. This is also the phase where the solution can evolve with time. It passes into ongoing operations. Finally, this phase serves as the starting point for future Question Phases and processes.

Preparing a Backup Plan

Always prepare a backup plan. This plan should use a smaller project scope and adjusted objectives. It can be used as a fallback plan if the original goes awry.

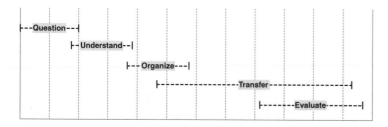

FIGURE 7.5 QUOTE System Timelines. The QUOTE System is divided into five phases that address critical stages of the project.

The scope of each phase can be either large or small. If a project stage is large, the QUOTE System can be reused within it. QUOTEs within QUOTEs provide structure to massive projects.

Inventorying the Organization (Question Phase)

Chapter 2 introduced the concept of a Global Architecture. This architecture is based on specific inventories of the IT situation within the organization.

In the Question Phase of a deployment project, you'll need to review these inventories and refine them if the information you need isn't available. Using a global architecture means that you're always ready for change within your organization. If you don't use a global architecture, ensure that you take advantage of the situation review to put in place an inventory tracking process.

In deployment projects, the Question Phase is usually initiated by a series of situations.

- Software product owners have identified that new versions of the technologies they are responsible for have arrived and meet the organization's criteria for project initiation.
- Users have identified that new technologies are available and they want to take advantage of them.
- Business objectives have changed and new technologies are required to support them.
- The organization is ready for change and requires the introduction of new technologies.
- The manufacturer or software publisher has indicated to the organization that new technologies are available.

These situations initiate a project's planning phase. A needs analysis is performed to identify the benefits that could be acquired through the integration of the new technology. The needs analysis provides the initial project evaluation.

The needs analysis should focus on a list of potential benefits, including problems that could be solved by the technology. It should include the initial scope definition—who will be affected, what the impact of the change will be, and how it should be approached—and initial budget estimates with a plus or minus 25-percent error margin.

The Question Phase

This phase includes

- Situation review, including
  - Internal inventories/problem identification
  - External review of new technologies
- Needs analysis
- Initial project evaluation, including
  - Potential benefits
  - Initial budget estimates
  - Initial project scope
- Cost/benefit analysis
- Go/no go for the project

Inventory Contents

Refer to Appendix A for a complete list of the items required in the inventory.

Finally, a cost/benefit analysis should be performed to en-sure that the organization will profit from the change.

This phase culminates in a go/no go decision for the project (see Figure 7.6).

Creating a Learning Environment (Understand Phase)

The Understand Phase begins the mastery of the new tech-nology and identifies potential solutions. The first step is to list the new features of the technology to be implemented. For Windows 2000 or XP, this is easy. Microsoft offers sev-eral versions of this list in several languages. Then, using

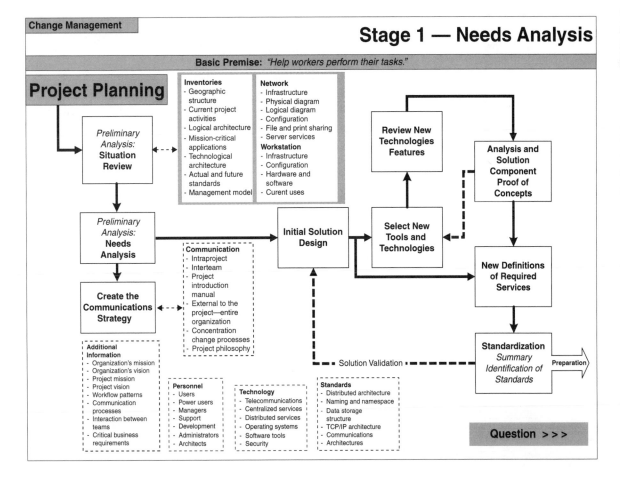

FIGURE 7.6 The Question Phase. The Question Phase focuses on inventories and initial solution design.

Evaluating the Impact of New Features

Evaluating the impact of new features helps you identify the scope of a change. Take, for example, printing in Windows 2000.

Several items have changed from previous versions of Windows. First, all printer hardware must be on the HCL. Second, printer drivers must be certified for Windows 2000. Third, shared printers are published and assigned through Active Directory, so sharing processes must change. Information about printers is also stored in Active Directory. Technicians will have to fill it in. Fourth, user interaction with shared printers is through Active Directory, so users will have to learn new ways of doing things. Finally, users cannot install local printers—they must use networked printers.[4]

The Scope of the Proof of Concept

The proof of concept (POC) can eventually cover about 1 percent of your user population. In fact, you'll have several POCs—some will focus on individual features; others will focus on portions of the solutions and eventually the population sample. It is a good idea to treat POCs the same way you treat software development, with Alpha, Beta, and Gold code stages.

the results of the needs analysis, you can begin to map features to problems or issues that will serve as the basis for your initial solutions.

Next is the project definition. It should include many of the elements covered in this chapter—vision, objectives, scope, structure, teams, tools, and timelines—in order to create the project plan. In addition, the project definition should include a refined budget estimate within a plus or minus 10-percent error margin, which will form the official budget for the project.

This budget should be supplemented by two additional documents: the impact evaluation and the migration strategy. The impact evaluation covers the portions of the organization affected by the change. This document should include items such as work pattern and operational processes, user interaction with IT systems, systems changes, and so on. The migration strategy identifies the strategies that will be used for systems deployment, interactions with users during the deployment, training strategies, and so on. Some of the decisions you'll need to take with Windows 2000/XP and Active Directory are illustrated in Figure 7.7.

Once the project is officially in place, the project's communications program is designed and initiated. Its scope depends on the scope of the change the organization will bear.

At the same time, the initial solution definition can begin. This process includes the definition of the standards that will guide the solution architecture. It will use these standards to identify problem resolution strategies and eventually culminate with the initial solution architecture. It is at this stage that the training solution can begin to form[5] (see Figure 7.8).

This stage of the project requires the installation of a laboratory or its adaptation if you already have one in place. Some hardware and software acquisitions may be required. Because the laboratory will be used for the duration of the project, its operational and testing standards should be defined. This stage may include a working mock-up of the solution in place. This mock-up will greatly assist in budget definitions through initial testing of existing applications

---

4. For exceptions, such as confidential or specialized printing needs, technicians will have to perform the local printer installation.

5. See Chapter 9 for more information.

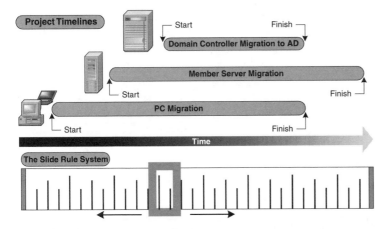

FIGURE 7.7 Migration Timings for Windows 2000/XP. Determining when to begin the migration of the core components of your network depends on your specific needs. You can deploy Windows 2000 or XP on PCs and Windows 2000 on application servers even though you haven't changed your domain or authentication environment. Servers can be deployed by service, and PCs can be deployed by direction. One thing is certain, though: When you begin to change the authentication environment, you need to do it as fast as possible. Thus, you can "slide rule" the deployment along the duration of your deployment project.

and systems. For example, with a migration to Windows 2000/XP Professional, you should use this lab to identify what the acceptable baseline is for existing hardware.

The laboratory serves two major functions: testing and training. The second role is as important to the success of the project as the first. Technical staff requiring retraining should have scheduled access to the lab. If not, this initial technical training program may have to be outsourced.

Finally, it may be necessary to perform a proof of concept to clearly demonstrate the benefits provided by the solution in order to get new budgets approved. Once again, the organization must issue a go/no go decision for the project.

Defining a Technology Transfer Methodology (Organize Phase)

This stage focuses on preparation. It begins with the finalization of the solution architecture, including the design of

The Understand Phase

This phase includes

- A review of the features of the new technology, including
  - Identification of features to be implemented
  - Mapping features to issues and problems
- Project definition, including
  - Vision/objectives
  - Scope
  - Structure
  - Teams
  - Tools
  - Budgets and impacts
  - Timelines
  - Plan
  - Project organization manual
- Initial communications program
- Initial solution definition, including
  - Naming and other standards that apply to the solution
  - Identification of problem resolution strategies
  - Initial solution architecture
  - Initial training solution
  - Deployment strategy
- Initial acquisitions
- Initial laboratory, including
  - Operating and testing standards
  - Initial tests
  - Solution mock-up
  - Technical training
- Proof of concept
- Go/no go for the project

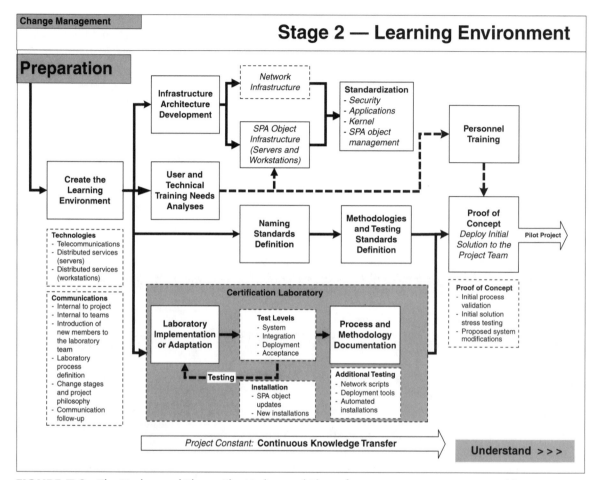

FIGURE 7.8   The Understand Phase. The Understand Phase focuses on creating an internal learning environment for the selected technologies.

Enterprise Project Planning

It is important to identify existing and ongoing projects during the Organize Phase because your project may conflict with other project schedules. If it is possible to synchronize delivery schedules, you should do everything to make it happen. After all, your driving principle is *little or no disruption to business operations*.

This is one of the principles of enterprise project planning.

the initial deployment strategy. These strategies can use a series of different approaches. You can deploy by line of business, affecting one business operation during its deployment but leaving others intact. You can use a geographic deployment strategy and perform everything at once in a given location. You can deploy by SPA object type, dealing with PCs all at once, then moving on to application servers and finishing with identity and security servers[6] (you can address these in a different order, if you wish). But one thing is clear: Your deployment strategy should aim to minimize impacts on users and business operations. This strat-

---

6. Domain controllers in Windows NT.

egy should be part of the communications program as soon as it has been approved.

It is during the finalization of the solution architecture that solution development should begin. Custom solutions will require large development subprojects. These subprojects will require extensive testing. Solutions focusing on infrastructure changes will require much less development, but developers should still be part of the team to support automation and ensure that their interests are preserved.

Once the solution is finalized, solution integration programs can be developed, including SPA object staging mechanisms, application testing and repackaging/certification, solution acceptance testing by appropriate clienteles, the definition of data recovery mechanisms, and the preparation of deployment infrastructures, such as mobile staging rooms and training facilities.

The preparation of the solution support program also occurs at this stage. It is integrated with the technical training program because affected technical personnel will need to be trained on the solution. In addition, it includes the preparation of special support mechanisms: Will the regular support team absorb support of the deployment, or should a special, separate team be put in place? How long will this special team be required? When does a migrated user move back to the regular support team?

The answers to all of the previous questions form the support mechanisms for the project. In most cases, deployment support is offered by the project for a period of 30 days before the user is returned to recurring support mechanisms. This 30-day period forms the project's deployment support guarantee.

Finally, there is the pilot project, which tests all of the facets of the solution to ensure quality of service for the deployment (see Figure 7.9). The pilot project should represent every deployment activity from user communications to machine deployment, including training.

The pilot project should deliberately test every deployment mechanism. For example, if the project aims for the replacement of PCs, applications should be forgotten *on purpose* at the PC staging process. This enables the testing of the support mechanisms for rapid application deployment during the pilot. This project should also include regular meetings with user representatives to determine the ongoing status of the pilot.

The Organize Phase

This phase includes

- Finalization of the solution architecture, including initial deployment strategies
- Solutions development (if required)
- Solution integration programs, including
  - Automated installation mechanisms
  - Application testing and packaging/certification
  - Refined user and hardware inventories
  - User data-recovery mechanisms
  - Deployment infrastructures
  - Acceptance testing
- Solution support program, including
  - Technical training program
  - Special support mechanisms
- Pilot project, including
  - User communications
  - Solution deployment
  - Training programs for users
  - Training programs for technical staff
  - Solution support
  - Pilot evaluation
  - Approach modifications (if required)
- Deployment strategy finalization and approval
- Final acquisitions

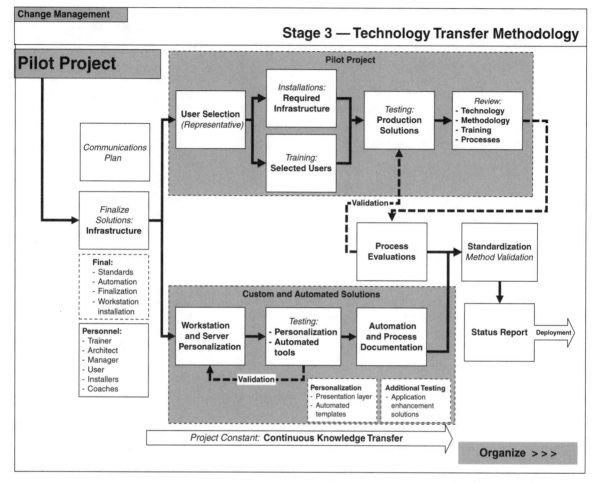

FIGURE 7.9 The Organize Phase. The Organize Phase focuses on stress testing every project solution.

The evaluation of the pilot should include comments from every pilot project participant: project managers, co-ordinators, administrators, technicians, users, trainers, support personnel (centralized and local), communicators, and any other personnel that participated in the pilot. Comments and recommendations should be used to modify deployment approaches to improve the quality of deployment services at the next stage.

If major architectural modifications are required, pilot project users should be first on the deployment list for the next stage. Pilot users agree to bear any inconveniences

The Scope of the Pilot

The pilot project should cover about 10 percent of your user population, including central and regional locations if your organization is decentralized.

the project may bring if its approaches and solutions are not completely fine-tuned. It is thus important to "reward" participants with the first receipt of the final solution.

The final modifications should be made to the deployment strategy. Management at all levels should accept this strategy before you can proceed.

The last step in this stage deals with acquisitions. Remember that in an EMF, you'll want to buy before you build and lease before you buy.

Evergreen Leases

Because change is a constant in IT, it is often better to lease than to buy. Evergreen leases are best because they include automatic upgrades on a scheduled basis. In addition, they cost the same over specific periods of time.

Deployment and Activation (Transfer Phase)

You're ready for deployment at last. All of your processes and solutions have been tested and approved. You'll need to finalize the preparation of your deployment infrastructures, and then proceed with the deployment itself.

Actual deployments tend to be quite complex. Users aren't available for training sessions, parts don't come in on time, technical staff fall ill. Sometimes it seems as if everything is going wrong, especially with massive deployments—deployments that affect the entire organization.

Two factors are important to your deployment's success: strong deployment coordination and deployment risk management. Because the deployment is in fact the coordination of a sequence of activities, the personnel you select require strong coordination skills. Communications systems will greatly help with the coordination programs, as you'll see in the next chapter.

As for risk management, it involves identifying potential project weaknesses and preparing for them. Before launching the deployment, ensure that you've covered all the bases. Your pilot project should have helped identify the majority of these risks. Remember: Always have a backup plan.

When you proceed with the deployment, you'll quickly see that after a while it becomes quite repetitive (see Figure 7.10). All the better—practice makes perfect! You'll soon be repeating all of the activities in your pilot project on an ongoing basis. Don't get lulled into a false sense of security by the monotony of the process. Always perform ongoing project status evaluations and be ready to modify approaches if something goes wrong.

The Transfer Phase

This phase includes

- Finalization of deployment infrastructures
- Deployment launch, including
  - Deployment coordination
  - Deployment risk management
  - User communications
  - Massive solution deployment
  - User training programs
  - Technical training programs
  - Deployment support
  - Ongoing evaluation

Proper Tools for User Support

Be sure you use the proper tools for user support. Microsoft found that a vast portion of their help desk calls were questions about the availability of their e-mail servers. They decided to post this information on a Web page and redirect users to this page.

This strategy reduced their help desk calls by 40 percent.

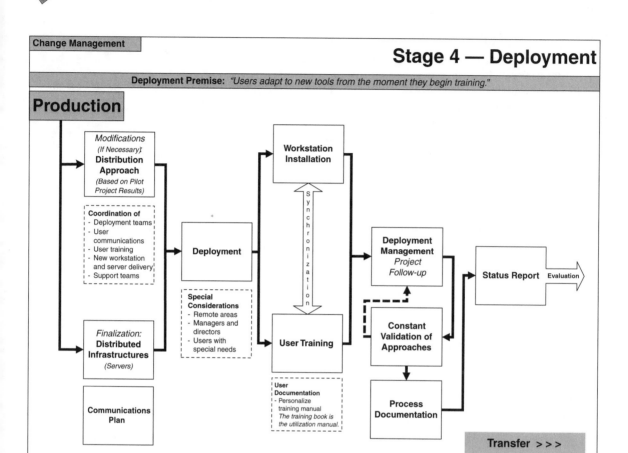

FIGURE 7.10   The Transfer Phase. The Transfer Phase focuses on repetitive deployment tasks.

Case Study
Supporting a Migration

Organization Type	Private Sector
Number of Users	2,500
Number of Computers	3,000
Project Focus	Migration to Windows NT
Project Duration	14 Months
Specific Project Focus	Migration from Multiple Environments to a Single SPA Object
Administrative Type	Centralized

An organization that moves to a new OS must use complete support mechanisms during the migration. Not only must these systems support the users during their familiarization with new tools, but they must also support the migration process itself and the teams that operate within it. This level of support is often more than an internal help desk can manage, because its staff is already occupied with other tasks. This organization chose to supplement its support program with special help for the duration of the migration. They increased staffing levels according to the following table.

Group	Increase
Technical Support Personnel	40 Percent
User Support Personnel	20 Percent
Project Information Support Personnel	10 Percent
Total Staff Increase	**70 Percent**

This staff increase was based on the following key elements:

- The architectural solution was very sound.
- The deployment was very well structured.
- The project used a very complete communications program.
- Appropriate levels of training were offered.
- The support team was given intensive training.
- The project included a data conversion program.
- Technicians were well prepared before the beginning of the deployment.

These key elements helped the organization control support costs during the migration.

Project Finalization (Evaluate Phase)

This phase includes three major activities. The first is to evaluate the project's performance against its objectives. Did it stay within budget? Did it meet every objective? Did it fit within defined timelines? Were there any overruns? Answers to these questions help form the rules for future projects.

The Evaluate Phase

This phase includes

- Project evaluation
- Solution integration into recurring administration, including
  - Final transfer of knowledge to operations staff
  - Deactivation of project support mechanisms
  - Final documentation
- Beginning of the solution evolution

The second activity is the absorption of the deployed solution into recurring operations. All documentation is finalized, and project personnel perform a final transfer of knowledge to administrative and operations staff. All project support mechanisms are deactivated.[7]

The third activity is the evolution of the solution. Once the operations staff has accepted delivery of the new technology, secondary evolutionary projects can begin. For example, after deploying and implementing Windows 2000/XP with Active Directory, you can begin to learn how to master it[8] and leverage its capabilities to increase quality of service within the IT infrastructure. This is the right starting point for this evolution because many of Windows 2000/XP's features are available only to a network that has completely migrated to this environment. You can often perform these modifications in the background with no further disruption of organizational activities.

As you can see in Figure 7.11, the Evaluate stage is the starting point of a new Question Phase and process.

Using Change Control

Microsoft uses a change control strategy to introduce new technologies or new versions of existing technologies into their network. This strategy uses three levels of integration called "projects" that are identified by three colors: gold, silver, and bronze.

The configuration contained in the gold project represents the current configuration for all servers, so the majority of their servers use this configuration. The silver project is used to represent proposed changes to the corporate standard such as new hardware, new service packs, new operating systems, and so on. It is introduced in a few production servers for testing purposes. These servers are constantly monitored for performance and stability improvements. If improvements are demonstrated over time, the silver configuration is upgraded to gold and all servers are migrated to this configuration.

The bronze project is for experimentation. Servers using this configuration are isolated from the production network and fully tested before they are graduated to silver.

Figure 7.12 illustrates Microsoft's change control strategy.

---

7. In an EMF, it is important to deactivate and not dismantle project support structures because you know they are required on a recurring basis.

8. Of course, a core team will already be familiar with it, but the entire enterprise needs to learn what it means to use a directory service.

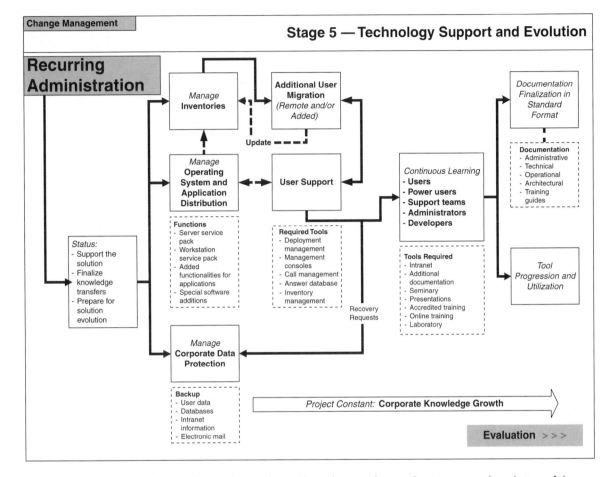

FIGURE 7.11 The Evaluate Phase. The Evaluate Phase begins the productive use and evolution of the solutions.

Using the QUOTE System

When designing an EMF, you follow the QUOTE System to discover and identify how to implement this Framework. Just as in the phases of a project, this system structures the way you approach change. In the implementation of an EMF, the Transfer Phase is used to prepare all of the mechanisms required to actually deploy the Framework in your organization.

Now that the project is ready, you'll need to learn about two more crucial activities: communications and training. These are two of the best agents of change, as you'll see in the following chapters.

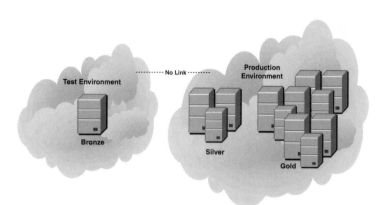

FIGURE 7.12   Microsoft's Change Control Strategy. Microsoft's change control strategy identifies projects with colors. This makes it easy for technicians to quickly identify the configurations they work with and introduces change gradually within the network. Note that there are never any links between bronze and silver or gold projects.

CHAPTER ROADMAP

Use this flowchart as a guide to understand the concepts covered in this chapter.

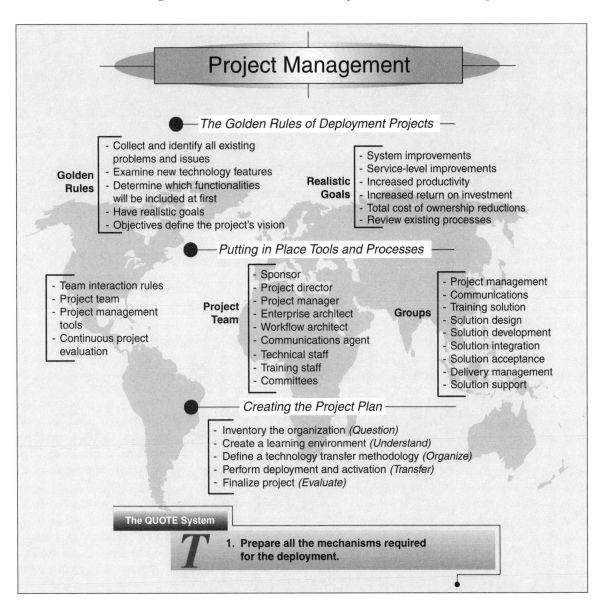

Project Management

● *The Golden Rules of Deployment Projects*

Golden Rules
- Collect and identify all existing problems and issues
- Examine new technology features
- Determine which functionalities will be included at first
- Have realistic goals
- Objectives define the project's vision

Realistic Goals
- System improvements
- Service-level improvements
- Increased productivity
- Increased return on investment
- Total cost of ownership reductions
- Review existing processes

● *Putting in Place Tools and Processes*

- Team interaction rules
- Project team
- Project management tools
- Continuous project evaluation

Project Team
- Sponsor
- Project director
- Project manager
- Enterprise architect
- Workflow architect
- Communications agent
- Technical staff
- Training staff
- Committees

Groups
- Project management
- Communications
- Training solution
- Solution design
- Solution development
- Solution integration
- Solution acceptance
- Delivery management
- Solution support

● *Creating the Project Plan*

- Inventory the organization *(Question)*
- Create a learning environment *(Understand)*
- Define a technology transfer methodology *(Organize)*
- Perform deployment and activation *(Transfer)*
- Finalize project *(Evaluate)*

The QUOTE System

T   1. **Prepare all the mechanisms required for the deployment.**

CHAPTER 8

Communications in an Enterprise Management Framework

A Critical Change Management Tool

> Communications is to the organization what oil is to a motor. A motor could not operate without oil. Given a minimum amount, it would work for perhaps a few minutes, but after a while, the entire motor would break down. Thus, this motor will only work properly with the appropriate amount of oil as per the manufacturer's recommendation.
>
> — *Pierre G. Bergeron,*
> *Translated from the original French*

Just like a motor, an organization is a fine-tuned machine that requires appropriate communication flows between its parts. Communication enables groups within the organization to work together and depend on each other.

Every organization requires an ongoing communications process. Sharing information is one of the cornerstones of change management within the organization. By announcing upcoming changes, the organization can limit their impact on the user base. Whether it is within their organization or in their personal lives, people have more opportunity to adapt to change when they are forewarned.

Communications is one of the critical processes of the EMF. Because the purpose of the Framework is to manage IT change within the organization and because change is the only constant in an IT world, communications is a process that must be constant and permanent.

IT personnel may have many skills, but in many cases, communications is a new field for them. How many IT organizations have complete documentation on their systems? How many have complete and up-to-date inventories?

The QUOTE System's Transfer Phase

We continue the Transfer Phase with a look at the tools that can assist change management processes within the organization. The first of these tools is communications.

The Maslow Model

Remember the Maslow Model for personal satisfaction from Chapter 1? Communications is one of the elements that can bring the most satisfaction in an IT world.

221

One of the most interesting games children play is the telephone game. They begin with a word or phrase and repeat it along a "telephone" chain. Invariably, the end result is not what they started with.

How many have nontechnical communications programs? Very few.

For modern IT, communications is a must. Managing the complex interactions of an enterprise IT system means communicating with several groups.

- The user base
- Other departments for non-IT issues
- Other departments for IT issues
- Groups within the IT department
- Partners
- Suppliers

But communications is not a simple process. When you communicate with a group, you must learn to quickly assess and understand the group's needs in order to respond appropriately. As a result, you'll need to fully understand the communications process and its principles, have a grasp of the tools required for a permanent communications program, and learn how to identify a message and the most appropriate vehicle for delivering a message. All of this is required to support the EMF communications program—the program that aims to support acceptance and integration of the .NET EMF within your organization.

The Communications Process

Communications is the process of broadcasting and receiving information, as illustrated in Figure 8.1. The information included in a message is processed according to factors such as confidence in the origin or the originator of a message, possible criticism, or the possibility of confrontation between people and ideas.

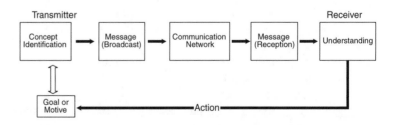

FIGURE 8.1 The Communications Process. Communications focuses on the transmission and reception of a message.

The definition of communications is "an action that enables a link with someone else." Communicating is establishing links with other people.

The word "communicate" comes from the Latin word *communicare,* or sharing. Communication can be a source of energy, of satisfaction, and of personal and professional empowerment. Communication is a means for multiplication. Without communication, there can be no association.

The Principles of Communications

Harold Pinter, a British playwright, is renowned for the focus on communications in his plays. Most of his pieces create the appearance of dialogue, but, in fact, each actor is delivering a monologue. An individual actor's monologue is interspersed with appropriate pauses, enabling the other actors to deliver theirs. The actors seem to be speaking with each other, but each is within his or her own little world and cannot seem to breach its walls. This is especially evident in *The Turtle Diary,* a 1984 film starring Ben Kingsley, which is perhaps Pinter's best-known work. It includes several scenes where you see the actors stare off into space while another person speaks his or her monologue.

In Pinter's plays, there is little communication because there is no listening. The first principle of communications is *learning to listen*—learning how to determine the mood of the audience, identify the needs of your listeners, and understand their preoccupations. Every good communicator is first and foremost a good listener.

Marshal McLuhan, a great Canadian communicator, is renowned for his concept of the Global Village. According to McLuhan, the evolution of communications technology and the reduction of distance in the modern world have a direct impact on the total amount of information people receive every day.

The Global Village concept is easily applied to the organization. The sum of information that is output by the organization in a single day is directly related to the size of the organization and the number of people participating in the communications process. What is important in communication is not the *amount* of information that is broadcast, but rather the *quality* of that information.

The second principle of communications is *learning to express yourself*—knowing how to build a bridge between yourself and your audience (see Figure 8.2).

Listening versus Hearing

There is a major difference between listening and hearing. Hearing means that you pay attention to what is said. Listening focuses on comprehension. When you listen, you pay complete attention to what is said and try to *understand* it.

Proactive Communications

Managers often underestimate the power of rumor in an organization. Because change situations awaken users' fears, it is always important to ensure that your communications program is proactive; that is, that you anticipate rumors and you ensure that the appropriate message is put forth.

FIGURE 8.2 Building Communications Links. A communications process builds a bridge between speaker and audience.

The Value of Paper

Paper is a traditional means of communication. Many people feel comfortable only when they have a piece of paper in hand. The age of the paperless office may still be far away—not because technologies cannot replace paper, but rather because people are not comfortable with today's paperless technologies.

Recent advances such as Adobe Acrobat, Microsoft Reader, and especially the Microsoft Tablet PC (to be released in 2002) are trying hard to displace paper in the near future.

Knowledge Management: The Internal Village

An example of communications within the enterprise is knowledge management. In order to share information among its personnel, the organization must put in place information-sharing technologies. These technologies must fulfill a specific need.

Today, few organizations have not yet tried to take advantage of intranet technologies. These technologies enable the indexing of all documents and the publication of pertinent information on Web-like pages. But the implementation of these technologies must follow a precise plan. In an EMF, technology is not a goal in and of itself.

Many organizations take the *Field of Dreams* approach to their intranets. In the film, Kevin Costner fulfills his dream when he begins to believe that "If I build it, they will come." Taking this approach when putting together an intranet does not translate into a winning strategy. As with every other aspect of the EMF, intranet technologies must respond to specific needs. Simply putting the technology in place does not fulfill the need.

The third principle of communications is *message content*—knowing what to include in your message.

When used properly, the intranet quickly becomes a great vehicle for communications. People quickly learn to rely on its content and use it every day because it is always up-to-date and completely indexed. But the intranet is not the only tool that is available for communications within the organization. There are several others: bulletins, newspapers, training manuals, e-mail, telephones, videoconferencing, meetings, and so on.

The fourth principle of communications is *choosing the proper vehicle*—learning to use the appropriate method of delivery for each message.

Communications is a change management tool. Be wary of changing traditional communications vehicles at the same time as you perform radical technological changes. For example, if you use a new electronic vehicle to distribute your message at the same time you modify computer systems on all desktops, you are compounding the changes you are introducing. Because people fear change situations, you must limit change as much as possible. Thus, you may choose to use traditional communications methods during the initial introduction of new technologies, and then later, when your personnel are comfortable with this initial change, you can move on to introduce new communications vehicles.

Communications in Migration Projects

Migration projects—projects whose focus is to migrate from one technological platform to another—are often projects that introduce massive change. As such, these projects disrupt daily operations and affect all users. Even though users welcome the changes introduced by these projects, they will still undergo the emotional cycle of change.

It is important to communicate with affected personnel beforehand to limit the impact of the change on business operations. Most projects will include a communications program whose purpose is to limit the impact of the change and to inform affected users about project status and objectives. But this is often not enough.

In many cases, the people who are in charge of communications within the project are also users who will be affected by the change. They are responsible for this critical change management tool at the same time as they are affected by it. It's a vicious circle. Because they are also affected by the change, they often tend to focus only on the project status. But it is also essential for people to understand the *reason* behind the change.

Communicating the Proper Message

Communications is especially important in a migration from Windows 95 to Windows 2000. In Windows 95, users are allowed to install components and software on their workstations. In Windows 2000, the average user does not have the capability to perform any installations. If the reasons behind the change from an "open" system to a "locked" system are not fully communicated, an organization will have a mutiny on its hands.

When you communicate the impact of a change, it is essential to include the objectives of the change. This part of the communications strategy must focus on the reasons behind the change—the reasoning used to justify every critical selection made during the elaboration of the solution. It must include at every level the information required for people affected by the change to fully understand the proposed changes. Comprehension ensures participation.

The communicator must create an environment supporting the desire to change. This is the point where communications becomes a marketing tool supporting the acceptance of the change. The success of a proposed change relies heavily on the quality of the communications during the transition period between the initial introduction of the change and the full integration of the change within organizational processes.

The negative impacts of a change are always reduced by a strong and effective communications program. This program must identify both favorable and unfavorable impacts of the change and design communications that put both in their best light. Proper communications makes the difference between the way people perceive the change: as welcome or unwelcome. If you implement an inappropriate communications program, your project will suffer the consequences.

A well-structured communications program includes information for each of the audiences affected by the change and identifies for them processes and methods they can use to reduce the impact of the change in their own situation. It's simple: The greater the change you intend to introduce, the more comprehensive your communications program must be.

The message needs to be simple and clear. It must be easy for people to understand; it must be at their level of comprehension. If it is intended for users, it shouldn't be too technical. If it is intended for managers, it needs to be in terms that they understand and that interest them. If the message is appropriate, it will invariably result in greater participation and easier acceptance of the change. Everything depends on content and method.

It is important to know at which stage of a change process communications should be introduced. During the change management implementation, communications provide ongoing risk management, as shown in Figure 8.3.

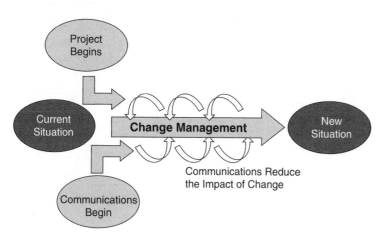

FIGURE 8.3   Communications and change management

In society, as in organizations, communications are essential. Every human interaction begins with communication. One piece of advice communicators should heed is to *listen* before they *speak*.

Case Study
Migrating to a "Locked" PC

Organization Type	Public Sector
Number of Users	2,000
Number of Computers	2,000
Project Focus	Migration to Windows NT
Project Duration	9 Months
Specific Project Focus	Migrate from a Variety of Operating Systems to a Standard
Administrative Type	Decentralized

This organization invested millions of dollars in a massive migration from a series of different operating systems to Windows NT version 4.0. The project was extremely well prepared and very well managed, but when it came to the communications program, the internal communications department refused to support or implement it because "no

IT project will communicate to the entire user base." As a result, the communications program was delayed until the actual deployment phase of the project, and no communications about the specific content of the migration program were made available to users. Nobody was forewarned of the content of the new system.

Like all projects, this one included an acceptance-testing phase. In this phase, end-user developers were invited by a different project group to come to the testing laboratory to install and test their own applications. The crunch came with the very first developer to arrive. Because his objective was to test his application on the new system, he began by installing it. It took less than two minutes for him to receive an Access Denied error message. At first, he thought he had made a mistake. Then he discovered that as a user, he did not have installation rights.

He immediately left and went to consult his peers. They called a special meeting with the project director and told him to put an immediate stop to the project. They refused the station as it was and refused to provide further support to the project.

In the end, the project went ahead and the station remained as it was, but only after some extensive risk management operations. Had the communications department been willing to support the initial communications program, this situation would never have occurred.

Managing Change through Communications

Chapter 6 introduced the cyclical nature of IT change. IT is constantly faced with change and must therefore constantly communicate with affected personnel. But it is not necessarily IT's responsibility within the organization to perform these communications. It is their responsibility to provide message content, but in most organizations, it is the responsibility of the communications department to manage the communications process.

In fact, it is within the communications department that the organization's communications experts are to be found. While most communications departments tend to focus on external communications, it is also their role to manage and provide internal communications. Just like the IT group, these experts provide a *service* to the organization.

As such, this department must also undergo a change with the implementation of the EMF. Its staff must create and provide a specialized IT communications service. Because IT tends to introduce technological changes through projects, the new communications services should be a project-oriented communications team. It should be designed to integrate with and support IT projects on an as needed basis.

In this manner, the organization will not have to reinvent the internal communications process every time a new IT project is initiated. This team will require a structured communications approach—a communications plan, in fact—that can be adapted to any IT change situation.

Case Study
Making People Listen

Organization Type	Private Sector
Number of Users	10,000
Number of Computers	9,000
Project Focus	Systems Deployment
Project Duration	6 Months
Specific Project Focus	Deploy a New Technology to Users
Administrative Type	Centralized

This large organization had done everything right. It was about to deploy a new technology to the entire user base. But this deployment called for users to perform some initial activities on their systems *beforehand*. This required an integration of a sound communications program into the project.

Project organizers began by warning users through an internal memo identifying what the project aimed to do, how users would be affected, and what benefits users would gain from the project. This memo was sent off one month before the project was to affect users. A second memo was sent two weeks later indicating the process used for the change and the dates involving users. Finally, a third memo sent out the week before the deployment indicated to users what procedures they would have to perform in order to ensure protection of their information.

The day of the deployment, IT personnel found that very few people had performed their operations themselves. Most people had read and understood the contents of the memo, but they had simply decided that it would be IT personnel who would perform these tasks and not themselves. They felt sure that IT personnel would do it anyway, even if they had asked users to perform the tasks.

What went wrong? What can this organization do to correct the problem? It is clear that users read the memos, but they simply didn't take them seriously. The cost to the organization was a longer deployment time and a frustrated IT group.

IT brought in some communications experts to see if they could correct the problem. Following are a few of the changes that were suggested and implemented:

- Demonstration rooms were set up to provide more information to users and to promote the results of the project *before* its implementation.
- Presentations were delivered to the user base to identify what would change and how users would be affected. These presentations also focused on the user's role during the change. The presentations treated the user as a partner in the process.
- Coaching personnel were introduced before, during, and after the change to assist users with their activities.
- A common vocabulary was identified to ensure that users understood everything in the messages sent by IT.
- Key users were identified in each department and included in the project team. These project user representatives were empowered to act in the name of the users they represented. They were also involved in the acceptance process of all of the deliverables of the project. These representatives were always the first to receive and review the change to assist in making messages clearer.
- A special program was initiated within the IT department to ensure that technical personnel would learn to include the user's point of view when examining new technologies.
- Another program was designed to incite administrators and managers to become more involved in the technological change management process.

All of these programs were designed to help form a bond between IT and other representative groups within the organization. Users learned to take IT processes more seriously. IT learned to pay more attention to user requirements when designing solutions. And management learned to treat IT as a strategic asset.

The result was a better integration of all of the IT processes inside the organization and the inclusion of members of every level of the IT organization in change management processes. Today, IT projects are more unified and users are treated as partners with IT. In addition, users have learned to respect IT. They have learned that when they have specific responsibilities in a project, it is important for the organization that they perform them.

A Structured Communications Plan

A massive deployment project's communications plan must include the following elements:

- A *project name* to identify the project.
- A *project logo* to enable users to quickly and easily identify every project intervention.
- A *series of bulletins* to the user base that include information about project scope, project objectives, advantages for users, changes brought about by the project, user responsibilities, and so on. This series of bulletins should begin at the very start of the project and last until the very end of the project.
- A *user committee* that serves as a two-way communications vehicle between IT and the user base.
- A *user survey* focusing on user needs, current issues, and general user comments.
- A *series of presentations* demonstrating the upcoming changes to the user base.
- *Regular meetings* with user committees to collect comments and suggestions.
- A *demonstration room* or rooms containing the new tool set. This room should be open to users so that they may judge for themselves the impact of the change. This room should also be staffed with a project representative who can help users understand the scope of the change.

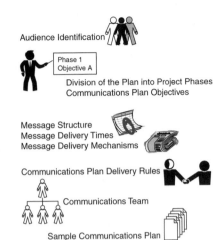

Audience Identification

Division of the Plan into Project Phases
Communications Plan Objectives

Message Structure
Message Delivery Times
Message Delivery Mechanisms

Communications Plan Delivery Rules

Communications Team

Sample Communications Plan

This image illustrates the structure of a project communications plan.

• A *pilot project* that tests and identifies the impact on the user base during deployment.

The structure of the communications plan is detailed in the sections that follow.

Communications Plan Structure

A project communications plan must be structured. It must include several elements that need to interact with each other, and it must provide information to all affected users. It should contain the following elements:

• Audience identification
• Division of the plan into project phases
• Communications plan objectives
• Message structure
• Message delivery times
• Message delivery mechanisms
• Communications plan delivery rules
• A communications team
• A sample communications plan

These elements are described in the sections that follow.

Audience Identification

The first objective of a project communications plan is to identify its audiences. Different audiences require different messages, and different messages require different delivery mechanisms. The project scope will also have an impact on audiences and delivery mechanisms. It is important for the communications planning team to quickly develop a sound understanding of the project's content, its objectives, and the user base it will affect.

For example, a Windows 2000/XP deployment on both servers and PCs will affect *everyone* in the enterprise, but its specific audiences would include the following:

• Project sponsor
• Project director
• Project manager
• IT project team, including

- Technicians/integrators
- Administrators for systems, security, performance, printers, inventories, data, and communications
- User/problem support
- System developers
- Planners
- Architects
- Software owners

- Human resources and communications personnel, including
  - Team leader
  - Trainers
  - Team communications coordinator
  - Message delivery personnel

- Localized teams,[1] including
  - Localized developers
  - Trainers
  - Local support personnel
  - Local technicians

- Team action owners

- End users

Audiences also include committees because committees regroup audience representatives. In fact, committees provide a multiplication factor for the communications process, enabling message delivery personnel to deliver their message once to key representatives who in turn can rebroadcast it to other members of the organization.

Committees should include

- *Management:* Key representatives of management at all levels of the organization should be included in this committee. It may be necessary to create two management committees, one for upper management and one for middle management, depending on the size of the organization.

- *Training coordinators:* Large organizations often tend to perform training internally. In these cases, they will

---

1. These team members will be present in a decentralized organization.

Change Management Committee

Identification of the members of the change management committee can be performed in two ways.

- First, this committee should include representatives of each one of the IT roles identified during role categorization (see Chapter 5).
- Second, the committee should include representatives from each of the key job functions identified in the organization. These should include management, administrative assistance, technical personnel, production personnel, and so on.

This committee is the one with which you sound out all of your solutions. It must be representative of the organization.

Participating in Meetings

One of the first messages you must deliver to any committee member, especially if he or she has never participated in such a process before, is that the member must express his or her opinion. There is no point in including people in a committee if they do not express themselves, even if they think what they have to say may not be appropriate. Sometimes the best project ideas come from the most incongruous sources.

require a committee of training coordinators. More on this subject is covered in Chapter 9.

- *Technical staff:* A change such as a move to Windows 2000 or Windows XP directly affects technical personnel. They should definitely be a targeted audience.
- *Change management:* This committee is made of key representatives of the user base at all levels. This committee should include personnel that play each of the different IT roles in the organization.
- *Union representatives:* If your organization includes unions, you should ensure that all changes that will affect the way people work within the organization are communicated to official union representatives.

The communications plan should reach each and every one of the audiences in the preceding list. The same message should be broadcast to each audience with variations on audience requirements. For example, management will be interested in budgets and deadlines as well as operation disruptions, while end users will be interested in changes that affect them personally.

The Project Introduction Guide

One of the first objectives of the communications team is to create a project introduction manual. Such a manual is often the most overlooked facet of communications in any project. Yet, if the project has a scope of several months or even years, such as would be the case for the deployment of Windows 2000/XP in medium to large organizations, it is certain that team members will change during the course of the project.

It is thus essential for the project to have a special introductory process for new team members. This process should be supplemented with a project introduction guide. The guide should include

- Initial project presentations
- Project scope manual
- Project status report
- Project organization chart
- Contact list for team members
- Team member roles and responsibilities
- Specific team member activity list

An introductory process for each new team member should support this manual. This process alone will save considerable time and expense for the project and will ensure that team members know precisely what their responsibilities are as soon as they become members of the project.

Dividing the Plan into Project Phases

Because the purpose of a project communications plan is to provide information to all audiences during all phases of the project, the best way to attack the project is to divide it into the same phases as the project itself.

Once again, this means using the QUOTE System for the communications plan. The plan will be divided into five phases:

- *Question:* This is the planning phase for the project. Communications must focus on planning activities and begin preparing the user base for the changes to come.
- *Understand:* This is the preparation phase. In this phase, the initial solutions are tested and prepared for the rollout. Communications must focus on preparation activities while continuing to identify benefits to users.
- *Organize:* This is the pilot phase. This may well include a pre-pilot program or a proof of concept. Then it follows with the pilot project itself. A *pilot* is defined as a complete delivery to a limited group of users who represent as many aspects of the organization's diverse user population as possible. At the end of the pilot, participants provide their comments on the overall delivery process. Communications must begin direct activities with users and communicate to users any positive comments provided by pilot participants.
- *Transfer:* This is the massive deployment phase. In this phase, the repetitive delivery of the solution begins and moves into full production. Communications must focus on the rate of delivery, project advances, and status updates. Any positive comments from users and managers must be communicated to the user base.
- *Evaluate:* The evaluation process begins during the massive deployment and continues after deployment is complete. Communications must focus on project status, relationship to project milestones and objectives, and

overall project performance. In addition, a project review must be completed and its results communicated to all interested parties.

The communications content of each phase is described in more detail in the last section of this chapter.

Defining Clear Objectives for the Plan

First and foremost, the communications team needs to define the objectives of the communications plan. Just like the project plan, the communications plan has a purpose that must be clearly defined and must meet specific goals.

Examples of the objectives of a project communications plan include the following:

- Communicate information between the teams within the project.
- Communicate information between members of the internal project teams and associated organizational teams.
- Inform the affected user base with the proper message at the right time.
- Minimize impacts on the user base.
- Ensure the harmonious deployment of the new tools associated with the project.
- Minimize impacts on business operations (communicate with partners, clients, and other external audiences if required).

Each project will have its own specific objectives. When you design the objectives of your communications plan, remember that the plan's goal first and foremost is to perform change management and minimize the impacts of change.

Message Structure

Communication is performed through *messages*. Each message must meet one of the plan's specific objectives. To facilitate the communications process, each message must be structured in a similar fashion by the communications team. This will greatly assist the team in the preparation of the specific content of the message. It will also facilitate interpretation of the message by its readers.

Messages should be structured in the following manner:

- Identification of the phase of the project
- Goal of the message
- Generic content of the message (summary)
- Identification of the specific audiences for the message
- Flowchart demonstrating the message source and the delivery times to specific audiences
- Message timing (when to start the communications process for this message, which audience is targeted first, which is second, and so on)
- Delivery mechanism for the message for each audience
- Specific content of the message for each audience
- Additional comments about the message

In fact, it is a good idea for the communications team to create a message boilerplate they can reuse each time a message must be delivered. This boilerplate provides an underlying structure to the process of managing the impact of change within the organization.

Message Delivery Timings

Communication is a flow of information from one person or group to another. In large organizations, communications teams will have to use *multiplication agents*—project team members who carry messages to other audiences within the organization. In this case, proper identification of the flow of a message becomes crucial. This is why messages must be divided into delivery timings.

Delivery timings help communicators identify when the message process begins, who its initiator is, who the audience is, and who performs the delivery of the message to this audience.

Figure 8.4 illustrates the use of timings in a flowchart demonstrating message flows.

The notion of timings (1, 2, 3, 4, and so on) helps create a generic communications plan. This enables organizations to create a specific communications project plan with specific dates as they are defined by the overall project. The organization has two tools to define specific dates for the communications plan: the project phase and the message timings. Each tool can be tied to specific phases of the project itself.

Being Heard

In large organizations, people are sometimes swamped with information. In this type of situation, how can you get them to hear your message among the myriad messages they receive each day?

Structure is important: A good logo and a well-designed message go a long way toward distinguishing your message from the masses. Also, a powerful communicator who knows how to direct readers' eyes toward your message and capture their interest is definitely a plus. It also helps if your communicator is familiar with the audience; thus there is an argument for an internal person to play the role.

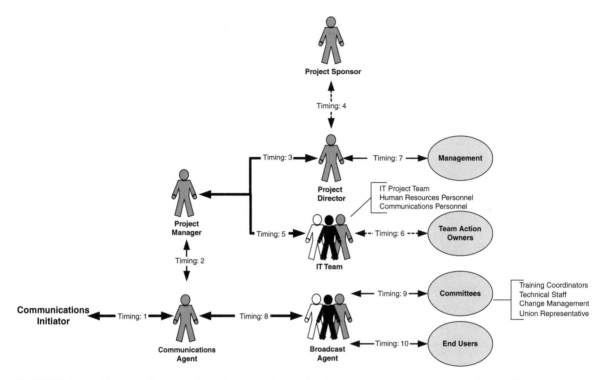

FIGURE 8.4   Message Timings. This diagram illustrates the communications process for an IT project. Every communications event must follow this process. Every communication within this diagram is bidirectional. Dotted arrows indicate that the audiences (project sponsor and team action owners) are not always involved in the process.

Communications Plan Delivery Rules

The communications plan operates according to a given set of rules and guidelines that affect both the general and the specific operation of the communications plan. Communication timings and message flows are illustrated in Figure 8.4.

General Rules

- A *communications initiator* is defined as a person or a group that has information to broadcast. For example, architects are initiators of the information on the operating system and application configurations, technicians initiate information regarding staging approaches, trainers cover the training strategy, and so on.

- *Information* that is to be broadcast must cover project activities, plans, approaches, and any other items that will impact either the project or a specific group. This includes information that may be of a technical, budgetary, operational, or temporal nature, especially if it can impact the project as a whole.
- The *broadcast agent* is responsible for delivering the message. There may be several broadcast agents. For example, for technical committees, the broadcast agent should be someone from IT; for management groups, the agent must be a manager; for users, the agent should be a trainer or someone from human resources; and so on.
- The *communications agent* is the person who receives messages from the communications initiators. This agent is the center of the communications system. He or she is in a direct relationship with the project manager. The agent can call upon assistance from the IT, human resources, or communications department to broadcast messages. He or she is in direct relationship with all broadcast agents.
- The *communications plan* should identify the scope of the audience for each message. The general message delivery flows are illustrated in Figure 8.4, but this does not mean that every message covers all audiences. For example, during the preparation phase, it is not necessary to communicate the specific status of the project to users because they still have months to go before they are directly impacted.
- *Message content* is modified for each audience. Generic message content must be the same for everyone, but specific message content will vary according to audience. For example, managers will want information that is pertinent to their operations and budgets, while users will want information that is pertinent to their own personal situations.
- *Unexpected messages* must still follow the generic communications process. It will be the communications agent's responsibility to identify specific audiences for these messages.
- Each *committee* is composed of information relaters. Committee members are responsible for relaying information to their own specific groups. They assist the communications agent by providing a multiplication factor.

Operational Rules

- The communications agent is always the first point of interaction—the point of entry for all messages.
- The project manager is always the second point of interaction. The communications agent must always discuss upcoming messages with the project manager.
- The project director is always the third point of interaction. The project manager must always keep the project director abreast of the messages to be broadcast and the status of the project. It is at this stage that the project director will identify if the project sponsor is to be involved in the message.
- The project sponsor is always the fourth point of interaction. The project director must communicate with the project sponsor on an as-needed basis during the course of the project. If this communication is necessary, it should be at the fourth point of interaction.
- The project team is always the fifth point of interaction. The project manager must communicate the message to them, especially if they are required to take action on the message.
- Team action owners are always the sixth point of interaction if direct action is required by the nature of the message. Team leaders manage these communications.
- Message delivery agents are always the seventh point of interaction. The communications agent is responsible for coordinating message delivery with these agents.
- Management committees are always the eighth point of interaction. The project director is often responsible for this message delivery with the assistance of the communications agent and/or the project manager.
- Other committees are always the ninth point of interaction. The communications team is responsible for this delivery.
- Users are always the final point of interaction. Once again, the communications team is responsible for message delivery.

The Communications Team

The communications team is composed of two types of personnel: the communications agent and message delivery personnel.

The Communications Agent

The communications agent is responsible for all communications activities within the project. This person is a journalist, a reporter who must search for and identify the nature of each message. Ideally, this agent is a member of the communications department specifically assigned to project-support activities.

This agent uses a communications plan to identify message delivery timings, specific message content, and information sources, as well as targeted audiences to simplify and assist the change management process.

This agent must work in close relationship with the project manager.

Message Delivery Personnel

Message delivery personnel are responsible for the specific delivery of a message and the means of delivery. They work in close relationship with the communications agent to prepare each message before delivery. Depending on the size of the project, a delivery agent may sometimes actually be the communications agent, but in larger projects, delivery personnel or agents are communications relaters that have a particular affinity to their audience.

For example, the project manager is the relater to the project team, the project director is the relater to the management committee, team leaders are the relaters to their team members, and so on.

Each message will have a specific delivery mechanism that is often related to message type and content.

Message Delivery Mechanisms

Organizations have several delivery mechanisms available to them. Each of these falls into one of three categories.

- *Paper-based mechanisms:* Bulletins, newsletters, posters, and so on.
- *Electronic mechanisms:* E-mail, presentations, the intranet, bulletin boards, and so on.
- *Word of mouth:* The importance of this factor in communications cannot be overlooked.

What is important to keep in mind is that each mechanism has its own purpose. For example, e-mail is often used to deliver short messages to large audiences. Bulletins

---

Poster Example

Posters are a very powerful way to create anticipation, especially if your project aims to repair long-term problems that users may have had to face.

For example, in a situation where users had little or no stability, you might create a poster with the following message: "Zero percent downtime! That's our goal. Believe it!"

There is no doubt that this message will get people talking about your project. Though their reactions may not always be positive, people will be anxious to see if you live up to your message.

are used to deliver messages that may take some time for the audience to absorb—a paper format requires the audience to take the time to stop what they are doing, pick up the paper bulletin, and give it more attention than they would a simple e-mail. Posters are used to foster anticipation, especially if their message is designed to "shock" the audience.

Think about message content before you decide which delivery mechanism to use (see Figure 8.5).

The Intranet

The intranet has a special place within the delivery mechanisms. As we are all learning through the use of the Internet, a well-designed Web site can provide a world of information to users. So can an advanced e-mail system. Both are used to support the intranet project site.

An intranet project site can include several different types of information such as

- The purpose of the project
- A layperson's description of the project objectives

Microsoft Project Central

In addition to being a very strong project management tool, Microsoft Project 2000 enables you to link everything and everyone through your company intranet. Remember to save a special place on the intranet site for your very own Project Central.

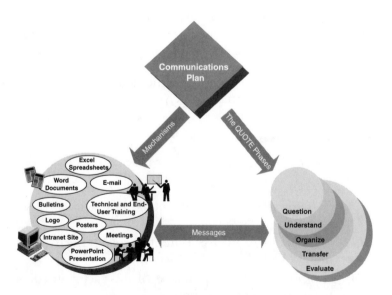

FIGURE 8.5 Message Delivery Interactions. Communications mechanisms support the communications process. Different messages need to be delivered during different phases of the QUOTE System.

- What the project proposes to change
  - At the user level
  - At the functional level
  - Tools to be changed
  - Other affected areas such as IT management and administration
- Training and deployment information, including
  - Deployment phases
  - Content of the training program
  - Deployment and training calendars
- Preparatory information
  - What users need to do beforehand
  - Time frames describing when the project team will contact them
- A project "goodwill" section
  - Chronicles describing a typical user experience
  - Comments and acclaims by users, managers, and IT personnel
  - Project performance and achievements
- Project frequently asked questions (FAQs)
- Tips and tricks for the use of the new products
- Project contact area
  - Identification of all user representatives including descriptions of their roles within the project
  - Identification of key project personnel
  - Help line for the project
  - Additional information sources
- Finally, as the project advances, use the intranet site to cater to specific audiences. To do this, you will need to apply specific security settings to each area because the messages they contain are for a certain audience's eyes only. These areas could include
  - Project management and administration information (Microsoft Project Central)
  - Committee communications, such as PowerPoint presentations[2]

> ### Project Goodwill Messages
>
> It is important for a project to generate goodwill toward the changes it brings. A special element of the communications program must focus on this goodwill. Milestones such as "1,000 users served!", personal commentaries by users and others that have already been through the program, and a clear description of what people can expect will go a long way toward fostering positive change management.

---

2. It is key that these areas be secured because a presentation delivered to management will not be disclosed to the general public, presentations to technicians should not be disclosed to users, and so on.

- Special groups and/or committee exchange areas
- A project glossary to enable everyone to establish a common vocabulary

The intranet is a new communications tool that can provide valuable assistance during the change management process. Make sure you use it as thoroughly as you can.

Information Sources

All of the messages that you need to deliver during the project communications program must originate somewhere. Following is a list of sources that most any project will require.

- Project deliverables, including
  - Current situation review
  - Needs analysis and problem identification
  - Project scoping document
  - Project organization manual
  - Project plan
  - Architectural objectives and guidelines
  - Global Architecture
  - Technical configuration documents
  - Security architecture
  - Transition and change management strategies
  - Laboratory and testing strategies
  - Deployment plan
  - Deployment calendar
  - Training and support plan
  - User needs analysis results[3]
  - User activity guides
  - Application testing and compatibility lists including conversion programs for application replacements
  - Risk management approaches
- External information sources, such as
  - Manufacturer's information sources

---

3. The user needs analysis is described in more detail in a later section of this chapter.

- Industry best practices
- Industry evaluations of the products
- Consulting firm analyses (from Gartner Group, Giga Information Group, META Group, and so on)
- Commercial training guides
- Related books and other technical papers

These information sources will assist communicators in putting together the messages required during the different phases of the project. They will also greatly assist in the evaluation of the impact of the change on the organization and the identification of the approaches required to manage it.

A Sample EMF Communications Plan

The following is a sample EMF communications plan. It provides an example of the focus of communications for each of the five project phases. Once again, it is based on the QUOTE System.

Question Phase (Planning)

This is the planning phase for the project. Here, the communications plan must focus on project planning activities and begin preparing the user base for the changes to come.

Activities during this phase should include the following:

- *Name the project.* The project name should be short and catchy, and it should form an acronym if possible. For example, the acronym "BIOS" could stand for "Better Information, Organization, and Structure," outlining the objectives for the project in its very name. It is easy to recognize because BIOS is also a well-known computer term.[4]
- *Design the project logo.* The project logo's design should enable audiences to quickly and easily identify every project intervention. This logo should reflect the nature of the project and its impacts on the user base. Because

---

The Question Phase

Communications activities
- Name the project
- Design the project logo
- Identify the project philosophy
- Prepare initial communications
- Create template documents
- Form committees
- Conduct a user survey
- Create a project introduction manual

Messages
- Project objectives
- Project structure
- Project status
- Project activities

Mechanisms
- PowerPoint presentations
- Meetings
- Technical training
- E-mail messages
- Word documents
- Excel spreadsheets

---

4. BIOS refers to the instruction set that is responsible for the early stages of the PC start-up sequence.

The Project Logo

The project logo is a key component of the communications strategy. It should be simple and easy to identify. The following image presents an example of such a logo.

This logo includes the following features:

- The project name, making it easily recognizable
- An image of a person, which indicates the user
- A globe to indicate the global nature of the organization
- A subtitle, PC Standardization, which is a secondary focus of the project
- The corporate logo (in this case, a portion of Resolution's logo) to identify the corporation-wide nature of the project

technology projects are often migration projects, the use of migratory birds in the logo is often very representative.

- *Identify the project philosophy.* The project philosophy must include information such as new capabilities based on new technologies, problems to be solved by the project, and the driving factors of the EMF.

- *Prepare initial communications.* The initial communication to the user base should be in the form of bulletins including information about project scope, project objectives, advantages for users, changes brought about by the project, user responsibilities, and so on. This series of bulletins must begin at the very start of the project and last until the very end of the project.

- *Create project templates.* The project will require templates for architectural and configuration documents, presentations to committees, bulletins, spreadsheets, and project plans. Each should include the project name and logo.

- *Form project committees.* The implementation of project committees that can serve as two-way communications vehicles between the project and specific audiences.

- *Conduct a user survey.* A user survey focusing on user needs, current issues, and general user comments (more on this later).

- *Conduct a series of presentations demonstrating the coming changes to the user base.* These presentations should be delivered to every committee at first. This should form the basis of regular meetings with the committees in order to collect comments and suggestions.

- *Create a project introduction manual.* The project introduction manual should be designed at this stage. This manual will be modified throughout the project phases to reflect the changing objectives for each phase.

- *Identify project activities.* These activities should be identified and communicated to all team members.

- *Design and implement the structure of project status meetings.* Internal project communications are crucial at this stage, so a mechanism should be designed for regular project status updates as well as an escalation method for specific project issues.

The User Analysis Survey

One of the major objectives of the EMF is to increase user productivity, not only through user knowledge but also through the implementation of systems that truly meet user requirements. The starting point of this intervention is a user analysis survey.

Organizations using the EMF must understand user needs and requirements at all times. Thus, the communications plan for this implementation must perform an analysis of user habits and activities.

This survey should cover a significant sample of the user base—between 5 and 10 percent of the user population.

Surveys often have very little success[5] because people are not necessarily interested in the survey. Your project should use a different approach. The best way to have valid and correct response to a survey is to identify survey officers within your organization. These are often members of the user or change management committees. You should select enough committee members to ensure that each member will not be responsible for more than 20 questionnaires.

The survey officer role then becomes one of direct intervention with users. Survey officers will be involved in

- The preparation and validation of the user survey questionnaire

- The selection of a number of users (up to 20) according to the user population sample parameters set by the project

- The distribution of the survey questionnaire

- The collection of the survey questionnaire

- The validation of the survey with the user before its return to the project

- The validation of survey results once the questionnaire is returned

- The validation of the solutions outlined in response to survey results

---

User Population Sampling

When you define the user population sample, it is important to identify user categories within the organization. This is best done with the job categories that already exist within the organization. The human resources department is the best source for this information.

Proceed as follows to identify user categories:

1. Identify the five major employee categories. These should include management, administration personnel, operations personnel, technical personnel, and planning personnel.
2. Identify the percentage of population covered by each category.
3. Select the appropriate number of people in each category to represent the user population. For example, if 5 percent of the staff is in management, 5 percent of your sample should be managers.

---

5. An industry survey is often deemed successful when it has a response rate of 3 percent!

The user survey questionnaire itself must focus on the following elements:

- Current software usage patterns
- Current issues and problems in the use of IT
- Workflow patterns
- User communication patterns
- Documentation and output patterns
- Support methods and patterns
- Personal knowledge levels for specific applications
- General user comments

User Survey Questionnaire

For an example of a user survey questionnaire, see Appendix E.

The information gathered from the user survey will provide the foundation for the customized solutions you will design when implementing your EMF.

In addition, the results of this survey will form the basis for new communication patterns between IT and the user base. Specifically, this aspect of the project should result in

- Improved user satisfaction because users will feel they have some say in the design of the new system
- Improved relationships because it fosters a spirit of partnership between IT and users
- Better solutions because the needs of users are specifically identified
- Additional functionalities because their requirements are clearly identified
- Better automation because documentation patterns are identified
- Direct implication of the client in the solutions process

The user survey is worth its weight in gold during an EMF implementation. Users especially appreciate it because it enables them to vent their frustrations with current systems and hope that these frustrations will not be carried over into new systems.

The results of this survey should influence architectural and configuration decisions. For example, application usage patterns help determine the layout of the most common toolset icons in the Presentation layer of the SPA object. The survey results should also influence communication patterns because they may identify immediate problems.

Understand Phase (Preparation)

During the preparation phase there is little on project status that must be communicated to users. Because the bulk of the work at this phase is preparation and acceptance of the solutions, most of the communications process deals with internal project communications. Communications must focus on preparation activities while continuing to identify the upcoming benefits to users.

Communications at this phase should include

- *Project status:* It is crucial at this stage that the entire project team is kept abreast of all project activities. The project manager must hold regular update meetings with all key project personnel. These people must, in turn, keep their own teams up-to-date. This communication must flow in both directions.

- *Project escalation method:* Any issues must be escalated and dealt with rapidly. The communicator must ensure that there is a proper issue escalation method. The resolution methods are the responsibility of the project manager.

- *Project intranet site:* The intranet site can be created at this stage. It should include such elements as project objectives, project status, results of the user survey, and other general project information. The Web site address should be communicated to users through a global e-mail message. It should then be included in all communications.

- *Project philosophy:* This is the ideal time to begin the communication of all major changes to users. These communications must focus on user and organizational benefits, especially if a "locked" system is on its way. The focus should be on showing users what is personal on the computer and what is corporate property. Several mechanisms can be used at this stage:

  - Bulletins with a series of articles on the changing nature of computing needs within the organization, a day in the life of a user using the new system, management and administration examples featuring user configuration management, and so on.

  - A demonstration room or rooms including the new tool set. This room should be open to users so that they may judge for themselves the impact of the change.

The Understand Phase
Communications activities
- Design project escalation method
- Design project intranet site
- Prepare demonstration room
- Create user guides
- Prepare training solution
- Prepare support solution

Messages
- Project philosophy
- User survey results
- Project status
- Project activities

Mechanisms
- PowerPoint presentations
- Meetings
- Bulletins
- Technical training
- E-mail messages
- Word documents
- Intranet site

This room should also be staffed with a project representative that can help users understand the scope of the change. This room should be available until the deployment of the solution.

- In addition, the communications program should focus on the following project activities:
  - System preparation and testing
  - Preparation of the training solution
  - Preparation of the support solution
  - Preparation of the deployment methods
  - Preparation of the user guides required during deployment
  - Preparation of the various teams affected by the deployment

All of the activities listed previously will be in their initial stages. They will be finalized during the next phase of the project.

Organize Phase (Pilot)

This phase deals with the finalization of all preparatory activities and the initial testing of all of the solutions through a pilot deployment. It may be necessary to perform a pre-pilot program or a proof of concept (POC) to validate that the project is moving in the right direction. If this is the case, the activities should include

- Finalization of all approaches
- POC (pre-pilot)
- Pilot program
- Pilot program evaluation
- Modification of the approaches (if required)

Both the POC and the pilot are deployments to controlled user populations. The major difference between the two is the scope of the population (about 1 percent for the POC and about 10 percent for the pilot). Both are defined as a complete delivery to a limited group of users who represent as many aspects of the organization's diverse user populations as possible. At the end of both tests, participants provide their comments on the overall delivery process.

The Proof of Concept

Proof of concepts (POCs) can serve several purposes during a project. Some organizations may also require a POC at the Understand Phase. For them, the POC serves to validate that a specific technical idea works. Others may want a POC at the Organize Phase. At that stage, it can serve as a test with a smaller scope of all of the pilot project's activities.

It is at this stage that the communications team begins direct activities with targeted users. It is also important for this team to communicate to the entire user base any positive comments provided by test participants.

- *Project status:* Project status communications within the project team must continue at all times.
- *Project intranet site:* The effective use of the Web site during deployment is tested here. This means that the intranet site should begin to include information specific to users targeted by the deployment. Users will want to know when their systems will be deployed, when they should take training, what they need to do beforehand, what they need to do afterward, and so on. They will also want to find their own names on the lists.
- *Project philosophy:* The project philosophy information should continue to be disseminated. It is at this stage that the project can begin to use posters to create a positive change atmosphere within the organization.
- *Preparatory activities:* In addition, the communications program should focus on the finalization of all project preparatory activities:
  - System preparation and testing
  - Training solution
  - Support solution
  - Deployment methods
  - User guides required during deployment (activities before, activities after, and training guides)
  - Preparation of the user representatives for direct interaction with their user base
  - Testing and finalization of the coaching team

  All of these processes will be thoroughly tested during both the POC and the pilot. The communications team will have to prepare POC and pilot evaluation forms and ensure that they are collected at the end of each test.
- *POC and pilot evaluations:* Finally, the communications team will be responsible for summarizing all of the results of the POC and pilot evaluations and communicating results to all audiences.

The Organize Phase

Communications activities
- Finalize intranet site
- Design project approaches
- Prepare POC and pilot evaluation forms
- Finalize user guides
- Finalize training solution
- Finalize support solution

Messages
- Project philosophy
- Project status
- Project activities
- Activities for users
- Project training
- POC results
- Pilot results

Mechanisms
- PowerPoint presentations
- Meetings
- Bulletins
- Technical and end-user training
- E-mail messages
- Word documents
- Intranet site
- Infoline
- Coaches

Using Onsite Coaches

One of the resources you should consider during a massive migration project is the onsite coach. These people are project personnel whose purpose is to assist users during their activities before and after the migration.

During migration projects, especially projects that migrate from one operating system to another, users are required to perform certain project activities. Validating their inventory is one such activity. Cleaning up their PC files is another. They may even have to move all of their documents to a special directory if the project has determined that only information in this special directory will be conserved.

After the migration, users finalize the personalization of their system, validate that their old files were transferred to the new system, and start using the new technologies.

For many users, these tasks are a challenge. Onsite coaches can greatly facilitate the process by moving through the deployment along with the project and providing before and after assistance.

The communications team has to ensure that all of its processes are completely tested and ready for moving on to the next phase: the massive deployment.

Using an Infoline

One of the most successful communications tools for migration projects is the *infoline,* a help line that is specific to the project. The infoline serves to directly provide information to users about the migration process. It can help them find their training and/or migration dates. It can assist them by directing them to other sources of help and assistance.

The infoline relieves the pressure of project coordination communications with users from normal help desk staff. It provides comfort to the user base because it shows that the project team cares to hear them.

Transfer Phase (Deployment)

During the massive deployment phase, communications move to full production mode. Communications at this phase should focus on:

- Repetitive communication with targeted user populations
- Success story publication (any positive comments on the solution or the deployment methods should be regularly conveyed to the user base)
- Project progress information (communicated to all audiences)

The communications process should be simpler to manage at this stage because it becomes very repetitive. Communications help support users during this process, as illustrated in Figure 8.6.

Evaluate Phase (Project Review)

The final project phase is the project review. The communications team must review and identify project successes, such as project milestones at the proper dates, objectives set and met by the project, budget results, and overall project performance.

The results of this review must be identified and communicated to all interested parties.

The Transfer Phase

Communications activities
- Begin repetitive communications
- Write success stories
- Follow project progress

Messages
- Project status
- Project activities
- Activities for users
- Project training
- Success stories

Mechanisms
- PowerPoint presentations
- Posters
- Meetings
- Bulletins
- Technical and end-user training
- E-mail messages
- Word documents
- Intranet site
- Infoline
- Coaches

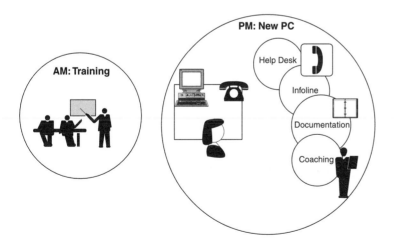

FIGURE 8.6 Message Delivery Mechanisms. User activities during the migration include, for example, attending training in the morning, and then using the new system in the afternoon. Various communication mechanisms should be used to support this process.

The Evaluate Phase

Communications activities
- Perform project review
- Identify project strengths and weaknesses

Messages
- Project review
- Success stories

Mechanisms
- PowerPoint presentations
- Meetings
- Bulletins
- Word documents
- Intranet site

Recurring Communications

Because the implementation of a project-based communications program is a significant undertaking, the organization should ensure that this new mechanism between users and IT be maintained on a recurring basis. Thus, communicators should endeavor to identify information that can be broadcast to the user base on a regular basis. This can include information such as upcoming software and hardware evolution, new function introductions, and so on. It is important to ensure that this kind of information is translated in a manner that is understandable and significant to users.

Using the QUOTE System

During the Transfer Phase, the organization changes the very infrastructure of the IT environment. Communications is one of the best agents of change. It is a significant process, but it cannot stand alone. Training and proper solution design are required to support the communications process.

Communications is one of the most important aspects of a project, yet it is often forgotten or simply not deemed important during the initial phases of a project. In an EMF, a solid relationship between IT and users is crucial. The best way to build this relationship is through a strong communications program. During your deployment, you'll have to ensure that the communications program does not fall through the cracks.

Case Study
Implementing a Project Communications Program

Organization Type	Public Sector
Number of Users	5,000
Number of Computers	5,500
Project Focus	Windows 2000 Deployment
Project Duration	1 Year
Specific Project Focus	Deploy a New System Management Structure with Windows 2000
Administrative Type	Decentralized

This organization chose to manage the entire deployment program internally with the support of key consultants. As such, the majority of the project was managed and delivered by internal personnel.

A consulting firm was hired to design the communications program for the project. Because the project seemed to be lacking structure, the communications team designed the communications plan as a deployment plan, listing all the activities required at each phase.

The project team also identified that they did not have the appropriate communications agents within the team, so they requested help from the human resources and communications departments. Both departments created special project support teams to respond to the technical project's requirements.

Using the communications plan, the new project personnel (from the communications department) supported the project throughout its delivery. This enabled them to identify additional impacts on the user base and proactively manage them through targeted communications to specific audiences.

In addition, they were able to transform the plan into a generic project implementation communications plan.

They were thus able not only to manage change during the initial deployment project, but also to be ready and prepared for any future technological innovation or change within their organization.

CHAPTER ROADMAP

Use this flowchart as a guide to understand the concepts covered in this chapter.

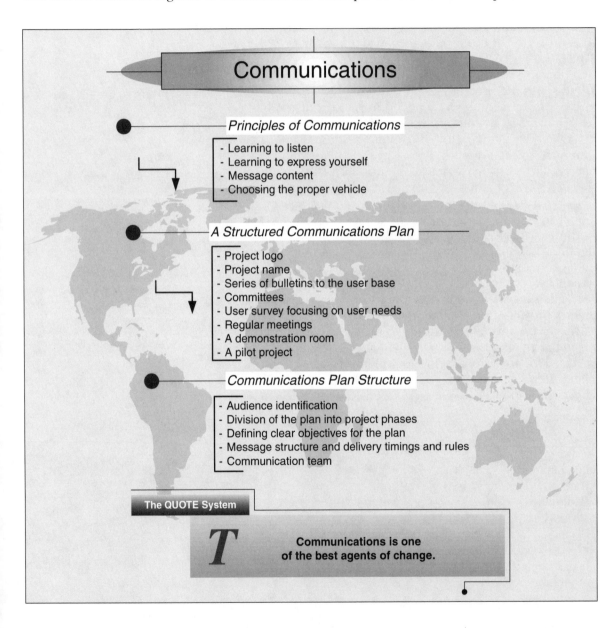

Communications

Principles of Communications

- Learning to listen
- Learning to express yourself
- Message content
- Choosing the proper vehicle

A Structured Communications Plan

- Project logo
- Project name
- Series of bulletins to the user base
- Committees
- User survey focusing on user needs
- Regular meetings
- A demonstration room
- A pilot project

Communications Plan Structure

- Audience identification
- Division of the plan into project phases
- Defining clear objectives for the plan
- Message structure and delivery timings and rules
- Communication team

The QUOTE System

T **Communications is one of the best agents of change.**

CHAPTER 9

Training: A Change Management Tool

Training Is a Very Powerful Change Management Tool That Must Harness Resources to Enable the Organization's Personnel to Adapt to Change

> It is up to our society to assimilate the idea that from now on, change is the rule and put an end to the illusion of stability that we have all been trying to maintain.
>
> — *John Whitmore*, Coaching for Performance

Using Training to Manage Change

While communications is the tool to use to maintain harmony within the organization during a change process, training is the tool that enables the organization's personnel to absorb the change and make it theirs.

The success of any technological implementation depends on the quality of the tools used to manage the change. The migration to the EMF requires thorough and complete change management strategies, especially if it is coupled with a major technological migration, such as that from Windows NT to Windows 2000/XP.

Remember, Microsoft claims that the difference between the previous families of Windows products (95, 98, NT, ME) and Windows 2000/XP is greater than the difference between Windows 3.*x* and Windows 95. This is quite significant because the latter was a major training challenge.

Remember also that there is an evolution in the graphics world. When users moved from DOS to Windows 3.*x*, they discovered that there was a progression between the environments. In DOS, they had to know the command and its proper syntax to use the system. In Windows 3.*x* the focus moved from memorized commands to the proper tool for

The QUOTE System's Transfer Phase

We finish the Transfer Phase with a look at how organizations can adapt to the EMF. The supporting processes we examine in this chapter identify the ways in which the organization can make the EMF implementation as easy as possible for their personnel.

The Evolution of the User with Windows

The way users perform their work changes with graphical environments. Take, for example, formatting a diskette.

In DOS, the user must know the Format command. It gets worse when he or she has diskettes of different densities.

In Windows 3.x, the user must know to use the File Manager, because a diskette is one of the objects it can work with.

In Windows 95, the user must use the disk drive because one of its properties is to format diskettes.

In Windows 2000, the system tells the user when the diskette isn't formatted[1] or diskettes arrive preformatted.

object management. In this environment, users needed to know which tool to use to perform an action. It was easier for them to remember the tool than the command itself.

In Windows 95, the focus moved from the tool to the object itself. With the Windows 95 interface, users can click the right mouse button on any object and expect that an appropriate command will be available in a context menu.

With Windows 2000, the system gains intelligence with a move to "managed" objects. The system itself knows when actions are required and proposes them to users. Windows Update, a tool that tells a user when new, critical updates are available for his or her system, is an excellent example of this capability. The manufacturer manages the OS state for the user.

The same thing applies to new productivity tools. Everyone who moved from WordPerfect for DOS to Microsoft Word for Windows faced major challenges. Imagine moving from a computer screen with absolutely no information on it except the position of your cursor at the bottom left to a system with graphic layout, menus, toolbars, status bars, scroll bars, a mouse, and much more.

Most people were lost at first because Word offered too much information. WordPerfect experts had to memorize every single available command to be able to use them. In addition, they had to learn to "program" text. Every formatting command inserted codes at the beginning and at the end of its application. WordPerfect experts were masters in the art of "reveal codes." Secretaries were program debuggers that could fix anything when the codes were revealed.

In Word, little or no memorization was required and no reveal code mode was available because Word did not have the programming approach that WordPerfect used. Most WordPerfect users were lost at first especially if they didn't understand the philosophy of Word. This philosophy did not change in Office 95 or 97.

In Office 2000, Microsoft changed the office automation suite to provide stronger, centralized management tools, but the user interface and interaction with Office programs

---

1. Of course, Macintosh enthusiasts will tell you that they have been formatting disks because the system has been telling them it needs to be done since the very first appearance of this computer.

barely changed. Because of this, most organizations didn't adopt the new standard. They didn't see immediate advantages for their user base.

This will not be the case with Office XP. In this version, Microsoft introduces the concept of *task pads*. For the first time, Microsoft moves from the concept of a generalized office automation suite to task-oriented tools. When you use Word XP to create a document, a specialized task pad will display to help you through the various tasks required to make the document, as shown in Figure 9.1. This task orientation is the key to increased productivity.

Managing Change through Training

The training industry itself had to undergo the same change Microsoft did with Office XP. The traditional computer training approach focuses on the tool itself. How many organizations have sent users to one or two days of generic training on Word? After this training blitz, users come back to work and must then apply this generic training to their own work situations. They have to learn how to use Word to create their own version of the corporate memo, or the corporate letter, or even the corporate envelope. When it comes to

The Philosophy of Word

WordPerfect and Word were very different products. WordPerfect was, in fact, an electronic typewriter because its operation emulated a mechanical typewriter. If you wanted to move text to a given location on the page, you had to insert multiple tabs horizontally or multiple "enters" vertically. This inserted all sorts of extra characters in documents. Page breaks were manual, as were section breaks.

In Word, text is treated as an object. This means that as an object, you can apply attributes or rules to control its appearance. It also offered a What You See Is What You Get (WYSIWYG) interface. If you want a word in boldface, you select it with the mouse, click the Bold button, and the word appears in boldface on the screen.

People who migrated to Word from WordPerfect and did not understand the differences had many difficulties. First, they did not know how to believe their own eyes. If text is bold on a page, it is bold on paper—you don't need codes to tell you that. Second, the documents they converted had all sorts of extra characters in them that threw off the documents' formatting when inside Word because Word applies rules to every object: tabs, paragraph marks, extra spaces, page breaks, and so on.

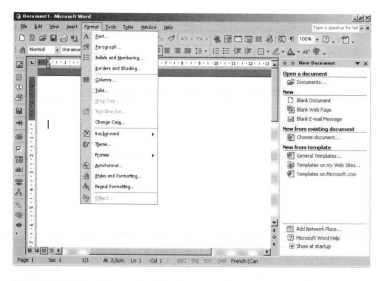

FIGURE 9.1 Microsoft Word XP. Word XP uses a task-oriented approach to document creation that assists users with the task of creating documents.

more complex documents, they are completely on their own.[2] Does this make sense?

Even though training methods themselves are varied—traditional methods such as classroom training, static information broadcast through the intranet, and virtual methods such as streaming technologies for live video presentations on the intranet—the content of this training hasn't varied very much from classic, generic approaches. Organizations still pay to have their users learn all there is to know about Word, Excel, or PowerPoint. Traditional training focuses on the tool itself (see Figure 9.2).

Organizations spend significant amounts of money to design world-class logos and corporate images that enable customers and partners alike to immediately recognize materials originating from within the organization. But with a generic training approach and no document controls, organizations throw the whole thing out the window when they let users create their own designs. Tools such as Word can create virtually any type of document a user wants. So organizations find themselves with as many letter formats as there are people using Word.

In addition, users spend a significant amount of time developing these formats. This is one of the indirect costs of TCO. Why should it be the user's responsibility to decide how to use his or her new knowledge? Even though a word-processing training program shows the user how to create a fax cover page, it will still not apply to the user's situation because his or her organization's corporate fax cover page will be different.

Software Knowledge → User Is the Expert ← Daily Tasks

FIGURE 9.2   The Traditional Training Approach. In a traditional training approach, the user is the expert on both program operation and task definition.

2. At least for the former document types, the user has a paper model; that may not be the case for complex long documents.

Invariably, users return to their older program if an emergency arises. Why? Because they are familiar with it and don't need to think in order to use it. Often, users continue to use older applications because they are more familiar with them, unless, of course, these tools have been removed from the system or they no longer work. But *forcing* a change is not the way to have it become accepted.

Change is facilitated when users *want* to change. For this, the new tool must be easier to use than the previous one. The reason someone uses a tool such as a word processor is simple—it is for *writing* documents, not *creating* them. This is especially true in today's empowered user world, where people type their own documents. Managers are an excellent example. They are already very busy. When they prepare a document, it is because they need to *write* something, not format it or perform page layout.

The Learning Process

People learn through stages—four stages, in fact.

The first is the Unconscious Incompetent stage. People do not know what they do not know. Take, for example, a new driver. Having never driven a car, the new driver is not aware of all of the factors required to have a good driving experience. He or she looks at others driving and everything seems easy to them. The new driver doesn't know that he or she doesn't know how to drive.

The second is the Conscious Incompetent stage. People know what they don't know. The new driver gets behind the wheel of a manual transmission car and tries to make it go. The new driver immediately learns that he or she didn't know what driving really was.

The third is the Conscious Competent stage. After some practice, the new driver can make the car go more or less smoothly, but the new driver needs to think about every action before he or she can perform it. The new driver is competent, but he or she needs to be conscious of the actions he or she has to take to drive the car.

The fourth is the Unconscious Competent stage. After much practice, the new driver is no longer new. Driving has become second nature to the new driver, and he or she can drive without having to think as much about each action. Actions have become reflexes, and the knowledge is now fully absorbed.

Each person undergoes this four-stage process whenever he or she learns something new.

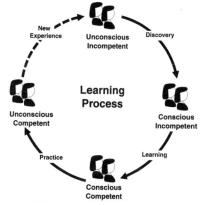

There are four stages to the learning process.

The problem with traditional training methods is that they do not take into account a particular organization's needs. Migrating from one OS to another means more than just changing work tools. Migrations often have direct impacts on how people do things. In a Windows 2000/XP migration, this impact is not only at the user level, but also, and more important, at the IT level. Operations are different. Programming is different. System management is different. Organizations must take this massive change process and reduce its impact by making the change work for them.

The best way to achieve this is by integrating and embedding operations and procedures within the new architecture and providing a personalized training program that takes this architecture into consideration. Taking these steps will greatly assist in the organization's primary migration goal: *increased productivity*. The training program must take these principles into consideration if the organization wants the migration to be a complete success.

A Migration Project Training Program

A recent study by the Canadian International Development Research Centre identifies that "organizations use a major portion of their time for the acquisition of knowledge." It goes on to state: "The best tool to acquire knowledge is training. Training investments must be continuous and must meet precise organizational and personnel requirements. An organization that wants to rely on knowledge management must include the principle of continuous learning into its business values."

The most important aspect of a migration program must be training if the organization wants to master the change. In fact, the success of a migration project is often based on the quality of its training program and of the knowledge transfer derived from it.

In an EMF, it makes more sense to have training focus on performing work for the organization rather than having the user become an expert. A successful training program should include

- A complete needs analysis to identify workflow patterns and knowledge levels within the organization. The results from this analysis will also be used to design the IT solution itself.

User Needs Analysis

See Chapter 8 for an example of a user needs analysis.

- The integration of needs and work habits into the technological solution.
- A custom training program that is focused on the technological solution.

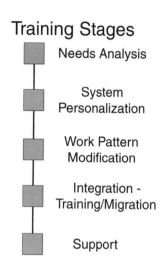

Training Stages

Needs Analysis

System Personalization

Work Pattern Modification

Integration - Training/Migration

Support

The result is a training program focused on organizational requirements, not generic application operation. This is *task-oriented training*.

The training plan should begin with a comprehensive look at organizational habits and existing productivity or operational issues. For example, if the new tool is a word processor, some immediate questions arise: Which documents are the most used within the organization? Do document-creation standards exist? How does the organization propose to organize information and how does it want to share this information? What are employee work habits in regard to word processing? The answers to these questions will assist the application of automation in the system migration.

The second step is performed with individual users. What tasks do they perform on a regular basis, and are there any relationships between groups of tasks? How can these tasks be assisted by information systems? Do users have specific communication patterns? With whom? At what rate? How? The answers to these questions will aid in the design of solutions that specifically meet users' needs.

The comparison is easy. If a person wants to write a letter without a computer, he or she finds a pencil and a pad of paper and then writes the letter. The use of a computer system should be as easy as that.

Why should organizations invest in the development of a multitude of word-processing experts? Why should organizations think that users are interested in seeing their work habits and methods integrated into an office automation application or that they should be responsible for this integration? Why imagine that this approach can possibly lead to increased productivity? Nevertheless, this is exactly what many corporations think today because they still use traditional training approaches.

It is, in fact, trainers and technicians that are the subject-matter experts. It should be their responsibility to analyze organizational and user needs in order to adapt office automation tools to business requirements. The training program can then focus on demonstrating how to use the tool

The Anatomy of an Automated Letter

Writing a letter is easy. You need the current date, the address of the person you're writing to, a salutation, the body of the text, a closing, and your signature. Automating a letter means re-creating this process (see Figure 9.3).

The user begins with the selection of the corporate letter template that includes

- The company logo
- Automated date insertion
- Return address
- The subject of the letter
- Salutations
- Letter closing
- Signature block

The user must then answer a series of questions:

- Who are you writing to? A client? A partner? Someone else?
- Did you write to this person before?
  - If yes, the system should permit the lookup of the person's name and address.
  - If no, it should offer to save the new address for future use. The user can save the address in the contact list.

The address is inserted into the letter as well as all other variable information, and the user is ready to write the letter.

The user writes the letter.
The user proofs the letter.
The user prints or e-mails the letter.
That's it! Easy, isn't it?

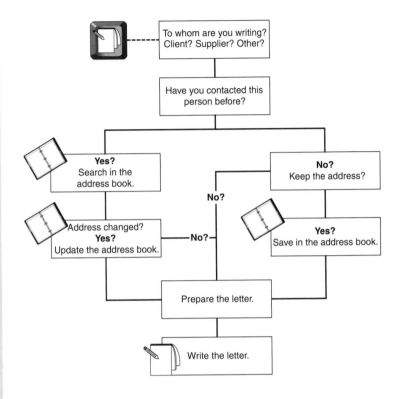

FIGURE 9.3 The Anatomy of an Automated Letter. An automated letter should include all of the steps identified here.

within the specific organization, not how the tool works generically. Users learn how to write a letter for Corporation XYZ, not how to create their own formats.

In this instance, the office automation tool becomes secondary to the task. It is the task that matters; the tool used to perform it can be any tool.

The Positive Impact of Automation in Training

In graphical environments such as Microsoft Windows, office automation applications give users and organizations the means to "tailor" their behavior to meet specific requirements. No longer do users have to compose *and* design each letter they write in Word for Windows. No longer do they need to design *and* create each budget spreadsheet. Excel, Word, Access, and Outlook all give organizations the ability to create template documents that store commonly used formats. In this regard, Office XP goes even further than any of its predecessors.

In addition, these template formats can store commonly repeated procedures to automate document creation. Word letter templates store the letter format, and Outlook gives them a user-definable bank of commonly used addresses. Excel templates store both formulas and formats. Windows and Exchange automatically mail-enable each of these applications.

Automating workflows and work patterns enables users and organizations to free themselves from nonproductive work. Users are more productive because they can concentrate on the task at hand, not the creation of tools and techniques that bend an office automation tool to their needs. It accelerates user training. It minimizes frustration because users are immediately productive.

Finally, it brings considerable savings to training budgets because training times are considerably shorter. Learning how to write an automated letter is much easier and faster than learning everything there is to know about Word. In addition, a course based on true office automation will incite users to change because they will see immediate advantages. Figure 9.4 illustrates the .NET training approach.

The enterprise reaps all the benefits. Users are immediately productive. Budgets are smaller. Migrations are successful. In today's business world, you are constantly faced with new information. It is through the interpretation of this information that you acquire knowledge. If you can automate some of your internal processes, you will have more time for the interpretation of new information and gain an edge in knowledge management.

In a recent series of articles on knowledge management, André Boudreau states, "Embedding knowledge means liberating this knowledge from individuals and groups and integrating it into information systems, work processes, and infrastructures." This is one of the ways organizations can achieve success. Automation techniques enable organizations to embed internal knowledge into the tools they use. This is one of the keys to any knowledge management strategy.

Making "Safe" Macros

Remember that today's technologies include code signing. This means that you can safely make use of office automation macros by including digital certificates within them. Your macros are safe and accepted while others are not.

The Application Enhancer

The role of the application enhancer is just that: to enhance or automate applications to meet corporate requirements.

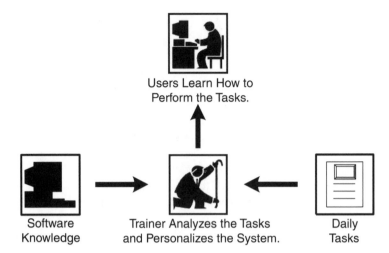

Users Learn How to
Perform the Tasks.

Software
Knowledge

Trainer Analyzes the Tasks
and Personalizes the System.

Daily
Tasks

FIGURE 9.4   The .NET Training Approach. In a .NET training approach, the expert designs an automated solution. The training program is then focused on how to perform the corporate task.

The Validity of a Testing Program

A testing program is only as good as its tests. It's true that if all you have to do to pass a test is memorize some information, the test isn't a valid knowledge evaluation method. Microsoft has endeavored to create a testing program that is difficult to bypass.

Test questions are secret. People taking the tests cannot copy any questions during the test. They are given a plastic pad and a felt pen—no paper. This worked until people started memorizing questions.

Microsoft then came up with an adaptive testing process. The test adapts to your answers and stops as soon as it has evaluated that you either know or don't know what you're talking about.

Today, Microsoft is trying to further enhance its tests by using real-world examples and situations. This is significant progress for them. Book knowledge should no longer be enough to pass tests.

Support for Continuous Learning

In a constantly changing universe, you must find innovative training and knowledge-validation methods. Several methods are available. For users, you have already seen that automation is such a method. For technicians, the challenge is greater because they must understand not only the way the organization works but also the ins and outs of the technologies they implement. For them, you must use a structured approach that provides an evolving learning environment.

Like other technology manufacturers, such as Novell and Cisco, Microsoft has designed training programs oriented toward technical certification. The Microsoft Certified Professional (MCP) program forms a "litmus test" for technicians of all levels because it offers a testing strategy. It covers several areas of technical expertise:

- *Microsoft Certified Professionals* are technicians that operate in a given area of technology. In this program, a technician must only pass one exam. As such, technicians can become certified in operating systems, database administration, Internet technology management, electronic mail systems, security, and so on. Application enhancers can also become certified through this program because it covers Microsoft Office Automation Development technologies.

- For administrators, Microsoft offers the *Microsoft Certified Systems Engineer* (MCSE) program. This program requires an engineer to pass seven different exams: four mandatory exams and three electives. Using the electives, MCSEs can become certified in a variety of fields.

- For developers, Microsoft offers the *Microsoft Certified Systems Developer* (MCSD) program. This program focuses on core exams on the Windows operating system followed by certification on various development technologies.

- Microsoft also offers the *Microsoft Certified Database Administrator* (MCDBA) program. It focuses on database administration, operation, and management.

- Finally, Microsoft offers programs for support personnel through the *Microsoft Office User Specialist* (MOUS) program. MOUS offers exams on all of Microsoft's office automation applications: Word, Excel, PowerPoint, Access, FrontPage, and Project. Several levels of expertise are available within the program to support different levels of proficiency.

Official trainer certification programs support all of these programs. This means that if you choose to use a certified training and education center (CTEC), you can ensure the quality of the training program to a certain degree.

Microsoft CTECs provide authorized training programs on Microsoft technologies.

Selecting a CTEC partner isn't easy, because several are available in most cities. At the very least your CTEC partner should offer the following, in addition to meeting all of Microsoft's requirements for certification:

- High-caliber trainers with real-world experience

- Practice tests to allow your professionals to prepare for certification exams

- A student-tracking program to provide you with regular training program updates

- A post-training support program

Selecting a Training Partner

When selecting a training partner, ask yourself these questions in addition to all the others you already ask:

- Is the training center a CTEC? If so, can Microsoft provide a reference for this partner?

- How many years has the center been in business? Is it stable?

- What makes this center different from all the others? What is its competitive advantage?

- How many people successfully passed their exams after taking training in this center in the last year? How many people took training?

- Does the center offer more than just technical training? Is user training also available?

- Does the center offer certification package deals?

- Does the center tailor programs to reflect specific organizational environments?

- Does the center offer special training programs such as new technology or new software version introductions?

- What are its hours of operation? Are night or weekend classes available?

- Does the center offer a student-tracking program?

- Does the center offer a train-the-trainer program for internal trainers?

- Does the center publish trainer resumes? Are these complete?

- Is the trainer's work profile available in order to assess real-world experience?

- Are complementary programs available to cover sister technologies?

- Are practice exams included? What is their validity?

- Does the center offer practice laboratories? If yes, how many? How many students can practice at the same time?

- Can students retake a course for free if they don't pass the exam the first time?

- What do the center's post-training support programs offer?

- Is student financial assistance available?

- Are the center's training programs income-tax deductible?

Though the Microsoft certification program is one of the best in the world, it still doesn't cover everything. For example, the arrival of Windows 2000 and Windows XP has demonstrated to businesses around the world that architects at all levels are rare commodities.

Microsoft does not offer any testing means for this category of personnel. The MCSE program could be close, but it seems too focused on specifics to be truly effective. MCSEs tend to be systems administrators rather than architects, and as such, the testing program includes too many questions on specific details of Microsoft's technologies.

With the coming of the Microsoft Solutions Framework (MSF), Microsoft has identified that different information is required for the elaboration of architectural designs, especially when it concerns Active Directory Services. It can't be long before an architectural testing program is put in place.

Classroom training is not the only approach to certification. For Windows 2000, Microsoft offered a basic training program that took five weeks of technical in-class training to professionals new to the platform. It's not every corporation that can afford to send its IT staff to such a program!

Once again, training programs that use personalized content can greatly reduce training costs and implementation delays. In addition, Microsoft Press and most other technical book publishers offer self-learning guides as well as exam support tools. Technicians who are more autonomous can learn at their own pace. But in order to do so, they require a testing environment.

An Internal Support Program

The training challenge is significant. It is not easy to implement a continuous learning program that supports learning at all levels. The internal training program must support classroom training (internal and external as required), e-learning techniques, self-learning techniques, testing programs, knowledge evaluation programs, and much more.

For technical staff, one of the best ways to support continuous learning is to implement an internal training and testing environment. Whatever the means they choose to learn, all technical staff will require a laboratory and testing environment to prove and improve their skills. In addition, the program should include

Answering Student Needs

One of the questions you must ask when evaluating a training partner relates to the training approach the partner uses.

Chapter 1 identified the four types of personalities: director, expressive, amiable, and analytic. All have their own needs in terms of training. The question to ask is, "Do the center's trainers know how to personalize each course to support individual needs?"

If so, each instructor will begin each class with a "discovery session" that asks students for their specific needs in the course. The instructor should write down the responses for all to see and check them off as they are met throughout the delivery of the course.

Selecting a Consulting Partner

The questions you ask yourself about your training partner should be the same you ask when evaluating a consulting partner.

- What is their approach toward certification?
- Do they provide a continuous learning program to their own staff?
- What is their internal rate of technological adoption? Are they market leaders or followers?
- Is their internal network using the technology they claim expertise in? If not, why not?

- An intermixing of skills to provide better technological coverage
- Access to software technologies
- A technical reference library
- Specific "learning times" for technical staff
- An internal learning support policy

Each of these elements is required to support learning. Organizations invest heavily in training. Each employee that leaves after taking a training program at the organization's expense should be considered a loss of potential profit. If organizations want to retain trained personnel, they need to provide more than just a salary.

A structured approach to continuous learning and personal improvement goes a long way toward personnel retention.

Intermixing Technical Skills

The first step in a continuous technical learning program is to intermix expertise. Take, for example, Microsoft .NET Enterprise Servers. This series of products includes various technologies all relying on Windows 2000 or XP to operate. Each technology meets a specific IT need. Organizations must often use several of these technologies to create an IT system that meets all of their business requirements. Training personnel on these technologies can be expensive unless the organization intermixes technologies.

By having personnel focus on specific technologies and ensuring that a minimum number of technicians cover each technology, the organization can ensure a complete level of support for each technology.

For example, if you use Exchange 2000, Internet Security and Acceleration Server, Host Integration Server, and Application Center Server 2000, as well as Windows 2000 or XP, you should ensure that at least two people study two of these technologies. Then you should ensure that each person knows the other's expertise so that if they need help with the technology, they know whom to contact. Finally, you need to make sure that each person can always be contacted. If these people are very mobile in your organization, this will mean pagers and/or cellular phones for everyone.

The best approach is to divide technologies into two categories, just like the Microsoft Certified Systems Engi-

---

Continuing User Training

One of the best ways to support ongoing user training is to provide functional workshops. These workshops focus on a key category of personnel. For example, a workshop could show project managers how to create a project using Microsoft Project and your internal project start-up manual. Another could show technical writers how to create and manage long documents. These workshops are short and to the point. As such, they fully support the task-oriented training approach of the EMF.

neer program does. The first focuses on operating systems. Everyone needs to be proficient in it. The second covers additional services, or the MCSE program's electives. Here, ensure that each technician covers at least two different technologies.

Microsoft .NET Enterprise Server technologies cover a broad spectrum of services. Technicians must cover as many aspects of this spectrum as they can. Each can focus on a specific certification program so that the team can cover them all, as shown in Figure 9.5.

This approach will provide you with a complete support program for all technologies. In addition, in the EMF,

The Microsoft Management Console

With Windows 2000, Microsoft unified the way administrators interact with technical environments. This is the Microsoft Management Console. This console makes it easier for technicians to learn more than one Microsoft technology because it is the same on all systems.

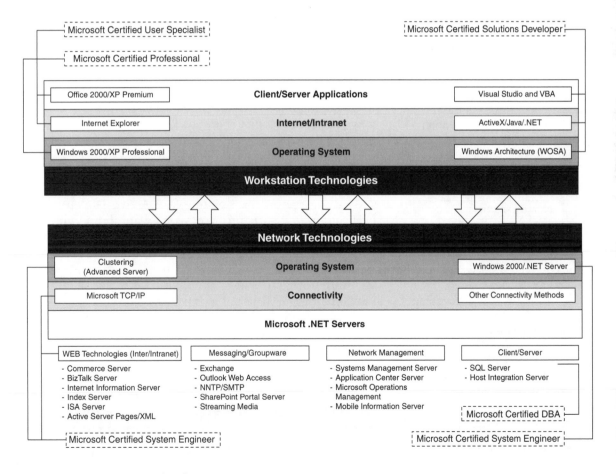

FIGURE 9.5   An example of a .NET Enterprise Server intermix

IT managers must follow and coordinate training activities for their professional staff.

Creating a Laboratory Environment

Chapter 5 identified the necessity of making use of a testing laboratory for the certification of all SPA object components. This laboratory has a second role in the EMF: technical training.

A technical training laboratory is necessary for two reasons.

- Internal trainers require a complete testing environment to identify user and process training solutions.
- Technicians at all levels require a complete testing environment to practice their skills.

The laboratory should contain enough technologies to be able to properly reproduce the organization's IT infrastructure. It should include technologies that are as recent as possible. Most often, organizations use recovered equipment that is not the latest and greatest. This only limits the potential benefits of this lab, because its purpose is to work with new technologies. New technologies always require more powerful hardware.

Figure 9.6 illustrates a training lab.

The lab must also include quick setup and recovery strategies. For example, if technicians are working on a case study that requires the staging of an Active Directory and .NET Server infrastructure, you won't want them to have to rebuild it from scratch every time they return to the laboratory. One of the best ways to provide this capability is to use interchangeable disk drives. This enables each technical group to prepare and store their own working environments. It saves considerable time when they return.

Another method is to use disk-imaging technologies. This requires a powerful storage server because each environment must be stored independently for the duration of the tests.

In addition, the laboratory will require a special station or stations that are disconnected from the laboratory network and connected to the internal network and the Internet. These stations are for documentation, research, and software downloads. Ideally, these stations are positioned throughout the lab.

Rate of Adoption of New Technologies

Organizations with varying business objectives will adopt new technologies at different rates.

Aggressive corporations adopt technologies as soon as they become available on the market. They are risk takers and industry leaders.

Aggressive followers let others take the first risks and will follow with a rule of "version minus 1." This means that they will always be one version away from the newest technologies. For example, with Windows 2000, these people waited for Service Pack 1 to become available.

Moderate adopters wait until industry experts say that it is completely safe to adopt new technologies before they do so.

Stable organizations wait until a majority of the industry has moved to the new technology before migrating.

Late followers wait until the last minute to migrate.

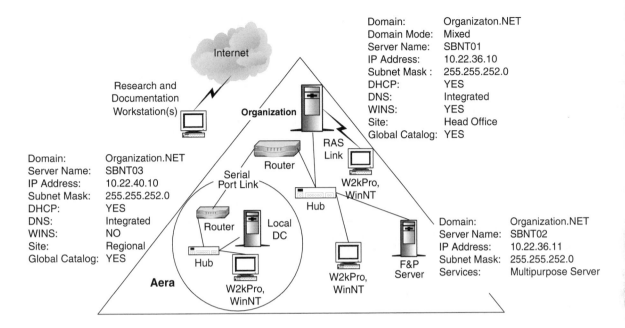

FIGURE 9.6 A Training Lab. Your training lab should be as complete as possible. This lab reproduces a typical internal network. Internal TCP/IP addresses are used because the lab does not connect to the external world.

The most important aspect of the lab is its activity coordination and resource sharing. As a result, it should include the same processes as the certification lab.[3]

Access to Software Technologies

Depending on the size of your organization and the amount of components within your network, you may decide that for these secondary purposes, you will require an additional laboratory dedicated to meeting training requirements. This laboratory should provide technicians and training design personnel with all the hardware and software resources that are currently in use within the existing network.

Whatever your organization's rate of technological adoption, you will also want to provide the laboratory with the very newest technologies in the market. This will enable technicians and trainers to become familiar with upcoming technologies before they are introduced into your network. Your staff will always be ready when new technologies are introduced.

---

3. See Chapter 4.

Depending on your adoption strategies, you may also want to provide access to *beta* technologies—technologies that are still in development and not yet on the market. This gives you a leading edge in technological adoption.

Microsoft has several programs that offer you both. The Select and Large Account Sales Agreements include access to every Microsoft technology, including public beta programs. For original equipment manufacturers and consulting and service firms, Microsoft offers the Microsoft Certified Solutions Provider (MCSP) program. It provides the same access to Microsoft software. Development firms and small technological firms can subscribe to the Microsoft Systems Developer Network and/or Microsoft TechNet. All of these programs offer a series of software evaluation programs ensuring access to the latest and greatest from Microsoft.

When you subscribe to one of these programs, Microsoft sends you its technologies in regular shipments. Each includes at least ten trial licenses for every Microsoft technology.

Building a Reference Library

The lab should also include a complete reference library. Almost every technical publisher provides information on Microsoft technologies. Many of them are leaders in the field. For example, many titles became available before the release of Windows 2000.

Essential library elements include the following:

- *Operations manuals:* The online help files and manuals for every technology should be stored in a central location within the lab.

- *Microsoft Press Resource Kits:* The Microsoft Press Resource Kit for every technology in use in your network should be on hand at all times. For new technologies still under evaluation, you can use the software version of the Resource Kit located most often in the support directory of Microsoft's CDs.

- *MCP training materials:* Several publishers offer Microsoft Certified Professional self-study guides. These are excellent resources because they include practical exercises. These exercises demonstrate the steps required to work with any given technology.

- *Development guides:* Some publishers specialize in documenting development strategies with Microsoft technologies.
- *Administration guides:* Several publishers focus on systems administration. These provide real-world knowledge on working and operating Microsoft technologies.
- *Internet connection:* The Internet is a great source of information and system updates.

A library tracking system should be used to manage the materials in this library. This ensures that its materials are available to personnel when required.

Freeing Up Personnel for Continuous Learning

It is also important to ensure that your personnel have the opportunity to use the lab. It goes without saying that technical professionals, like all professionals, must invest some of their own time to improve their skills. But if the organization wants the continuous learning program to work, it must be ready to invest in it as well. Several strategies are available.

- *A half-and-half arrangement* enables professionals to study during paid hours if they are prepared to invest the same amount of their own time.
- *Replaced time* lets professionals replace portions of study time with holidays.
- *Global study time* gives professionals a set amount of paid study time on a yearly basis.

In every case, you will need to develop study goals and strategies with each of your technical and training staff members. Your staff will greatly appreciate a serious corporate commitment to learning.

An Internal Support Policy

The final element of the continuous learning program is the internal support policy. Technical staff members must be ready to share their knowledge. This must be a specific objective of the program formalized into a self-supporting and information-sharing strategy.

Attending Technological Conferences

Many organizations send their technical staff to technical conferences. While these conferences are rich in information, they are also costly. Organizations should ensure that any technician that attends such a conference shares his or her knowledge when he or she returns. This can be done through a summary presentation of the gathered information to other technical staff. This can be the employee's repayment for attending the conference.

This program is supported by the publication of technical areas of expertise that clearly identify who is an expert in which technology. This information should also include how the experts can be reached both during normal operations and during emergencies.

Table 9.1 summarizes the costs of certification on a per-exam basis. Table 9.2 summarizes the components of the technical continuous learning program.

TABLE 9.1   Calculating Certification Costs

Component	Cost	
Training material/program	Self-study training guide or course cost	$ _____
	Practice exam	$ _____
Study time	Technician pay rate sharing policy	$ _____
Shared laboratory time	Laboratory cost/number of users	$ _____
Reference tools	Software licenses	$ _____
	TechNet subscription	$ _____
	Resource Kits	$ _____
	Reference books	$ _____
Certification exam	$100 U.S. per trial	$ _____
Total		**$** _____

TABLE 9.2   A Technical Continuous Learning Program Checklist

Component	Questions	Status
Technologies	Does your continuous learning program focus on a mix of technologies?	Yes .... ☐ No .... ☐
Laboratory	Is there a laboratory available for continuous learning?	Yes .... ☐ No .... ☐
Hardware technologies	Does the lab provide new technologies and resource-sharing mechanisms?	Yes .... ☐ No .... ☐
Software technologies	Are all required software products available?	Yes .... ☐ No .... ☐
Reference library	Does the lab include a comprehensive reference library?	Yes .... ☐ No .... ☐
Staff learning time	Do staff members have the time, the inclination, and the incentive to learn?	Yes .... ☐ No .... ☐
Internal support	Is there a knowledge-sharing strategy in place?	Yes .... ☐ No .... ☐

Continuous Learning Management

The continuous learning program should be supported by strong management policies clearly identifying the program's goals and objectives. Its structure, its availability to technical staff, its processes, and its obligations should also be clear.

This program, coupled with a similar program for users, will ensure that the organization stays abreast of the technologies it uses. It will also ensure that operations staff fully master these technologies. Finally, it will enable self-actualization for users and technical and training staff. It is an essential component of the EMF. This program is in place when you can answer all of the questions in Table 9.2 in the affirmative.

Preparing for a Microsoft Certification Exam

Use the following checklist to see if you're ready for your exam.

- *Be prepared.* It is useless to try an exam if you don't think you're ready. Practice a lot and ensure that you are familiar not only with the technology itself, but also with how it interacts with other Microsoft technologies.
- *Practice.* New exams include software simulations that mimic the activities you perform in the actual software program. If you don't have the opportunity to practice with this tool, you'll never be able to answer the questions.

When you take the exam, remember the following:

- If it is a traditional exam, *mark your questions.* Several questions are very detailed. If you see that a question is too time-consuming, mark it and move on to the next one.
- *Mark your time.* Make sure you have enough time for the exam. It would be sad if you didn't pass because you didn't have enough time to at least read every question.
- *Read each question carefully.* Questions often include a lot of clutter—information that is there to confuse you. Make sure you read the beginning and the end of each question before you answer.
- If time allows, *return to previous questions.* An exam often includes several questions on the same subject. One question can often provide the answer to another.
- *The first answer you come up with is most often right.* If you don't know, follow your intuition.
- *It's better to answer than leave blanks.* Blank answers are worth nothing.
- *Don't stress yourself out.* After all, it's just an exam, and if you know your stuff, there's no need to sweat it.

The Migration Training Plan

When migrating to new technologies, the organization must define ways to absorb and appropriate the change. One of the key strategies is the training strategy.

The migration-training plan must be complete. In addition to "new" user training approaches, the training plan must address all levels. This is especially important if you're migrating to Windows XP and Office XP as well as implementing the EMF.

The training program must meet the needs of the following audiences:

- End users
- Managers
- Systems administrators
- Operations and technical staff
- Training staff
- Support staff
- End-user support personnel
- Developers
- Application enhancers
- Project team members

It must make use of innovative and modern training approaches in order to provide a solid cost/benefit ratio. This is how the training QUOTE works.

The Training QUOTE

The training QUOTE divides the migration training plan into five basic phases.

Question Phase (Planning)

The project begins with the planning phase. In this phase, the training plan must focus on project-planning activities and begin identifying the changes to come.

It should include the following activities:

- *Define the initial project plan.* This plan should cover the first two phases of the QUOTE System in detail and broadly outline the last three phases.

The Question Phase

Training activities
- Identify impacts of change
- Identify audiences
- Design initial strategy
- Estimate budget
- Conduct user survey

Deliverables
- Initial project plan
- Impact study, including audience identification
- Initial transition strategy
- Budget estimate
- User survey results
- Initial technical training

Mechanisms
- PowerPoint presentations and meetings
- Word documents
- Excel spreadsheets
- External classroom training
- Internal continuous learning center

- *Identify the impacts of change.* This should include a review of the technology's new features, a review of proposed architectural structures and system configurations, and a comparison to existing infrastructures.
- *Begin initial technical training for key project personnel.* This is most easily done through outside sources because the organization isn't ready for the technology yet. It may also be done in the continuous learning center, if it exists.
- *Identify impacted audiences.* This is covered in more detail in the following section.
- *Design a training strategy.* The training team must begin an initial strategy design based on factors such as the amount of change, the objectives of the training program, the number of people to train, the number of training programs to run concurrently, available resources, and current skill levels within the organization.
- *Prepare a budget estimation.* The training team must perform an initial budget evaluation of total training costs.
- *Conduct a user survey if knowledge levels are unknown.* This survey is done in conjunction with the communications team.

This training plan should be divided into four categories. Each category concentrates on a specific type of audience.

- User training
  - End users
  - Managers
  - End-user support personnel
  - Training staff
- Technical training
  - Systems architects
  - Systems administrators
  - Operations and technical staff
  - Support staff
- Development training
  - Development architects
  - Developers
  - Application enhancers

The Understand Phase

Training activities

- Design a training solution
- Analyze training logistics
- Implement a train-the-trainer program
- Publish training information on the intranet
- Complete and validate user guides
- Design office automation and workflow solutions

Deliverables

- Complete training solution including logistics and costs (project plan as well)
- Train-the-trainer sessions
- The training offer (to communications team)
- User guides for internal use
- Continued technical training
- Automated templates and other systems
- Training coordination

Mechanisms

- PowerPoint presentations and meetings
- Word documents
- Excel spreadsheets
- Microsoft Project plans
- Office programming tools
- External classroom training
- Intranet training solutions information

- Project training
  - Project team members

The training strategy must cover all four aspects of training. With projects such as the migration to Windows 2000 or XP, this training strategy can become a project in and of itself.

Understand Phase (Preparation)

The preparation phase is the creative phase for the training team. Because the bulk of the work at this phase is preparation and acceptance of the solutions, most of the training process deals with the design of appropriate approaches for each of the four audience types.

This phase should include the following activities:

- *Design a training solution.* A complete training solution should be designed for each of the training audiences. This should include a mix of internal and external training sources. It should be timely and cost-effective. Internal methods should include classroom training, migration training, and self-study.

- *Analyze training logistics.* This analysis should include the logistics of every aspect of the training program: training room preparation, trainer preparation, regional solutions, and solution preparation. Every physical element and supporting activity must be identified and prepared.

- *Implement a train-the-trainer program.* The trainers' technical training program should begin at this stage. It should include advanced usage training on every aspect of the new user tools. If technical training is part of the internal offering, the train-the-trainer program should include advanced technical training.

- *Publish training information on the intranet.* The training team must make its training solution known to all audiences. It may choose to publish it on the project intranet Web site. This will be determined in conjunction with the communications team.

- *Design office automation and workflow solutions.* The training team must use the results of the user survey to automate and personalize the solution to organizational requirements. This is done in conjunction with application enhancers and developers. It is at this stage that key personnel in both these audiences begin technical training.

- *Design user guides*. The training team must begin the design of every user guide that will be used for internal training purposes. They will also act as evaluators for the user activity guides prepared by the communications team.

Preparing the Training Solution

The training solution is a complex set of processes whose objective is to mitigate the negative aspects of change. As mentioned previously, it must provide a solution for each of its four audience types. Its objective should be to perform just-in-time training. This means that the training program should focus on getting people up and running as fast as possible. The method used to meet this goal for each audience type is examined in the sections that follow.

Audience Type 1: Users   User training programs are often the most expensive for an organization. The challenges are big. You must provide training at all skill levels, for a variety of tools, and in a timely manner so that users can profit from their new systems as soon as possible.

In addition, training deadlines are often defined by other project imperatives. If the organization needs to train 500 people per week because that is the rate of migration the project can sustain, training teams have no choice but to follow this deadline. As a result, user training solutions should be innovative and adaptive.

For end users, a migration-training program will often be enough, especially if automation is part of the technical solution. This type of program is not your classic classroom session. Most classrooms can support only 12 users at a time because that is the maximum a single trainer can properly train. At 12 per room, it takes a lot of rooms and a lot of sessions to train 500 people per week. Figure 9.7 illustrates the .NET user training approach.

If you design your migration program to meet and replace existing user skills with some improvements, you can change the training venue and greatly reduce costs. Here's how it works:

Migration Presentation Design

The migration presentation should outline all of the activities users will undergo during the migration. Because it is very much like "a day in the life of a user," it can be short and to the point. For example, a migration to Windows 2000/XP Professional requires about one hour of presentation. Include Outlook XP and you have a half-day presentation. A combined migration to Windows 2000/XP and Office XP can be done in two half-day sessions, especially if personalization and automation are included in the technical solution.

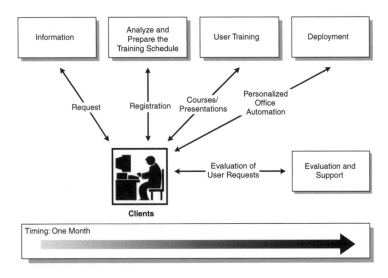

FIGURE 9.7   .NET User Training. In a .NET training approach, the user training program must be continued.

Migration Presentation Computer Setup

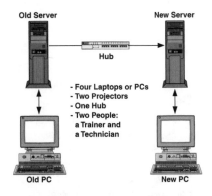

Four laptops are ideal for the presentation system setup. Two will be used as servers, old and new, and two will be used to represent client computers.

The first client computer is used to project the presentation and to demonstrate the "old" way. The second is used mainly for the demonstration of the new system.

Two presenters are also ideal because one can present while the other demonstrates.

1. Begin with the elaboration of your traditional training manuals. These manuals should completely cover every new feature at the beginning, intermediate, and advanced levels. Because your audiences for each training level diminish as they become more advanced, you can start with the beginner guides first.

2. Next, design a PowerPoint presentation that demonstrates every activity the user will undergo during the migration process. Include new product features and automation solutions into your presentation. Ensure that your presentation includes page numbers referencing your traditional guide so users can look up how to perform an operation.

3. Deliver your presentation making sure that users have access to both the presentation and the reference guide. Several delivery mechanisms are available. If your network supports multimedia streaming, you can broadcast the presentation on the network and place the reference guides on the intranet. But the most successful mechanism to date is a live presentation.

   This means performing the presentation in an auditorium to between 50 and 100 users. People will enjoy the break from their everyday routines. The project can profit from users' absences and work at their desks to migrate their systems. People can socialize with others in a non-threatening environment. The live presentation's cost is greater than an intranet broadcast, but its benefits are far greater in a change management situation.

4. In addition, you'll need to create local support teams—subject matter experts, in fact—so that users can have localized support directly where they are.

5. For most users, the two solutions, the migration presentation and the local support teams, provide everything they need, but for at least 20 percent of your staff, these solutions aren't enough. These people will either require hands-on training because they are not comfortable with the presentation solution or they will simply require more advanced training. The solution for these more traditional classes can be internal or external, depending on your internal training resources. You can also hire external trainers to supplement your internal team. But if you do so, ensure they are completely familiar with your internal training manuals and approaches before they deliver training for you.

Managers will require smaller groups. They will be comfortable with the training approach, but they will want shorter and more focused sessions. Figure 9.8 illustrates grouping users.

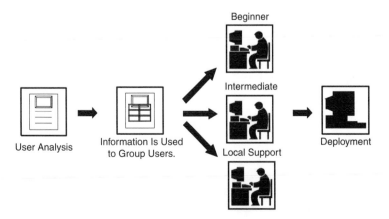

FIGURE 9.8 Grouping Users. Both the user survey and the user inventory will help group users for training.

Local End-User Support

One of the best groups for this role is the secretarial group. Through the very nature of their job function, they must often be advanced users of office automation software. Yet, with the move to self-typed documents, their workloads have decreased. Secretarial and administrative assistance staff members are also usually well liked by their peers. Assigning them the role of local end-user support is often an ideal way to realign their functions within the organization.

End-user support personnel will require comprehensive training on the personalized technical solution. Their training program should be more traditional and should cover both personalization and generic program features. The support population should represent about 5 percent of your user base.

Training staff members need train-the-trainer programs on both generic program features and personalized solutions. Their training is similar to end-user support training, but it arrives at a much earlier stage in the project because these are the people who will design other training solutions.

Audience Types 2 and 3: Technicians and Developers

Technical and development training are extremely similar, so they are treated in the same manner. This training should address the following audiences:

- *Technical training:* This should focus on general training on the new technologies. This will assist staff in making appropriate design decisions. But for most of your technical staff, this training should focus on the specific features of the new technology that have been selected for your particular environment.

  - Systems architects will require most of the generic training because they will be the ones to design the personalized solution for your environment. Architects who do not participate in the solution design will require specific training.

  - Systems administrators require some degree of generic training to assist in solution design. But for the most part, they will require specific training.

  - Operations and technical staff require specific training.

  - Support staff require specific training to support your custom solutions.

- *Development Training:* Training should focus on the potential of the new technologies as well as on the specific content of your custom solution.

  - Development architects require the same training as the systems architects because they should participate in solution design.

  - Developers require training on conversion techniques and specifically on new programming techniques based on your custom solution.

- Application enhancers require the same type of training as central developers, but their training should focus on desktop and office automation rather than on central systems.

This type of training requires a strong certified training partner, whatever the technology you decide to use. This will be especially important for the delivery of courses with custom content.

Microsoft, for example, allows certified centers to create custom programs by picking and choosing specific modules from different courses. CTECs don't normally offer these custom programs because they are complex and difficult to manage. But these types of programs are exactly what customers need. Don't take no for an answer. If your partner does not want to offer specific content, you might consider looking elsewhere.

All technical and development staff should also participate in the migration-training program. It is important for them to be aware of the details of the training program being delivered to users.

Procedural Training One of the most important aspects of technical and development training is the design and definition of new procedures, especially with the EMF. Because the Framework is based on standardization, it is important to implement standard operating procedures (SOPs).

If you migrate to Windows 2000/XP and implement the EMF, you will have to define the areas of interaction for all IT staff. You will also need to identify and write SOPs for each area of interaction. The best way to write these procedures is to do it while the project is in its preparation stages. This is done during the workload assessment activities, so the project team has a large responsibility in this activity.

Once the SOPs are defined, you will need to add an internal training activity for every technical and/or development staff member. This activity is probably the most important training activity for the EMF.

Audience Type 4: Project Training Project training focuses on the project team itself. This training must in-

---

Sample SOP

For an example of how to write a standard operating procedure (SOP), see Appendix F.

SOPs for Windows 2000/XP

In a large deployment project for Windows 2000/XP with 12,000 users, the number of SOPs that were required exceeded 100.

Fortunately, the customer already had several on hand so that only minor modifications were required. In addition, several of the procedures were included in automated scripts using the Windows Scripting Host, making it easy to write and easy to follow.

Mapping and Adapting Public Programs

If you find that you have a large initial training group and that external classroom training is too expensive, consider using custom, in-house courses. Training partners can map course content to your needs and deliver special courses within your own classrooms.

clude two types of training: generic technical training and project-specific training.

Project team members are responsible for designing and validating the solution as well as putting it in place. They must begin by mastering the upcoming technologies. On projects such as the migration to Windows 2000/XP, organizations should begin with significant amounts of technical training and information because these technologies are so different from the ones that are already in place. It is only after this initial training program that architects and administrators can begin to design the solution. Integrators will require initial generic training because they will be responsible for laboratory environments and solution testing. Project team members will be the first to test all training solutions developed internally for users.

During the course of the project, the size of the project team will fluctuate. The degree of fluctuation will depend on the stability of the team you select initially and whether your project is designed to use departmental or regional teams for deployment. Project-specific training concentrates on these issues. If you must integrate other personnel into the project, it may be necessary to design a project introduction program that includes project information[4] and some generic technical training. This will help bring new team members quickly up to speed and ease their integration into the project team.

Finally, project team members are responsible for the elaboration of new procedures for recurring technological management. It will be their responsibility to work with internal teams to design these procedures and work with the training team to develop training programs to deliver them to recurrent administrative staff. In this case, members of the project technical team become the training providers.

Training Coordination   All of the activities listed previously will be in their initial stages. They will be finalized during the next phase of the project. But it is at this stage that a training coordinator will become necessary. The detailed coordination of all training activity is one of the responsibilities of the project. This should be based on existing in-house training asset management tools, but if none are available or if current tools are inadequate, the project should

---

4. Based mostly on the project introduction guide.

either acquire or develop supporting technologies for this responsibility.

Because a global migration project touches every member of the organization with regard to training, it is important for the project to deliver a training solution review at the end of the project. This review is the training coordinator's responsibility.

Organize Phase (Pilot)

This phase deals with the finalization of all preparatory activities and the initial testing of all of the solutions through a Proof of Concept (POC) and/or a pilot deployment. The activities in this phase should include

- Finalization of all materials and logistic approaches
- POC (pre-pilot) training
- Pilot program training
- POC and/or pilot program evaluation
- Modification of the approaches (if required)

Both the POC and the pilot change the environments of user and technical populations. Both are defined as a complete delivery of the training solution to a select group of users who represent as many aspects of the organization's diverse user populations as possible. At the end of both tests, participants must provide their comments on the overall training solution and delivery process.

The project team is also responsible for the training of support personnel in preparation for the pilot program and the deployment. These courses should include some degree of generic training as discussed previously, but they should also include the details of every technical solution to be put in place.

It is at this stage that training coordination techniques are tested and evaluated. It is crucial to make any changes deemed necessary to these techniques.

A portion of the traditional classroom environments will be migrated by the project at this stage because the training team has to begin addressing traditional training to a minority group as part of the overall training strategy.

The Organize Phase

Training activities
- Finalize training solution
- Test user guides and training solution
- Evaluate quality of training solution
- Evaluate quality of office automation and workflow solution
- Migrate traditional classrooms to new technologies

Deliverables
- POC user and technical training
- Pilot project user and technical training
- Integration of automated templates and other systems with deployment
- Support group training
- POC and/or pilot evaluation
- Migration of the systems environments for a portion of the traditional classrooms

Mechanisms
- PowerPoint presentations and meetings
- Word documents
- Excel spreadsheets
- Microsoft Project plans
- Office deployment tools
- External classroom training
- Intranet training solutions

The Transfer Phase

Training activities

- Begin repetitive user and technical training
- Continuously reevaluate quality of training solution
- Continuously reevaluate quality of office automation and workflow solution

Deliverables

- User and technical training
- Integration of automated templates and other systems with deployment
- Support group training

Mechanisms

- PowerPoint presentations and meetings
- Word documents
- Microsoft Project plans
- Office deployment tools
- External classroom training
- Intranet training solutions

The Evaluate Phase

Training activities

- Perform project review
- Identify solution strengths and weaknesses

Deliverables

- Project review
- Training inventory

Mechanisms

- PowerPoint presentations
- Meetings
- Word documents
- Access/SQL databases
- Intranet site

Transfer Phase (Deployment)

During the massive deployment phase, training moves to full production mode. Training should now focus on

- Repetitive training of targeted user populations
- Training project progress and coordination information provided to all audiences

The training program should be simpler to manage at this stage because it becomes very repetitive. But the quality of the solution should be constantly reevaluated in order to ensure that the program continues to meet project objectives.

Training for the Transfer Phase tends to focus mainly on users, but it is also important for the training team to ensure that proper technical training is delivered to IT staff as the deployment progresses. The percentage of IT staff taking training should be consistent with the percentage of migrated users. If 40 percent of the users are migrated, 40 percent of IT staff should be trained on the new solution; when you reach 60 percent of the users, you should have 60 percent of support staff trained; and so on.

Evaluate Phase (Project Review)

The final phase of the project for the training team is the project review. Team members must review and identify key success areas of the overall solution as well as weaknesses. The results of this review are documented and provided to all interested parties.

In addition, the project should deliver a complete training inventory to the organization. This training inventory is derived from the training coordination database that was used during the project. These results should then be integrated into the organization's project start-up kit so that during the next deployment or migration project, the organization will have ready-made training solutions.

Recurring Training

The intent of the training solution for the migration project is to provide just-in-time training. This means that its goal is to ensure the rapid development of functional skills with the new products for targeted audiences. Once the project is complete, it is important to continue building on these skills with recurring training through the continuous learning program described previously (see Figure 9.9).

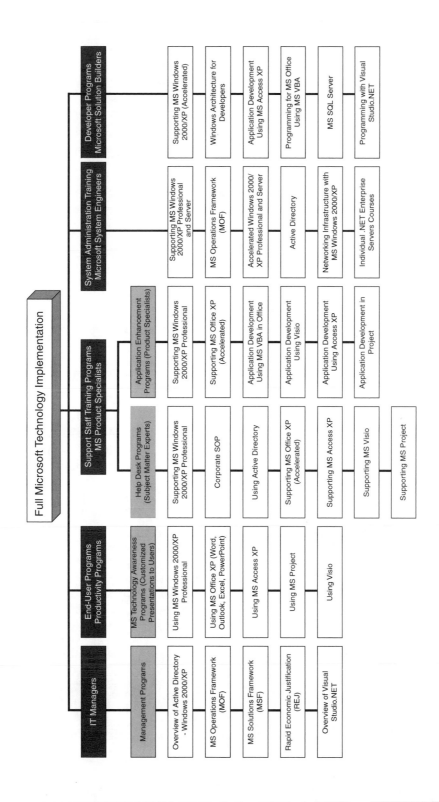

FIGURE 9.9 A Recurring Training Program. A complete recurring training program must cover all the bases.

This chart demonstrates a possible training program covering a variety of audiences: managers, users, support personnel, application enhancers, systems administrators, and developers. It also integrates corporate standard practices and manufacturer's best practices.

Using the QUOTE System

With the training program, we complete coverage of all of the change management tools required to put in place the EMF. This information was designed to assist you through the Transfer Phase of your EMF deployment. Now you are ready to complete the .NET QUOTE with the Evaluate Phase.

Case Study
Implementing a Complete Training Program

Organization Type	Public Sector
Number of Users	2,500
Number of Computers	2,500
Project Focus	Migration to Windows NT
Project Duration	9 Months
Specific Project Focus	Migrate to a Secure Operating System
Administrative Type	Centralized

This organization began a migration project to change from Windows 95 to Windows NT Workstation 4.0 as well as Microsoft Office 97. Because this migration would affect all users, including technical and support staff, they designed a comprehensive training program.

The program included presentation-style migration training to users. All users and technical staff took this training. The program was delivered in one day and covered Windows NT, Word, Outlook, and Excel. Advanced training on Word and Excel, as well as PowerPoint and Access training, was delivered to specific groups not exceeding 30 percent of the user base.

Windows NT training focused only on the differences between NT and Windows 95. This training took one hour.

Office training focused on the new interface and on the differences with existing products. Outlook training took two hours. Word training took two hours, and Excel training took one hour, for a total of six hours of training.

The migration presentation was based on automated document templates that were derived from the end-user survey analysis performed at the beginning stages of the project. The advantage of this approach was that users did not learn how to use Word, Excel, Outlook, or Windows NT—they learned how to perform word processing, financial management, communications, and operations within the organization's network.

This program was so successful that it became the introductory program for new employees in the organization at the end of the project.

CHAPTER ROADMAP

Use this flowchart as a guide to understand the concepts covered in this chapter.

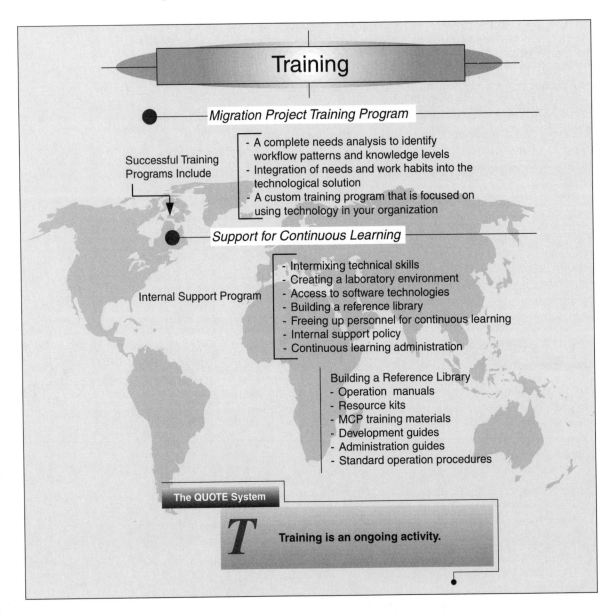

Training

Migration Project Training Program

Successful Training Programs Include

- A complete needs analysis to identify workflow patterns and knowledge levels
- Integration of needs and work habits into the technological solution
- A custom training program that is focused on using technology in your organization

Support for Continuous Learning

Internal Support Program

- Intermixing technical skills
- Creating a laboratory environment
- Access to software technologies
- Building a reference library
- Freeing up personnel for continuous learning
- Internal support policy
- Continuous learning administration

Building a Reference Library
- Operation manuals
- Resource kits
- MCP training materials
- Development guides
- Administration guides
- Standard operation procedures

The QUOTE System

T Training is an ongoing activity.

CHAPTER 10

Profiting from .NET Enterprise Technologies

Performing an Evaluation of the Enterprise Management Framework and Moving On to Recurrent Activities

In the EMF, change is no longer the only constant. Stability within an ever-changing world is the new constant. This stability is maintained through the application of structured change management practices. This is why it is important for your organization that you ensure that the management and evolution of the Framework become everyday practice.

The Evaluation of the Framework

The final stage of the implementation process begins with evaluation. Using the EMF structure, you began by identifying specific objectives and a vision, the vision to implement an enterprise infrastructure for .NET technologies. Now you must identify if you have met these goals. Here's how:

- *Review support calls:* Identify if the number of calls has decreased or if the nature of the calls has changed. The number of calls should be significantly smaller and the nature of the calls should be focused on usage rather than system problems.

- *Poll users:* Are users satisfied with the level and quality of IT service?

- *Review procedures:* Are IT staff using standard operating procedures and has the use of those procedures reduced the number of incidents?

> **The QUOTE System's Evaluate Phase**
>
> We complete the QUOTE for the EMF with the Evaluate Phase. This is where you can begin to reap the benefits of the Framework: increased stability, increased productivity, smoother operations, and much, much more.

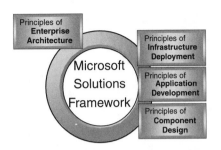

The MSF covers several aspects of Microsoft technology implementations.

- *Manage change:* Is your organization now ready to manage IT change on an ongoing basis?
- *Determine .NET scalability:* Is your IT infrastructure ready for .NET Enterprise Servers?

Completing the EMF

The implementation of the Framework isn't an easy process, but with the principles and practical examples of this guide and your manufacturer's recommended approaches, you will be able to put in place a complete continuous change management process within your enterprise.

Manufacturer-recommended approaches vary depending on the manufacturer. If you're using Windows, you can find these recommendations in the Microsoft Solutions Framework (MSF). The MSF covers several aspects of technology implementation: architectural design, operations management, structured development, and readiness review.

With its focus on people, PCs, and processes, the EMF brings together a series of principles and processes that surround and complement manufacturer approaches like the MSF. Figure 10.1 illustrates this concept.

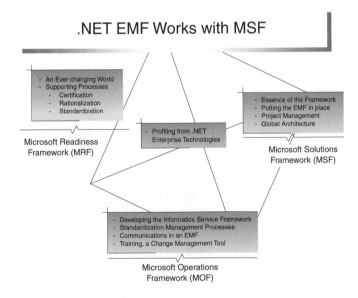

FIGURE 10.1 The EMF and MSF. In a technological migration toward a new Microsoft technology, the EMF and the MSF can work together to ease the process.

Your .NET implementation will require a combination of both approaches and a major effort on your part. Once you get there, you'll need to make sure that you maintain and fully integrate the processes of your own EMF into everyday operations. This is why the project evaluation is critical.

This project evaluation has several objectives. The first is to perform a *complete review* of all of the processes used in the project. This review should become the basis of your project start-up kit. A benefit of the start-up kit is that the next time you need to put a project in place for change management you will be ready and will not have to reinvent the process.

Second, this review serves to update your global architecture. As you saw in Chapter 2, the elaboration of a global architecture is a complex and time-consuming process. It is crucial for the project to use the review to update every modified element of the Global Architecture. It is important for you to keep this architecture up-to-date from this point on.

Third, this review and evaluation becomes critical because it is the starting point of the cyclical QUOTE System. The next time a technological implementation or update comes around, this evaluation will become source material for the Question Phase of the new implementation.

Change and the EMF

The EMF is about continuous change management. It describes and identifies the processes used to move from Situation A to Situation B. The starting point of any change management situation is always your *current* situation. Now that you have completed the implementation of the Framework, you should have and should maintain proper information on your current situation.

The next time a new technology arrives (take, for example, Longhorn, which is the code name for Microsoft's release of Windows after XP) you will be ready to absorb the change.

Change management starts with your current situation, reviews new product features, identifies industry and manufacturer best practices, identifies modifications to existing standards and potential problems, and uses these elements to perform change. During the change process, you can use risk management strategies to minimize impacts until you finally arrive at the new situation. This process is illustrated in Figure 10.2.

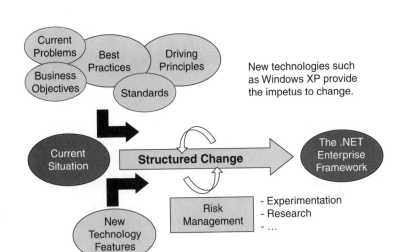

FIGURE 10.2 The Change Management Process. Going from the current situation to a changed situation is a change management process.

The amount of change brought about by new technologies determines how you implement the change. For example, a migration from Windows 2000 to Windows XP can simply be performed through the ongoing kernel management process described in Chapter 5 because the amount of change between the two platforms is minimal. It goes without saying that some training will be required, but as far as the technology goes, you can deploy it all remotely. This may well be the case for the next few years of your EMF.

Remember, when you implement change, try to do it in a controlled manner.

Taking Small Steps toward Change

This Framework is designed with evaluation and evolution in mind. The Framework is scalable. Its very structure is to implement a basic standard environment, and then, once it is in place, add functionality and capability as you need it.

For example, many organizations see the move to Windows 2000/XP as a major undertaking. And it is. But if you take it in stride and design your initial implementation project with reasonable objectives, you can take smaller steps toward the migration. How do you do this? It's simple.

The Big Picture

Even though it is easier to break a project or a technology into smaller components, it is always important to remember the big picture.

Windows 2000/XP includes at least 100 new and improved features. *You don't need to put them all in place at once!* Design your initial project with the objective of putting in place half or fewer of the features in the new feature set. Then, once the new technology is in place, scale your network by introducing specific features on a project-by-project basis. This process is illustrated in Figure 10.3.

Taking small steps is just what the QUOTE System is all about. As shown in Figure 10.3, you use the QUOTE System to perform your initial implementation of Windows 2000/XP. Then you use the Evaluate Phase of the QUOTE System to begin systems evolution. It is at this point that you begin to recover and reuse your .NET investments to start adding functionalities to the network environment. And because you now have a controlled IT environment, the changes you bring to your new network should no longer disrupt business operations.

Lessons Learned

During the implementation process for your own EMF, you will learn quite a bit of information about yourself and your organization. Here are a few final tips to ease the process.

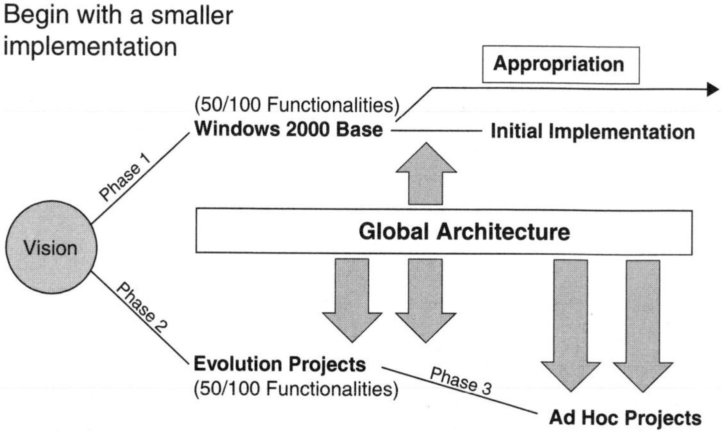

Remember Sun Tzu

In his book *The Art of War,* the ancient Chinese philosopher Sun Tzu wrote what would become one of the world's most famous proverbs: "Divide and conquer."

This is exactly what you should do when you implement major technological change. Divide it into smaller pieces. It will be much easier to conquer.

Begin with a smaller
implementation

FIGURE 10.3 The Steps toward a Migration. Migrating to Windows 2000/XP should be done in parts, not all at once. Your Global Architecture should provide structure at all times.

- Be sure you have clear objectives. And if you use teams that include both internal personnel and external consultants, be sure that these objectives are completely clear to both teams. Ensure that each team's objectives are identified and communicated to the other.
- Be sure to make it clear to your internal team what "project mode" means. Often, external project teams are in project mode while internal teams are still in recurrent management mode. Project mode means deadlines, deliverables, acceptance processes, and accountability.
- Your internal team may be disturbed by the external team because they do not necessarily have the same objectives or work at the same pace. It may be a very good idea to ensure that internal teams take a small project management course at the beginning of the project to ensure the smooth integration of both teams.
- If your internal teams have specific objectives that may not necessarily be covered by the project, make sure that these are identified at the very beginning of the project. If there can be some synchronicity between these specific objectives and the project's, map it right away.
- Make sure you design and use project user guides for each major project you implement. These are seldom created, yet they can provide so much because at the very least, they clearly identify everyone's roles and responsibilities.
- Make sure that your current situation analysis provides a summary report. The current situation is the starting point for any change. If you don't have a complete summary of the situation, it is very hard for external consultants to grasp the complexity of your environment. The summary also provides a clear picture of your organization to internal team members.
- Make sure you have regularly scheduled update meetings during your implementation project. Communications is the key to change and risk management. These updates are crucial to the complete success of your project.
- When you design the operational mode of your project, document it and make sure everyone sticks to it. If deliverables have a set time frame for acceptance, accept them within this set time frame. If escalation procedures work in a specific manner, use them in this manner. Do not deviate from set practices unless it becomes critical to do so.

- Make sure you have a very tight grasp on project activities. Slippage can put the project at risk. It's up to your team to make sure that this doesn't happen, and if it does that you're ready for it.

- Don't worry if you feel lonely as a change agent. Change agents have a tendency to quickly recognize each other and gather intuitively. You won't be alone for long.

- Select the right project manager. This person is probably the most critical person in the project.

- Learn to delegate. Too many projects use key internal personnel for every single critical activity. If you find yourself in this situation, learn to identify what is most important to you and delegate other tasks. Many projects put themselves at risk by relying on the same people for critical activities. This is a good way to burn out.

- Once you have rationalized technologies within your network, make sure managers stick to the rationalization processes. Make them understand the dollar value of accepting that their staffs use nonstandard products.

- If you use external consultants, make sure you team them up with internal personnel. Ask them the right questions and have them document their answers. Make sure you get the most from the knowledge transfer process.

- Learn to recover and reuse your investment in the EMF by continuing to scale your IT environment once it is implemented.

- Once you've implemented the EMF, don't lose it. This Framework is an ongoing process. Ensure that you follow its growth and learn to adapt it to changing business needs and technological environments.

- Don't forget that the first time is always the hardest. Practice helps you learn from your experiences.

- One final recommendation: In your implementation, don't try to adapt people to technology—adapt technology to people. You'll have much greater success.

This Framework is about a lot of things. It is about increased productivity, reduced support costs, and constant evolution. It is about constantly being up-to-date in terms of the technology you use in your network. It is about using IT as a strategic business tool. It is about providing continuous learning environments for continued increases

Tools for Any Use

As a change agent, you'll find that your tools are very versatile. In a recent project meeting including five highly paid consultants, we found that everyone there was trying to "invent" a project plan for the client.

We tried telling everyone that for a migration to Windows 2000, there are a number of different sources we could use to perform this exercise—all of which would be cheaper for the client. We even had the Windows 2000 Deployment Guide (from the Resource Kit) on hand, but no one would listen.

Eventually, the group did use the Deployment Guide—they put it under the projector they were using to raise it so everyone could see!

In some cases, the change agent simply can't win.

in people skills. It is about people, PCs, and processes interacting in your own IT environments to the profit of your enterprise.

The Final QUOTE

You finish the QUOTE for the EMF with the evaluation of our implementation. How successful were you? What are your new support activities? What are the tangible benefits?

The .NET EMF tries to cover many of the aspects of human, technological, and process activities in an enterprise. This is a major task. Putting people, PCs, and processes to work in a .NET world is really up to you. You determine the success of your own implementation. And, the value you place on IT helps determine the level of benefits you draw from it.

This book brings together the sum of our experience with people, PCs, and processes. We hope it helps you reflect on the relationship between the three, especially if you choose to follow its principles. Remember that you can find a lot of useful material on this book's companion Web site at http://www.Reso-Net.com/EMF, including forms, more complete appendixes, and original versions of some of the images we use (to let you print them in a bigger format).

If you start the implementation and need more information, don't hesitate to communicate with us at EMF@Reso-Net.com.

Now you're ready to manage IT change!

PART III

Appendixes

APPENDIX A

The Global Architecture Grid

Tools for Designing the Global Architecture

This appendix includes a series of tools to help you design your Global Architecture, including

- A Global Architecture grid filled in with explanations of what you should find in each cell
- An empty Global Architecture grid you can use during your design exercise
- A sample table of contents used to perform the situation review and identify inventories for the Global Architecture

Refer to Chapter 2 for more information on the Global Architecture.

TABLE A.1   Sample Global Architecture Grid

Global Architecture	Network	Data	People	Tasks
Scope	Breadth of coverage of the physical network.	Breadth of coverage of the information stored in corporate data.	Human resources requirements within the organization.	Goals and objectives of task management within the enterprise.
Enterprise	Type of service required from the physical network to support business objectives.	Type of information stored in the data systems. Organization of that information.	Functions and organization of people within the enterprise.	Type of activities required to support business processes.
Influences	Factors influencing the service aspects of the physical network.	Factors impacting data collection and retention.	Factors influencing how people interact with systems and technologies.	Factors influencing how people perform tasks within the organization.
Systems	Software used to control and manage all of the physical components of the network.	Software and processes used to control and manage the organization's data.	Systems used by people in the organization.	Systems designed to support the execution of tasks within the organization.
Technologies	Hardware components used in the network infrastructure (PCs, servers, mainframes, WAN components).	Hardware components used to support the organization's data, including both paper and information technologies.	Technologies used to support people and business processes within the organization.	Technologies provided to support people in the execution of their tasks. This can include information and non-information systems.

TABLE A.2 Global Architecture Grid

Global Architecture	Network	Data	People	Tasks
Scope				
Enterprise				
Influences				
Systems				
Technologies				

Table of Contents for Situation Review (Inventory)

When you perform a situation review, you will need to cover the areas identified in the grid in the following list.[1]

Technical Information

Identify the Network Infrastructure

- ❏ Identify responsible personnel for detailed network infrastructure information
- ❏ Obtain network diagrams
- ❏ Identify all WAN links (link speed, link type, and so on)
- ❏ Identify all LAN links (for all sites)
- ❏ Document network addressing scheme (addresses, subnet masks, VLANs)
- ❏ Identify the administration model for the network (sites including local administrators, remote management, and delegation policies)
- ❏ Document Internet connectivity
- ❏ Identify routes and security guidelines for all routers

Identify Directory Services and Their Infrastructures

- ❏ Identify responsible personnel for directory services and network operating system infrastructures
- ❏ Document all identity management or directory services within the network
- ❏ Document the logical structure for each directory service
- ❏ Document network operating system infrastructures (Windows NT, UNIX, NetWare, and so on)
- ❏ Document server topology
- ❏ Document network and directory access methods (Are there local components on workstations?)
- ❏ Document client platforms in use (Windows NT, Windows 9x, Windows 2000, Macintosh, UNIX, and so on)

---

1. This list can also be used to move to Active Directory.

Identify DNS Infrastructures

❏ Identify responsible personnel for DNS infrastructures

❏ Document name resolution systems

❏ Document the service type (software used, version, and compatibility)

❏ Document the logical structure of the DNS namespace (zones, transfers, and so on)

❏ Document server location within the organization

Identify DHCP Infrastructures

❏ Identify responsible personnel for DHCP infrastructures

❏ Document DHCP server topology and positioning

❏ Document logical DHCP structure (configuration, parameters, global and local options, and so on)

Identify WINS Infrastructures

❏ Identify responsible personnel for WINS infrastructures

❏ Document WINS server topology and positioning

❏ Document logical WINS structure (configuration, parameters, replication schema, and so on)

Identify Messaging Infrastructures

❏ Identify responsible personnel for messaging infrastructures

❏ Document the type and version of the messaging system

❏ Identify messaging server topology and positioning

❏ Identify server positioning and link types (MTA, SMTP, and so on)

❏ Identify global and local address book topologies

❏ Identify messaging load and replication parameters

Identify Other Infrastructure Relationships

❏ Document server administration infrastructures and processes

❏ Document PC or workstation administration infrastructures and processes

❏ Document software management infrastructures and processes

Identify Naming Conventions

❏ Identify naming conventions for users and groups (organizational units if they exist)

❏ Identify naming conventions for servers, PCs, and other physical network components

❏ Identify naming conventions for messaging services

❏ Identify naming conventions for other management systems

❏ Identify DNS naming conventions

❏ Identify UNIX/mainframe naming conventions (if applicable)

Identify the Security Model

❏ Identify responsible personnel for security management

❏ Locate/identify security policies

❏ Identify administrative security standards for each network operating system in use

Identify Line-of-Business Applications

❏ Identify responsible personnel for these applications

❏ Document line-of-business applications

❏ Identify identity management relationships between line-of-business applications

❏ Identify application growth

❏ Identify application structure (servers, services, components, and so on)

❏ Identify application delivery mechanisms

❏ Identify e-commerce applications and management systems

Identify User-Based Applications

❏ Identify responsible personnel for these applications

❏ Document user-based applications

❏ Identify user-based application populations and their locations

❏ Identify application delivery mechanisms

Organizational Information

Identify Organizational Objectives
- ❑ Obtain the organization's mission statement
- ❑ Obtain the organization's vision statement
- ❑ Identify organizational business objectives
- ❑ Identify corporate goals
- ❑ Identify the organization's business plan
- ❑ Identify the organization's key partners

Identify the Organizational Structure
- ❑ Obtain the organizational chart
- ❑ Identify key decision-making personnel for IT and organizational decisions
- ❑ Identify people and groups of influence within the organization (who to meet during projects)
- ❑ Identify workflows between users, departments, and regions

Identify Organizational Expansion Rates
- ❑ Determine evolution projections for the user population
- ❑ Determine evolution projections for network and local line-of-business applications
- ❑ Identify central and regional support and PC administration personnel
- ❑ Determine personnel mobility
- ❑ Identify temporary personnel requirements and patterns
- ❑ Identify seasonal personnel increases/decreases

Identify the Geographic Layout of the Organization
- ❑ Document the location and size of each facility
- ❑ Document client populations for each line-of-business within each facility
- ❑ Locate site maps for each facility
- ❑ Identify if the organization has an existing regional deployment pattern

Identify the Administrative Model

- ❏ Identify the user and group administrative model
- ❏ Identify the resource administrative model (printers, file services, servers, and so on)
- ❏ Identify the messaging service administrative model
- ❏ Identify any other relevant administrative model
- ❏ Identify operational principles

Identify the Human Support Patterns

- ❏ Identify user training services
- ❏ Identify technical training patterns
- ❏ Identify communications patterns within the organization
- ❏ Identify documentation, information, and knowledge management patterns within the organization
- ❏ Identify organizational information sources

Completing this list and then maintaining it is the best way to create and manage your Global Architecture.

APPENDIX B

Essential Standards
Standards for the .NET Enterprise Architecture

This appendix outlines the standards required to implement and support the global standardization effort in an organization. The standards outlined here make up the .NET EMF for SPA objects within the organization.

Each standard is clearly identified and numbered. Standards are grouped in sections based on area of activity. Five areas of activity are covered:

Generic: Covers general standards affecting every component of the network infrastructure

Directory services: Covers the conception, use, and management of the directory

Management and administration: Covers the management and administration of the network infrastructure

Use and operation: Covers usage, interoperability, and operation of the services offered by the network

Certification: Covers the preparation, use, delivery, conception, and operation of hardware and software components within the network

Merriam-Webster's online dictionary[1] defines a standard as follows: "Something established by authority, custom, or general consent as a model or example; a structure built for or serving as a base or support."

This appendix is a collection of elements that make up the model; these guidelines should be followed when designing, using, or managing SPA objects. All standards outlined here are based on the standardization targets elaborated in Chapter 3. These essential standards are, in fact, a list of

---

1. http://www.m-w.com/home.htm

rules and guidelines that enable IT to begin the standardization process and globally integrate the network.

This appendix covers all aspects of the standardization implementation. For each of the five elements covered, each standard is clearly described according to the structure displayed below. In the interest of brevity, only the standard number and title are included in this appendix.

A document including a copy of the standard number, name, statement, and justification is available at http://www.Reso-Net.com/EMF.

The standards outlined in the following tables control all aspects of the SPA object within the global network.

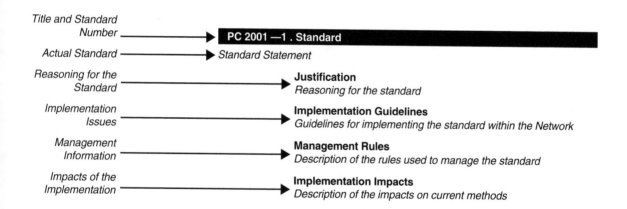

TABLE B.1 General Standards

Number	Title
PC2001 — 1.	System Title and Version Number
PC2001 — 2.	Minimum Hardware Requirements
PC2001 — 3.	Homogeneous Network for all SPA Objects
PC2001 — 4.	Unique Kernel — PC
PC2001 — 5.	Unique Kernel — Servers
PC2001 — 6.	Ongoing System Maintenance
PC2001 — 7.	SPA "Intelligent" File System
PC2001 — 8.	Standard Fonts for SPA Objects
PC2001 — 9.	Buy before Build
PC2001 — 10.	Industry Best Practices
PC2001 — 11.	Manufacturer Best Practices
PC2001 — 12.	Partner Strategic Vision
PC2001 — 13.	Full Use of the Core Operating System Feature Set
PC2001 — 14.	Component Rationalization
PC2001 — 15.	Certification Process
PC2001 — 16.	Secured Point of Access to Secure the Network
PC2001 — 17.	Standard Operating Procedures

TABLE B.2 Directory Services

Number	Title
PC2001 — 18.	Structured Directory Services Management
PC2001 — 19.	Directory Schema Extension and Modification Management
PC2001 — 20.	Directory Schema Management Committee
PC2001 — 21.	Directory-Enabled Application Evaluation Process
PC2001 — 22.	Core Directory Services in Protected Top-Level Domain
PC2001 — 23.	Site Structure and Management
PC2001 — 24.	Directory Replication Management — Quality of Service
PC2001 — 25.	Directory Service SLA — Quality of Service
PC2001 — 26.	Namespace Naming Standards
PC2001 — 27.	Directory-Enabled Namespace Management
PC2001 — 28.	Forests, Trees, Domains, and Workgroups
PC2001 — 29.	Organizational Unit Attribution
PC2001 — 30.	Delegated Directory Object Management
PC2001 — 31.	The Directory as Information Source
PC2001 — 32.	User Information Publication
PC2001 — 33.	Shared Folder Information Publication
PC2001 — 34.	SPA Object Information Publication
PC2001 — 35.	Shared Printer Information Publication
PC2001 — 36.	Directory Integration of Corporate Application
PC2001 — 37.	Directory-Enabled Application Delivery
PC2001 — 38.	Directory-Enabled Application Attribution
PC2001 — 39.	Group Policy Management
PC2001 — 40.	Exclusion of Local Disk Security from the Directory

TABLE B.3 Management and Administration

Number	Title
PC2001 — 41.	PC Identification Standards
PC2001 — 42.	Unique Network Protocol
PC2001 — 43.	Specialized SPA Object Functions
PC2001 — 44.	Limitations on PC Resource Sharing
PC2001 — 45.	Operating System Installation Methods
PC2001 — 46.	"Intelligent PC" Management
PC2001 — 47.	Non-Kernel Application Management
PC2001 — 48.	"Silent" Application Installations
PC2001 — 49.	Self-Healing Applications
PC2001 — 50.	Mobile and Stand-alone PC Installations
PC2001 — 51.	Client/Server Application Management
PC2001 — 52.	Unified Logon Scripts
PC2001 — 53.	Point 'n' Print Functionality
PC2001 — 54.	Electronic Messaging Configuration
PC2001 — 55.	System BIOS Protection
PC2001 — 56.	Secured Local SPA Object Configuration
PC2001 — 57.	SPA Object Access Rights and Permissions
PC2001 — 58.	Local SPA Object File Security
PC2001 — 59.	Mobile and Stand-alone PC Access Control
PC2001 — 60.	Identical Logical Disks — PCs
PC2001 — 61.	Identical Logical Disks — Servers
PC2001 — 62.	Local Disk Root Structure
PC2001 — 63.	Local Tree: Software
PC2001 — 64.	Local Tree: Data
PC2001 — 65.	Reserved Local Disk Space
PC2001 — 66.	Dial-Up Networking
PC2001 — 67.	Standard Network Map
PC2001 — 68.	Mirroring Process: User Data
PC2001 — 69.	Mirroring Process: Applications

Continued on next page

TABLE B.3   Management and Administration *(Continued)*

Number	Title
PC2001 — 70.	Mirroring Process: Profiles
PC2001 — 71.	Communication Tools to Users
PC2001 — 72.	Inclusion of Active Desktop Components
PC2001 — 73.	Remote Control Policy
PC2001 — 74.	PC Software Delivery Policy
PC2001 — 75.	PC Asset Management and Inventory Policy
PC2001 — 76.	Self-Service Application Installation and Management

TABLE B.4 Usage and Operations

Number	Title
PC2001 — 77.	Terminal Service-Mode Applications
PC2001 — 78.	Preference for .NET Server Applications
PC2001 — 79.	Requirements for Third-Party Applications
PC2001 — 80.	Dynamic Link Library (DLL) Management
PC2001 — 81.	Non-Certified Application Support
PC2001 — 82.	Scripting Language Local to the SPA
PC2001 — 83.	Graphical Logon Scripts
PC2001 — 84.	Multilingual Kernel and Regional Parameters
PC2001 — 85.	Complete Application Installation
PC2001 — 86.	Shared PC Construction
PC2001 — 87.	Shared PC Usage Policy
PC2001 — 88.	Secure Access to the PC
PC2001 — 89.	Encryption of Personal Data
PC2001 — 90.	Kernel Office Automation Components
PC2001 — 91.	Dictionaries and Enabled Languages
PC2001 — 92.	Office Automation Add-Ons
PC2001 — 93.	Standard Communications Tools
PC2001 — 94.	Personal Information Managers
PC2001 — 95.	Internet Browser Policy
PC2001 — 96.	Generic Drawing Tools
PC2001 — 97.	Terminal Emulation Tool
PC2001 — 98.	Mission-Critical and Mission-Support Applications
PC2001 — 99.	Presentation Layer Design
PC2001 — 100.	Start Menu Contents and Structure
PC2001 — 101.	Quick Launch Area and Tray Icons
PC2001 — 102.	Corporate Desktop Zone
PC2001 — 103.	Personal Desktop Zone
PC2001 — 104.	Centralized Client/Server Tool Access

Continued on next page

TABLE B.4   Usage and Operations *(Continued)*

Number	Title
PC2001 — 105.	Intranet Quick Search Access
PC2001 — 106.	Call Center and Help Desk Access
PC2001 — 107.	Automated Productivity Tools
PC2001 — 108.	Wallpaper and Screensavers
PC2001 — 109.	IT/IS Communications to the PC
PC2001 — 110.	Management Communications to the PC
PC2001 — 111.	Primary PC Usage Role — Generic User
PC2001 — 112.	Secondary PC Usage Roles

TABLE B.5 Certification

Number	Title
PC2001 — 113.	Exceptions to the Certification Process
PC2001 — 114.	Certified Hardware
PC2001 — 115.	Certified Drivers
PC2001 — 116.	Driver Code Signing
PC2001 — 117.	Certified In-house Development
PC2001 — 118.	End-User Development
PC2001 — 119.	Development Toolkit
PC2001 — 120.	Application Code Signing
PC2001 — 121.	Application Delivery Modes
PC2001 — 122.	End-User Application Delivery

APPENDIX C

Inventory Data Sheet
Collecting User Inventory Data

You can use this sheet to collect inventories from users' PCs before a migration.

User Inventory Data Sheet

Name of User Representative		Department	

IDENTIFICATION

PC Asset Number		User Name	
PC Name		User Access Code	
Division Number		Division Description	
Deployment Date		Network Link Number	
Training Date		"Before" Communication Date	
User Language		Regional Settings	

HARDWARE CONFIGURATION

Professional Computer (PC)

	Current Configuration		New Configuration	
Type	☐ Workstation	☐ Portable	☐ Workstation	☐ Portable
Brand				
Model & Speed				
Processor				
RAM				
Hard Disk				

Monitor

	Current Configuration		New Configuration	
Type	☐ Flat Screen	☐ CRT	☐ Flat Screen	☐ CRT
Model				
Size				

Printer Connections

	Current Configuration		New Configuration	
Type	☐ Network	☐ Local	☐ Network	☐ Local
Local	☐ LPT Ports	☐ USB Ports	☐ LPT Ports	☐ USB Ports
Connections	☐ Infrared Ports	☐ Wireless Ports	☐ Infrared Ports	☐ Wireless Ports

Additional Peripherals

	Current Configuration	New Configuration
CDR & CDRW		
Modem		
Zip Drive		
Video Card		
Network Card		
Scanner		
Mouse		
Keyboard		
Other		

Les Entreprises
Resolutions
Enterprises

User Inventory Data Sheet

HARDWARE CONFIGURATION

Standard Configuration

Type				
	☐ General User	☐ Management	☐ Information Worker	☐ Shared PC
	☐ Mission Critical	☐ Developer	☐ Support	☐ Systems Administration
	☐ Technical	☐ Production		

SOFTWARE CONFIGURATION

Product Number	Current Configuration	New Configuration
1.		
2.		
3.		
4.		
5.		
6.		
7.		
8.		
9.		
10.		
11.		
12.		
13.		
14.		
15.		
16.		
17.		
18.		
19.		
20.		

ADDITIONAL COMMENTS

Quality Control (Signature)	

— Please include any additional documentation deemed necessary —

INTEGRATOR:_____   USER DATASHEET.DOC   DATE :_____

APPENDIX D

SPA Object Content List
Sample Kernel Contents for PCs

This table displays what should be included in each layer of the SPA Object Model.

Layer	Suggested Contents	Actual Contents
Hardware	Acquisitions must meet minimum configuration requirements: • Processor and speed • RAM • Local hard disk space • Network interface card • Intelligent power management • Video card and monitor	Tested and validated in the lab: • Pentium 166 MMX • 96MB • 2GB • Netflex; Portables: 3Com/Xircom—10Mb with wake on LAN • Built-in video
Operating System	Provides basic PC services including: • Windows 2000 Professional (multilingual user interface) • Service packs and/or hot fixes, if applicable • Specific drivers (video, power management, printing, and so on) • DLLs (VBRun300.DLL, others) • TrueType fonts	Actual: • Windows 2000 Professional English MUI • 128 bit • Hot fixes: freeze on May 1 • Access runtimes: Version 97 and 2000 • DLLs: Visual Basic 3.0, 4.0, 5.0, and 6.0 • Basic Windows 2000 fonts
Networking	In order to apply network standards: • Unique protocol • Domains/workgroups in the network • PC identification (NetBIOS names, host names) • Logon scripts • Dial-up networking tools	Actual: • TCP/IP: from DCHP • Domains only • Asset number: from inventory • Windows Scripting Host • Dial-up components

Continued on next page

Layer	Suggested Contents	Actual Contents
Storage	In order to standardize the way information is presented: • Identical logical disks • Local tree: software • Local tree: data • Network tree • Local data replication to network tool	• Local disk tree • WinZip 7.0
Security	To standardize access control: • Owner of the PC • User profiles and system strategies • Local and network access rights and permissions • Central access control • Group policy management	• Basic network profiles
Communications	Both tools and procedures: • E-mail client • Agenda and contact lists • Browsers (home page, internal corporate favorites, proxy/firewall controls) • Communication tools to users (message from management, from IT, and so on) • Terminal emulation tools	Actual: • Outlook 2000, SP1 • PIM: Outlook • Internet Explorer 5.0 • Plug-ins (for Explorer, please list) • 128-bit encryption • Communication to users (basic network tools) • Attachmate Extra! • Windows Media Player 7.0
Generic Tools	Including office automation: • Office automation (Office 97 Standard [without Outlook] managed through groups and profiles) • Generic graphics tools • Service packs • Dictionaries • Utilities such as antivirus, DMI management, and SMS agent	Actual: • Office 2000 English: site configuration (assistant off by default) • Draw 2000 • Photo editor • SP1 plus Y2K • Dictionaries (all English if possible: British, Canadian, American) • Utilities: - Antivirus: McAfee - SMS agent - Acrobat Reader 4.05

Layer	Suggested Contents	Actual Contents
Presentation	Controls the desktop appearance and generic functionalities: • Active Desktop components • Menus and Quick Launch area • Shortcuts • Local versus central control of desktop elements	• See Presentation layer document
Corporate Applications	Includes mission-critical and mission-support applications: • PC roles (possible impact on the PC's hardware configuration) • Group-based identification • 32-bit tools • Client/server, if possible	• Corporate fonts • Corporate templates • Local and global templates

APPENDIX E

User Survey Questionnaire

This questionnaire has been used in a number of projects to identify user requirements. It is provided here as an example of the questions you need to ask.

You can automate this questionnaire in tools such as Microsoft Word or Outlook to collect information, though it works best on paper because it is easier for user representatives to validate before they return it to the project.

Your Name: _____   Date: _____

Direction: _____   Service: _____

Les Entreprises
Resolutions
Enterprises

Professional Category:
Management ☐ **Professional** ☐ **Administration** ☐ **Technician** ☐ **Administrative Assistant** ☐

Other: _____

End User Survey

The object of this survey is to properly assess the way people work with microcomputer technology within an organization. Its specific objective is as follows:

> *To help define user needs and requirements in regard to the use*
> *and operation of microcomputers and office automation software.*

This survey tries to identify the following information:

- The basic configuration of a standard workstation
- The current set of software tools you use today on your computer
- The basic software toolkit required for the most common tasks you perform
- Your current level of knowledge on microcomputer and office automation usage

This information is vital. It will serve in the design of a new, standard basic workstation for all users. Your help is greatly appreciated. Please answer all questions to the best of your ability. Leave blank questions that do not pertain to your situation. Thank you for your participation.

— Project Management Team

General Information — Microcomputer Usage

1 With respect to your general use of your workstation and its office automation software:

a. Which functions do you perform most often?

	Daily	Often	Rarely
Sample Document (e.g., memos)	☐	☐	☐
Automatic Correction	☐	☐	☐
Keyboard Shortcuts (e.g., F12 Save as)	☐	☐	☐
Movement Keys (e.g., arrows)	☐	☐	☐
Search and Replace	☐	☐	☐
Cut and Paste	☐	☐	☐
Thesaurus	☐	☐	☐
Electronic Forms (e.g., Expense Report)	☐	☐	☐
Wizard/Help	☐	☐	☐
Drag & Drop	☐	☐	☐

Other: _____

_____

2 When using Electronic Mail, which group or individuals do you communicate with the most?

	Daily	Often	Rarely
Personnel in the same branch			
Personnel in other branches			
Management within the same department			
Other personnel within the organization			
Personnel outside the organization			

.NET End User Survey

3 What do you use Electronic Mail for?

	Daily	Often	Rarely
Replacement of paper memos and paper trail			
To send brief messages to others			
Replacement of verbal work order requests			

Other: *Please explain* _____

_____

4 Do you receive/send Facsimiles?

	Daily	Often	Rarely
Please indicate your rate of usage...			

5 What type of documents do (or have) you create(d)?

☐ Letters	☐ Memos	☐ Fax Cover Pages	☐ Operating Procedures
☐ Reports	☐ Long Documents	☐ Financial Summaries	☐ Other: *Please explain*

Do you type your own documents?   Yes ☐ No ☐

6 Do you use personalized applications?   Yes ☐ No ☐ Not applicable ☐
(Examples of personalized applications are listed below.)
If yes, what type of personalized application do you use?

☐ Word Processing Macros	☐ Spreadsheet Macros	☐ Database Macros
☐ Databases	☐ Source Documents	☐ Image Banks
☐ Automated Document Templates	☐ Other: *Please explain*	

7 In the following list, please indicate if these tools are (or would be) useful in your work.
Please prioritize those that you feel are useful using a scale from 1 (most useful) to 12
(least useful).

	Very Useful	Useful	Not needed		Priority
Word Processing					
Spreadsheet					
Presentation Graphics					
Personal Database					
Graphics/Illustration					
Page Layout					
Electronic Mail					
Electronic Fax					
Calendaring Tool					
Document Management & Indexing					
Internet/Intranet Browsing					
Other: *Please explain*					

Do you create your own personalized applications? Yes ☐ No ☐ Not applicable ☐

.NET End User Survey

8 Which of the following methods do you prefer to use when you encounter a computer problem? Please prioritize your answer on a scale of 1 (favorite method) to 5 (least favorite).

	Priority
☐ Help Desk	
☐ Self–directed search	
☐ Online Help (F1 or Windows Help)	
☐ Colleague	
☐ Other: *Please explain.*	

Mobility & Accessibility

9 Do you share your PC workstation with others?   Yes ☐   No ☐   Not applicable ☐

Do you share your Mailbox with others?   Yes ☐   No ☐   Not applicable ☐

Do you telecommute?   Yes ☐   No ☐   Not applicable ☐

If yes, how? _____

_____

10 Do you use a portable PC?   Yes ☐   No ☐   Not applicable ☐

11 Do you require special accessibility features on your   Yes ☐   No ☐   Not applicable ☐
PC? (Magnifying Glass, On–screen Keyboard, Sticky
Keys, etc...)

Automation & Shortcuts

12 Which item among the following list would you find useful?

☐ *Automated Letters* (Store and Reuse Addresses, Choice of signature blocks, Formats with or without Letterhead)

☐ *Automated Memos* (Select To and From fields, Insert Subjects, Use Automated Formats)

☐ *Automated Fax Cover Page* (Auto Insertion of Destination Information, Automatic Calculation of enclosed Pages, Automated Format)

☐ *Quick Access to Help Desk* (A Single Click to Submit a Call or View the Status of a Call)

☐ *Quick Search Tool* (Single Click to Search Entire Information Base)

☐ *Other Quick Access or Automated Tools* (If you have suggestions for automated tools or components to which you would like rapid access, please feel free to suggest them below.)

_____

_____

_____

_____

.NET End User Survey

Current Knowledge Level

Software Usage

13 Which Software Products are you familiar with? (Please answer to the best of your ability.)

Operating System: Windows 95/98 ☐   Windows NT ☐   Unix ☐   Other: _____   version:__

Word processing: WordPerfect ☐   MS Word ☐   Ami Pro ☐   Other: _____   version:__

Spreadsheet: Lotus 1-2-3 ..... ☐   MS Excel ..... ☐ Other: _____   version:__

Database: MS Access .... ☐   dBase..... ☐ Other: _____   version:__

Presentations: MS PowerPoint.. ☐   Lotus Freelance ..... ☐ Other: _____   version:__

Graphics: Visio .... ☐   Windows Draw ..... ☐ Other: _____   version:__

Publishing: PageMaker .... ☐ Ventura Publisher .... ☐ Other: _____   version:__

Internet Browsing: Netscape .... ☐   Internet Explorer ..... ☐ Other: _____   version:__

Scheduling: Notes .... ☐   Organizer ..... ☐ Other: _____   version:__

Please indicate your level of experience with the following:

	None	Some	Medium	Advanced
MS Windows [version ___]				
Word processing				
Spreadsheet				
Database				
Graphics/Presentations				
Electronic Mail				
Page Layout				
Calendar/Scheduling Facility				

Please indicate your preference for the following:

Training Language: English ☐ French ☐   *Software Language:* English ☐ French ☐

Comments and Suggestions

14 Do you have suggestions for general system improvement?

_____
_____
_____
_____
_____
_____

Please return the completed questionnaire to _____
Thank you for your help!

APPENDIX F

Sample Standard Operating Procedures

Standard Operating Procedures Are at the Core of the .NET EMF

A *standard operating procedure (SOP)* is a written set of instructions that someone should follow to complete a given task. It focuses on maximizing efficiency during operational and production requirements. Once implemented, SOPs can help provide guaranteed service levels and thus are the basis for the elaboration of Service Level Agreements.

When well defined, SOPs enable an organization to measure the time it takes to perform a given task. SOPs are also used to simplify problem troubleshooting because every process is the same everywhere. Finally, SOPs provide redundancy and reduced costs in administration because all network technicians and administrators use the same processes wherever they are located, and no retraining is required. The SOPs you write will become the core of any technical training program you provide.

This appendix provides SOP best practices, a structure for SOPs, and a blank SOP form.

SOP Best Practices

The following are some concepts to keep in mind when you write SOPs.

- Incorporate safety and environment variables into the traditional how-to-do steps or how-to-operate steps.
- All SOPs must meet the definition of an SOP.
- An SOP should include no more than 6 to 12 steps. If an SOP goes beyond 10 steps, consider these solutions:

- Break the long SOP into several logical subjob SOPs.
- Write an accompanying shortened SOP that lists only the steps but does not provide detailed explanations of those steps.
- Prepare the longer comprehensive-training SOP first to provide a picture of what training is required. Then decide how to break it into shorter, subjob SOPs. Alternatively, make the long-form SOP a training document or manual to supplement the shorter, subjob SOPs.
- If you write shortcut SOPs, explain the reasons behind certain steps to provide an understanding of the importance of following all the steps in the proper order.

- Write SOPs for people who perform under different interpersonal circumstances.
  - For people who work alone
  - For two or more people who work together as a team
  - For people who will supervise other people doing a job
  - For people who are not familiar with rules generally understood by your employees

- Consider the age, education, knowledge, skill, experience and training, and work culture of the individuals who will be performing the SOP steps.

- Forecast future effects and steps at certain points in the SOP to tell readers things they should know in advance (upcoming steps that require caution, precision, timing, and personal attention).

- Once the SOP is complete, have several workers test it and give you feedback.

- Review the effectiveness of SOPs after a few weeks and make necessary changes if in-the-field practice suggests that descriptions should be improved.
  - Review SOPs when processes and equipment are changed.
  - When new equipment is installed, take the opportunity to write a new SOP, incorporating the good from the old and adding what is necessary with regard to the new equipment.

- Keep SOPs short as much as possible. This will ensure that they are followed.

- Rely on the expertise of your staff to create and test the SOPs.

SAMPLE SOP — TITLE

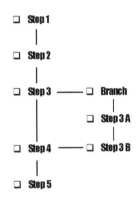

- ❏ **Step 1**
- ❏ **Step 2**
- ❏ **Step 3** —— ❏ **Branch**
  - ❏ **Step 3 A**
- ❏ **Step 4** —— ❏ **Step 3 B**
- ❏ **Step 5**

Graphically illustrate the steps of the SOP if possible. A picture is worth a thousand words...

The title identifies the standard operating procedure. It should also define the purpose of the SOP as much as possible.

Category
Identifies which category the SOP falls into (network management, workstation management, etc.).

Use document reference numbers and revision dates on the title or cover page and a second page such as the table of contents or first page of text.

Purpose
State the purpose of the SOP including the intended audience in one or two sentences. Include information about process and regulatory standards, and the expected consequences of performing the SOP.

Write a "scope" statement that tells what related subjects the SOP will not cover. This way, there is no opportunity that someone will be confused and make a mistake. Use the scope to clarify things for the reader.

Responsible Department
Identify the business unit, department, or sub–department that is the owner of the SOP.

Task Owner
Identify the owner of the task. This person will be responsible for overseeing the use of the SOP and overseeing its evolution.

Task Operator
Identify the task writer and who it is aimed at: Network Administrator, Architect, Integrator, Support personnel, etc.

Task Coverage
Give an overview of the steps in the SOP that describes the process in terms of its major functions. Provide overall descriptions of the major system and its components.

Tools Required
List by category, items or tools required for the SOP.

Equipment	
Reference materials	
Training requirements	
General materials	
Specific materials	
Tools	

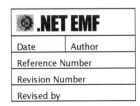

⚙ **.NET EMF**	
Date	Author
Reference Number	
Revision Number	
Revised by	

Other lists can include:

- Environmental conditions
- Time conditions
- Information sources

Describe the machinery, processing system and other major components, if required.

Terms and Concepts

Define these terms and concepts in their own paragraph so the readers know that they are unusual words or concepts and can find them easily for use when needed.

Warnings!

Place safety warnings, cautions and notes prominently within the SOP before the actual steps are described. Never place safety items or cautions at the end of a step.

Task Summary

Provide a short overview of the tasks to be performed. This allows personnel to understand the overall process.

Service Level Agreement

Identify the SLA this SOP is designed to meet.

Steps to Perform

List and explain the process steps in sequential order.

- Remember to limit the number of steps (6 to 12 max.).
- If two steps must be done at once, explain them in a sentence that clearly says so.
- Provide a more detailed explanation if a reader needs more information to fully understand the reason for performing a step.
- Provide readers with alternative steps to take in case a desired step does not work.
- When a SOP is time-dependent, indicate the times clearly.
- When an SOP depends on informational input, include the source with reference document number and date, if possible.
- Decide where to use graphics to communicate clearly.
- List all references.
- Test the SOP in the field and then develop troubleshooting instructions.

Additional Comments

Provide any comments deemed necessary to increase comprehension by the Task Operators.

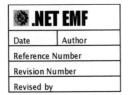

⚙ .NET EMF	
Date	Author
Reference Number	
Revision Number	
Revised by	

**APPENDIX A —
BLANK SOP
WORKSHEET**

❑ Step 1
|
❑ Step 2
|
❑ Step 3 ——— ❑ Branch
| |
| ❑ Step 3 A
| |
❑ Step 4 ——— ❑ Step 3 B
|
❑ Step 5

SOP Title
_____
_____

Category
_____

Purpose
_____
_____
_____

Responsible Department
_____

Task Owner
_____

Task Operator
_____

Task Coverage
_____
_____
_____

Tools Required
_____
_____
_____

Terms and Concepts
_____
_____
_____

Warnings
_____
_____
_____

Task Summary
_____
_____
_____

Service Level Agreement
_____
_____
_____

⚙ **.NET EMF**	
Date	Author
Reference Number	
Revision Number	
Revised by	

Steps to Perform

_____
_____
_____
_____
_____
_____
_____
_____
_____
_____
_____
_____
_____
_____
_____
_____
_____
_____

Additional Comments

_____
_____
_____
_____
_____
_____
_____
_____
_____
_____
_____
_____
_____
_____
_____
_____
_____
_____
_____

.NET EMF

Date	Author
Reference Number	
Revision Number	
Revised by	

BIBLIOGRAPHY

Bergeron, Pierre G. *La gestion dynamique concepts, méthodes et applications*. Gaétan Morin éditeur, 1986.

Boudreau, André. *La gestion du Savoir*. Vol. 23 no.2, Vol. 23 no.3, Vol. 23 no.4. InfoQuébec, 1998.

Collerette, Pierre, and Gilles Delisle. *Le Changement Planifié*. Les Éditions Agence d'ARC Inc., 1982.

The Concise Oxford Dictionary of Current English, Seventh Edition. Oxford University Press, 1982.

Gates, Bill. *Business @ the Speed of Thought*. Warner Books, 1999.

Honeycutt, Jerry. *Introducing Microsoft Windows 2000 Professional*. Microsoft Press, 1999.

Iseminger, David. *Microsoft Win 32 Developer's Reference Library*. Microsoft Press, 2000.

Maslow, Abraham. *Motivation and Personality*. Longman Higher Education, 1954.

McLuhan, Marshal, and Bruce R. Powers. *Global Village*. Oxford University Press, 1967.

Northrup, Anthony. *Introducing Microsoft Windows 2000 Server*. Microsoft Press, 1999.

Sun Tzu, and Samuel B. Griffith. *The Art of War*. Oxford University Press, 1984.

Whitmore, John. *Coaching for Performance*. Nicholas Brealy Publishing Limited, 1992.

INDEX